CONFLICT ON THE NORTHWEST COAST

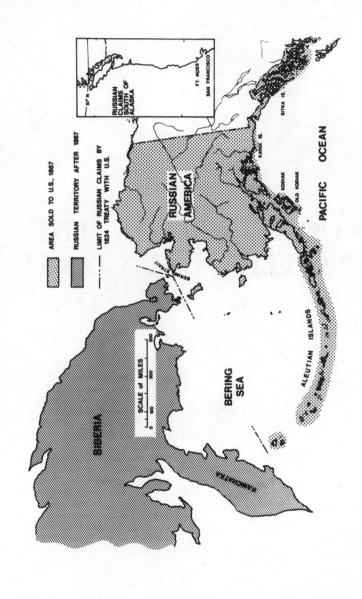

CONFLICT ON THE NORTHWEST COAST

American-Russian Rivalry in the Pacific Northwest, 1790-1867

Howard I. Kushner

Contributions in American History Number 41

GREENWOOD PRESS

Westport, Connecticut   •   London, England

Library of Congress Cataloging in Publication Data

Kushner, Howard I
 Conflict on the Northwest coast.

 (Contributions in American history; no. 41)
 Bibliography: p.
 Includes index.
  1. Alaska—Annexation. 2. United States—Foreign
relations—Russia. 3. Russia—Foreign relations—
United States. 4. United States—Territorial expan-
sion. I. Title.
 E669.K93   979.8'02   75-67
 ISBN 0-8371-7873-8

Library of Congress Catalog Card Number: 75-67
ISBN: 0-8371-7873-8

First published in 1975

Greenwood Press, a division of Williamhouse-Regency Inc.
51 Riverside Avenue, Westport, Connecticut 06880

Manufactured in the United States of America

FOR CAROL AND PETER

Contents

viii   Contents

Acknowledgments

Many people have given me aid and advice in the preparation of this book. To Walter LaFeber of Cornell University I owe the greatest debt. Also, Joel Silbey and Walter Pinter both of Cornell offered valuable criticism. Roger Daniels of State University of New York College at Fredonia read the entire manuscript, and I have incorporated several of his suggestions. Edward Saveth, also of State University of New York College at Fredonia, made many worthwhile criticisms. Carol Kushner of San Francisco and Fredonia helped edit the manuscript several times.

Mary Notaro, History Department secretary at State University of New York College at Fredonia, typed the manuscript at least three times and added immensely to its readability. I also wish to thank Dianne Litchfield, my departmental secretary at San Francisco State University, for her assistance. Frank Sloss of San Francisco provided me with valuable documents he obtained in Alaska and with information from his own vast personal knowledge about Alaskan commerce. Jon Wakelyn, the editor of this series, and Jeannette Lindsay, managing editor of Greenwood Press, also have been helpful and considerate. Beverly Miller improved the manuscript by her copyediting. The staffs of various libraries proved essential in my research. Particularly helpful were the staffs of the California Historical Society in San Francisco; Special Collections at Rush Rhees Library at the University of Rochester; the Bancroft Library at Berkeley; the Cornell University libraries; and, not least of all, the Reed Library at State University of New York College at Fredonia.

The material in Chapter 5 appeared in an earlier form in the *New England Quarterly* 45 (March 1972) under the title " 'Hellships': Yankee Whaling Along the Coasts of Russian-America, 1835-1852." Much of the material in Chapter 6 appears in the *Oregon Historical Quarterly* 75 (December 1974) under the title "The Oregon Question Is . . . a Massachusetts Question." The material in Chapter 7 appeared in the *Western Historical Quarterly* 4 (July 1973) under the title "Visions of the Northwest Coast, Gwin and Seward in the 1850's." Some of the material in Chapters 8 and 9 appears in the *California Historical Quarterly,* 54 (Spring 1975): " 'Seward's Folly'?: American Commerce in Russian-America and the Alaska Purchase."

Grants from the Research Foundation of Cornell University and the Fredonia Foundation made much of my travel possible.

Fredonia, New York
August 1974

Introduction

This book offers a new interpretation of the purchase of Alaska. My research led me to question two related aspects of American–Russian relations from 1790 to 1867. First, most scholarship on this period has concluded that relations between the two nations were amicable. This view seems to have developed because American–Russian relations are generally studied with an emphasis on European matters. On the other hand, American–Russian relations in the Pacific Northwest largely have been neglected. By tracing this relationship in the Pacific Northwest from 1790 to 1867, one uncovers a history of conflict and, at times, near hostility between the United States and Russia.

Second, the discovery of a rivalry between the two nations led me to question the thesis, held by consensus and revisionist historians alike, that Russia sold its North American possession to the United States because it was able to play upon traditional American friendship to rid itself of a worthless possession. While consensus historians—among them, Frank A. Golder, Victor J. Farrar, and Thomas A. Bailey—have argued that the purchase of Alaska resulted as well from Secretary of State William H. Seward's lust after territory, revisionist historians—for example, William A. Williams—alleged that Seward and other commercially minded leaders acquired Alaska because they saw it as a stepping-stone to Asia's markets. Nevertheless, both schools agree that the sale to the United States resulted from a traditional friendship between the United States and Russia.

My findings, however, lead me to conclude that conflict and rivalry over the Pacific Northwest, not amity, led the czar reluctantly to cede Russian-America to the United States. While my research, in part, tends to confirm the revisionist view that many American leaders desired Alaska as a stepping-stone to the Orient, this view must be extended to include the fact that long-term American enterprise and interest in Russian-America convinced many policy makers and businessmen that Alaska was valuable in its own right. The sea otter trade, whaling, the ice trade, interest in commercial fishing rights, and other commercial ventures all played a significant part in causing conflicts to arise between the Russian government, which tried to exclude United States citizens from Russian-America, and the United States government, which attempted to protect the rights of its citizens in their pursuit of commercial enterprise. American commercial activities in Russian-America and the federal support and protection they received were so persistent that the Russian government concluded it either had to sell its possessions in North America to the United States or see the United States take them.

In retrospect, this was a struggle between unequals. The Russians lacked both the power and the deeper interests in the area that Americans had displayed. No doubt, Russia ultimately sold Alaska because it found itself overextended. Yet, Russian policy makers reached the conclusion that retention of Russian-America was an overextension of Russian territorial interests only after eighty years of American pressure—and they reached that decision quite reluctantly.

CONFLICT ON THE NORTHWEST COAST

1

Background for a Rivalry
1790–1815

Scholars have argued that the primary reason Secretary of State William H. Seward was able to purchase Russian-America in 1867 was the intense Russian desire to sell the land.[1] To begin and end the story there, however, would be to miss its most important element: why did the Russians desire to sell? Edward de Stoeckl, the Russian minister to the United States and the man who negotiated the sale with Secretary of State Seward, thought Russia had a most compelling reason to dispose of this particular colony. In a July 1867 memorandum to Count de Westmann, assistant minister of foreign affairs in St. Petersburg, Stoeckl acknowledged that strong opposition to the sale of Russia's possessions in North America existed in certain quarters in Russia, especially among some of the influential press. "But that proves," added Stoeckl, "that our people do not have a fair idea of the state of our colonies. It was a question of our selling them or of our seeing them [the United States] seize it."[2]

The acquisition of Alaska by William H. Seward was the culmination of many years of interest in this area by the official American government and special business concerns in the East and Far West. By at least 1860, the Russian government realized it either had to sell its possessions or give them up to American commercial filibusterers and legislators. Only America's internal distress from 1860 to 1865 put off the seemingly inevitable change of ownership.

I

The roots of the Alaska purchase extend back to the days of Robert Gray's discovery of the Columbia River. Captain Gray and his ship, the *Columbia*, are known for the discovery and subsequent naming of the river which flows through Oregon and Washington to the Pacific Ocean. The Columbia River, however, was uncovered by Gray on his second voyage to the Pacific Northwest Coast. Gray's earlier voyage (1787–1790) was as significant as his second, more famous, journey. During this first voyage, Gray, along with Captain John Kendrick, began the northwest sea otter fur trade to China.

Until 1790, American trade with China, while lucrative, was nevertheless spotty and unpredictable. While American maritime merchants were allowed to trade in the Canton market, the only port in China open to foreign traders, they faced the problem of having no suitable medium of exchange with which to purchase Chinese products. Although specie was an acceptable medium, American traders could not always obtain it. Robert Morris had sponsored the successful voyage of the *Empress of China* in 1784 with a cargo of ginseng. This root was limited in quantity; moreover, the Chinese demand for this product was unpredictable. The *Grand Turk* of Salem, the first Massachusetts ship to reach Canton (1786), had made huge profits, but its cargo also mainly consisted of ginseng. The British were outdistancing their American cousins in the China trade because they could import such Canton favorites as opium, mumie, sharks' fins, and edible birds' nests from India and the Moluccas. The British were able to use silver specie for most of their tea and silk purchases.[3]

Gray and Kendrick had been sent to the Northwest Coast by a group of Boston merchants and shippers. Charles Bulfinch, the originator of the scheme, got the idea from reading Captain Cook's *Journals,* which were published in 1784. The *Journals* related Cook's success in selling sea otter fur he had obtained along the northwest shores of the American continent to the Chinese merchants at Canton. The *Journals* left no doubt that a substantial gain could be made from a very small investment. An

American who sailed with Cook, John Ledyard, had stormed up and down the eastern American seaboard making similar claims in the 1780s. Unfortunately for Ledyard, no one had listened to him. The two ships sent west by the Bulfinch group in 1787 traded for sea otter furs in the area around Nootka Sound. Gray took the *Columbia,* laden with furs, from Kendrick (who remained to obtain sea otters with the smaller vessel, the *Lady Washington*) and sailed to the Orient. Arriving in Canton, Captain Gray sold his cargo and returned to Boston harbor in August 1790. While the *Columbia*'s first voyage was not a financial success, it nevertheless indicated that the sea otter trade might solve the American need for an acceptable medium of exchange for Canton silks and teas.[4]

The news of the *Columbia*'s success in selling otter fur to China quickly spread. Before Bulfinch and Co. could refit the *Columbia* for a return voyage to the Northwest Coast, Thomas H. Perkins, a Boston merchant, sent the brigantine *Hope* to the Northwest Coast (September 1790) under Gray's former first mate, Joseph Ingraham. As the *Columbia* began its second voyage, many other Boston ships were being prepared to join in the promise of a new and lucrative triangular trade. Within two years, the Boston–Northwest Coast–Canton–Boston route was well established. The number of American ships engaged in the sea otter trade continued to grow, and by 1801 sixteen American vessels were trading for this fur along the Northwest Coast.[5]

Generally, the vessels left Boston in the summer and arrived in the North Pacific in the spring. The ships would trade chisels, shoes, knives, and firearms with the Indians in return for sea otter furs. After accumulating a sufficient number of furs, the ships would sail for Canton, stopping along the way in the Sandwich Islands for both relaxation and sandalwood. (The latter brought additional profit to the American shippers at the Canton market.) The profits of this triangular trade were lucrative. A net profit of more than $200,000 for a single voyage was typical. Many Boston fortunes, including that of William Sturgis, were made as a result of this trade. Sturgis left Boston for the Northwest Coast in 1798 as a sixteen-year-old foremost hand on one of Perkins' ships. By

1812, he headed the firm of Bryant and Sturgis, the leading trading firm in Boston during the next several decades. Perkins, Lamb, Dorr, Boardman, and Lyman are among the other names connected with firms that made their fortunes in this trade. The value of imports on American vessels at Canton rose to more than $5 million annually by 1805. This level was generally maintained in every year until 1812, with the exception of 1809, when the embargo had its effect.[6]

Americans were not alone in their search for wealth from the Northwest Coast. Spain, England, Russia, France, and Portugal had fur traders along the coast at various times. Nevertheless, from 1790 until 1815, American traders dominated the sea coast fur trade. The trade between the western coast of America and Canton was carried almost exclusively on Yankee vessels, for several reasons. First, during most of this period, the European nations were involved in war. In addition, the British, the greatest potential rival to the United States' predominance in the Pacific Northwest, were handicapped by the monopoly granted to the East India Company on all trade with China. The East India Company's charter forbade any other British company from trading in China before 1834. Until 1834, therefore, the British were unable to capitalize fully on their prior discoveries. The Russians, another potential rival, were restrained because their ships were not allowed to enter Canton or any other Chinese port. They either had to send their furs back to Siberia and then overland to China or else ship their furs to Canton in Yankee brigs. They chose the latter method.[7]

The Boston traders soon found that the great success they had trading with the Indians for furs had limited duration. The Indians of the Northwest Coast quickly grew tired of being cheated and often robbed by the Yankee traders. The Americans, on their part, had made the tactical error of trading the Indians firearms in exchange for furs. By 1800, the Indians, angered by the continued encroachments of the traders, grew increasingly hostile to all white men. In an uprising of 1802, the Tlingits (or Kholosh), using American guns, destroyed the Russian settlement at Sitka.[8]

As a result of the unrest, American sea captains participated in smuggling and illicit fur trading farther south along the coasts of Spanish California. The Spanish government in California, however, was not pleased by American incursion into its mercantile system. The Spanish were so annoyed by the continued Yankee violations of their coasts that, in 1803, the Spanish governor of California, José Joaquin Arrillaga, ordered all port commanders to halt the practice of giving aid to foreign ships in distress. The governor declared he was fully convinced the requests of American vessels for supplies were merely an excuse for stopping in order to procure furs. Not one of these ships in the last five years, noted the governor, had ever asked for enough supplies to take them to their avowed destination; rather, they obtained enough supplies to allow them to sail from port to port along the California coast in violation of Spanish law.[9]

With stronger Spanish restrictions imposed, the Yankee captains found smuggling along the California coast very difficult. They could no longer trade easily with the hostile Indians. The one alternative that seemed open to the Americans was to hunt the fur-bearing animals themselves. Searching out the sea otter, however, proved arduous and time-consuming, so the Americans soon gave up that tactic. Then, in 1803, Captain Joseph O'Cain found a suitable alternative and temporarily saved the sea otter trade for Yankee merchants.

O'Cain, in partnership with the Winship brothers of Boston, landed in Kodiak, Russian-America, in 1803. He proposed to the Russian governor, Alexander A. Baranov, a plan by which O'Cain would keep the colony supplied with necessities and even recruit skilled workmen if Baranov needed them. O'Cain would accept some of the company's furs as his price for supplying the colony as well as transport the remainder of Russian-America's furs to Canton where Russian vessels were not allowed. Baranov, who favored O'Cain's proposal, had just sent all the furs he had (worth 1.2 million rubles) to Siberia, however, so the Yankee captain suggested that he be lent a number of Aleuts, who were natives of Kodiak and skilled hunters. The Aleuts, moreover, had proved more peaceful than their southern brethren. These Indians would hunt the abundant sea otter along the California coast. By using the Aleuts and anchoring the ships off the coast and away from the Spanish patrols, O'Cain asserted, he could avoid the new Spanish regulations. The Russian-American company would be given shares for each voyage, and with its shares it could purchase the supplies it needed from O'Cain, Winship and Co. Baranov agreed to O'Cain's proposal. The first voyage under the Russian-American contract brought Baranov's colony $80,000, more than enough to buy O'Cain's entire cargo. O'Cain then sold the furs at Canton for a huge profit. A new era in sea otter trade began.[10]

As news of O'Cain's and Winship's success spread, more and more American sea captains joined forces with the Russian-American company. These ships did a large and profitable business[11] until the War of 1812 caused a stagnation in the maritime affairs of the Pacific Northwest. Even before 1812, the Russians, jealous of the Americans' incursions, began to think of various ways by which the Boston middleman could be eliminated.

II

The 1805 voyage of Nikolai Rezanov (grand chamberlain to the czar and former chief director of the Russian-American Company in St. Petersburg) signaled the first awareness in St. Petersburg of the American penetration into the Russian colonies. Rezanov feared an American takeover of the colonies. Arriving in the Pribilof Islands, Rezanov wrote to Czar Alexander in July 1805 that the islands "would be an unexhaustible source of wealth . . . were it not for the Bostonians who undermine our trade with China in furs, of which they obtain in large numbers on our coast." He warned that it was "necessary to take a stronger hold of the country else we shall leave it empty handed, since fifteen to twenty ships come here annually from Boston to trade." He suggested that the company "should build a small branch brig, and send out heavy ordinance for her armament." This, he assured the czar, would "compel the Bostonians to keep away, and the Chinese would get no furs but ours."[12]

At the end of August 1805, Rezanov's fact-finding mission arrived in Sitka. He wrote to the directors of the company that while the Tlingits, who had four years ago destroyed Sitka, "appear to be subdued," the peaceful situation could not last long. Rezanov lamented that the Tlingits "have been armed by the Bostonians with the best guns and pistols, and have even falconets." Nevertheless, Baranov was able to persuade Rezanov that the contract system with American sea captains was worth maintaining if only because it forced the Americans to deal with the Russian authorities rather than operate extralegally along the Russian–American coast. He agreed with Rezanov, nevertheless, that Russian ships should replace the Yankee vessels as soon as possible. The Russian governor noted he had always sent Russian commanders with the Aleuts in contract to the Americans, and these commanders had returned with detailed reports on quantities and habitats of the sea animals.[13]

Toward the end of his stay in Russian-America, Rezanov sent his views to the Russian-American company's directors on the course he believed the colony should take in the future. Most important, he urged, was the founding of a Russian establishment on the Columbia River: "To accomplish this it would be necessary to build as soon as possible an armed brig to drive away the Bostonians from this trade forever." Rezanov believed that a settlement on the Columbia could more easily attract Russian settlers than the company's establishments farther north. There was no time to lose since Rezanov had learned that sixty Americans were on their way from the United States overland to settle on the Columbia River. He warned that "the American States claim the right to those shores, saying that the headwaters of the Columbia are in their territory; but on the same principle they could extend their possessions all over the world, where there was no previous European settlement." The report ended with a plea: "Four Boston ships are at present cruising and trading in the sounds, . . . when shall we drive these unwelcome guests away?"[14]

Rezanov told Baranov that the most important object at the moment was territorial expansion and instructed him to move south as far as California. Rezanov had two immediate objectives: first, a port on the Columbia River and another just north of San Francisco, and, second, some type of Russian sphere of influence or trading station on the Sandwich Islands, which were the stepping-stone to Canton from Russian-America. Rezanov did more than instruct. On February 25, 1806, he took the ship *Juno* on an expedition to the Columbia River. An outbreak of scurvy, however, forced him to sail to San Francisco before any detailed exploration could take place. The first Russian attempt to secure the Columbia River ended in failure.[15]

The Russians believed that in order to secure their colonies several steps would be necessary along with expansion. They must limit American citizens to trading solely with the established Russian authorities along the Russian-American coast. The Russian colony then must work to supplant the Bostonians with Russian traders and Russian ships. Next, following Rezanov's advice, the imperial government should work through diplomatic channels to halt the American sales of arms to the natives and then to eliminate all Yankee activity in the Pacific Northwest around the Russian territories. Governor Baranov took the first steps in order to deprive the Yankees of the sea otter trade.

He had early planned "not to divide the profits of this business with anybody."[16] After five years of preparation, the Russians sent out their first hunting expedition in 1808. Baranov's chief assistant, Ivan Kuskov, commanded the voyage. Of the two Russian vessels that left New Archangel in October, only one arrived in California; the other was shipwrecked near the Columbia River. Baranov was unable to send another ship out until 1811. Even if the Russian colony had been successful in this endeavor at independent hunting, it would not have been rid of its Yankee visitors, for the Russians could not ship their furs directly to the Canton market in Russian bottoms. The company continued to send its independently procured skins to China (about two thousand per year) in American vessels.[17]

Baranov's attempts at expansion also met with failure. He sent an emissary to the Sandwich Islands in 1809–1810 to obtain permission for a Russian trading post. The envoy, Leontii Hagemeister, succeeded only in alienating the Hawaiian king. Kuskov was sent to make a settlement north of San Francisco; yet in 1811, two years after his departure, Baranov had heard nothing from his chief assistant.[18]

III

In St. Petersburg, both the Russian government and the directors of the Russian-American Company were finding it no easier to dislodge the Americans by diplomacy than Baranov had by his attempts at expansion and exclusion. Acting on Rezanov's urging, Count Nicholas Rumiantsev, the Russian minister of foreign affairs, wrote to the American consul in St. Petersburg, Levett Harris, on May 17, 1808. Rumiantsev informed Harris that the Russian-American Company had repeatedly complained to its government "that the ships of the United States, instead of trading with the Russian possessions in America, have there carried on a clandestine trade with the savages. . . ." He complained that the American traders furnished the Indians "firearms and powder" and noted that the Indians had used these very arms to destroy the Russian settlement on Sitka. Russia, maintained Rumiantsev, did not desire to terminate commerce with the United States in the Pacific Northwest; on the contrary, the Russians desired an increased trade between the company and the Americans. His imperial majesty insisted, however, that American traders trade solely at Kodiak and only with the agents of the Russian-American Company. In this way, everyone could "avoid the pernicious consequences of a clandestine trade with the savages." The Russian minister explained to Harris that, to attain these ends, the United States government could sign a convention with the Russian government attesting to such principles.[19]

Harris told the Russians he would bring the matter to the attention of his government—and there the matter rested. Washington officials, both unable and unwilling to stop its traders from selling to the natives of the Northwest Coast, did nothing. One of the major stumbling blocks to any convention between the two nations had been the absence of any official representative of the

Russian government in the United States. The Russian government, which had delayed sending an official representative, changed its mind in June 1808, realizing that if it wanted to deal with the American government on this question, it had to have an official in the United States who could negotiate. On June 13, 1808, Rumiantsev requested Harris to inform his government that the czar had appointed André Dashkov to serve as consul general at Philadelphia and chargé d'affaires "near the Congress of the United States."[20] An expanding American mercantile interest, which had resulted in conflict over Russian-America, had played an important part in convincing the Russian government to send its first accredited diplomatic representative to the United States.

When Dashkov arrived in the United States in June 1809, he wrote Secretary of State Robert Smith to request a reopening of the question of "illicit trade carried on by vessels of the United States" with the Indians of the Russian possessions in the Northwest Coast of America. Dashkov, citing Rumiantsev's May 17, 1808, note to Harris, essentially restated the earlier complaint. His note, however, was more specific in that it requested the United States government "to terminate, by proper and sufficient means, the illicit trade of some American speculators on the Northwest Coast of America and the adjacent islands." The Russian government added the charge that United States citizens had not only endangered Russian citizens but also had "violated" Russian territorial rights. The Russian consul's note suggested that the United States government pass a "law" that would forbid the continuance of the "illicit and irregular trade with the natives of the Northwest Coast of America" and "induce" American vessels "to trade in those countries exclusively with the factory or agents of the Russian Company." Again, the Russians suggested the signing of a convention "as the most proper means of preventing all future complaints."[21]

Secretary of State Smith[22] requested Dashkov to describe the precise boundaries of the area that the Russian government claimed as its possession in the Pacific Northwest. Dashkov admitted that he was not authorized to specify any exact demarcation line.[23] President James Madison used the Russian failure to denote a specific boundary as a convenient excuse to terminate the unwanted negotiations. This tactic apparently left Dashkov under the impression that if the Russian government could present a reasonable boundary line, the United States government would be willing to sign a convention limiting the commerce of American vessels in the area.[24]

Madison, however, instructed Secretary of State Smith to tell Dashkov that the problems which precluded the signing of a convention on this matter were more complex than the simple drawing of a boundary line. On May 5, 1810, Smith forwarded the American position to Dashkov. The Secretary of State noted that even if the Russian representative were authorized to fix a southern boundary, other difficulties "of a very delicate character" would be evident. First of all, Smith argued, if the Indians of the area were under Russian jurisdiction, the United States was bound only to leave its citizens to the penalties that Russian law prescribed. On the other hand, if the Indians were independent, the Russian government could not prohibit trading except in a state of war, which, at present, did not exist. Second, the United States could not restrain its citizens in their quest for enterprise simply out of friendship for the Russians. Third, Smith claimed that the President did not have the power to stop the American vessels even if he wished to do so, and the Congress, which did have the power, lacked the inclination.[25]

The negotiations then moved to St. Petersburg where John Quincy Adams was serving as the first American minister to Russia.[26] Madison and Smith realized that signing any convention with the Russians that restricted United States commerce in the Pacific Northwest was tantamount to recognition of Russian sovereignty over vast areas of North American territory. Smith informed Adams that the "United States being under no legal obligation to comply with the Russians" would not do so. He added that it would be difficult to stop American vessels from trading openly along the Russian–American coasts "without maintaining a right which this nation [Russia] has not yet asserted." Smith informed Adams that the American government held the view that "Russia has the means of enforcing its own rights" against those whom she considered American intruders. "It cannot be essential," he added, "that any foreign power should cooperate with her for the purpose." Smith closed with a statement of policy:

As it does not appear how far the Russians stretch their claim southwardly . . . it is material that some latitude should be fixed as the limit, and it is desirable, as the coast south of it will enter into the plan of Indian trade likely to be embraced by our citizens, that the limit should be as little advanced southwardly as may be.[27]

Adams reported that Russian Foreign Minister Rumiantsev hoped to reopen the question of the Pacific Northwest traders.[28] Rumiantsev claimed that he desired that "the trade from the Russian settlements on the Northwest Coast of America to China . . . be carried by the Americans." There was just one qualification he placed on that privilege: if American vessels were given the exclusive franchise of carrying Russian trade to Canton, the United States government must agree "to a restriction not to furnish warlike weapons and materials to the neighboring Indians." As for the southern boundary, Rumiantsev told Adams, the Russian possessions included Nootka Sound and went to the mouth of the Columbia River. Adams transmitted this conversation to his government, adding that he did not "imagine that it is the Count's serious intention to claim the mouth of the Columbia River."[29] Within two weeks, Adams changed this earlier appraisal. He told Smith that the Russians were seriously claiming that their possessions extended to the Columbia's mouth. Adams quickly made known the intention of his government to keep the Russian boundary in North America as far north as possible.[30]

With the negotiations at a virtual standoff, the Russians decided to give in for the time being; they believed their interest would be better served in avoiding conflict with the United States. The needs of the Russian-American Company would have to be temporarily deferred, for Russia was involved in Europe in a battle for survival. During 1810, the czar was an erstwhile ally of Napoleon and an enemy of Great Britain. America's friendship and its carriers were necessary to offset British control of the seas. Therefore, in October 1810, Rumiantsev told Adams that he realized the United States government could not control its traders in the Pacific Northwest, even if it wished, unless it passed special laws, which it seemed unlikely to do. The Russian foreign minister did not think the present was the appropriate time to set a boundary. His majesty, Rumiantsev concluded, did not desire a falling out with the United States over this issue. During this period of crisis, the czar wished "to bring all nations to pacific dispositions, and most carefully to avoid everything which could strike out a single spark of discord among them." The issue of American rivalry in the Pacific Northwest remained unresolved, the conflict merely postponed.[31]

During two years of negotiations with the United States, the Russian government failed to obtain its chief objective: limiting American traders in the Russian possessions to dealing solely with the Russian-American Company. The American government had not even recognized the Russian right to any exclusive control in the Pacific Northwest.

Instead of lessening, Yankee penetration of the Russian area increased. O'Cain had promised in 1804 to bring American craftsmen to the Russian colonies. By 1810, American artisans had a very important role in Russian-America. In 1809, the Russian governor, Alexander A. Baranov, put his children under the tutelage of a twenty-five-year-old American named Abram Jones. Jones quickly learned Russian and served for many years thereafter as Baranov's interpreter to American and British sea captains. The manager of New Archangel's shipyard was an American named Lincoln. Baranov's chief navigator was a naturalized American citizen of Prussian birth named Benzeman, whom O'Cain had brought to Russian-America. Boston captains supplied food to the colony and also provided the chief means of transporting the Russian goods to foreign markets.[32] Even the board of directors of the Russian-American Company in St. Petersburg had an American director—Benedict Kramer, Jr., representative in Russia of the American banking firm of Kramer, Smith and Co.[33]

Yankee presence in the Russian colony may have provided false hopes for some would-be Russian revolutionaries. In the summer of 1809, when nine Russian conspirators formed a revolutionary society, they expected the American citizens working for the company to join with them out of republican sympathy. They planned to kill Baranov and other officials and then sail to Easter Island to establish an American-type republic. The plotters were disappointed; the Yankees were too busy making profits to worry about revolutionary plots.[34]

Yankee influence was at its height in 1810 when Captain Vasilli Golovnin arrived in New Archangel as the commander of the first Russian war vessel ever to visit the Russian-American colony. As a military man, Golovnin was appalled at what he saw. He reported to his government that the Americans were about to take over the Russian possessions. Golovnin's fears were reinforced by the return from Canton of John Jacob Astor's agent, Captain John Ebbets, in the ship *Enterprise* (May 1811). Golovnin reported that Astor intended to seize Russian-America. The Russian captain wrote to his superiors that Ebbets was "told to obtain most minute details of the trade and conditions of the Russian colonies, their strength and means of protection, the actual power of Baranov and the relations between the company and the government." To Golovnin, only one conclusion could be drawn: "In brief, Astor wished to ascertain the feasibility of a seizure of the colonies by the United States."[35] That such a conclusion may have been absurd should not obscure Golovnin's belief in what he wrote. Moreover, the board of directors in St. Petersburg was not apt to ignore such a warning.

Golovnin's warning, Rezanov's earlier reports, and the growing American presence convinced the board and the government that something must be done before the Americans posed an even more serious threat to the colony's existence. In a memorandum to Alexander I on December 18, 1811, the governing board stated its problem: "It is impossible to ward off this danger except by issuing a determined warning to the North American navigators who, by reason of the spirit and liberty embodied in their constitution and the freedom to sail and do business wherever and however one pleases, will not heed any suggestions." The American penetration of the Columbia by John Jacob Astor's agents, reported the governing board, had intensified American competition. The board hoped the czar "will not allow . . . any further interference with Russian business on the part of private North American hucksters." The directors repeated the old charges that the Yankees were selling arms to the Indians. Astor, they alleged, and "other unmanageable fellow countrymen" were out "to crush every opportunity for [the Russians] developing more trade and to violate to all intents and purposes the tranquillity of the colonies."[36]

The Russian government, which since 1808 had tried unsuccessfully to get the United States government to sign a convention recognizing Russian sovereignty in the Pacific Northwest, knew it could do little or nothing to stop the American penetration. Minister of the Interior O. P. Kozodavlev, replying to the board's memorandum, argued this was not the proper occasion to alienate the American government. He noted that if Russia tried to use force (which seemed to be what the board was urging), a diplomatic break would most probably ensue and the Russian-American Company then would have more to worry about than American merchants. When Dashkov, the Russian chargé in the United States, heard about the board's memorandum, he proposed that the Russian-American Company try to use peaceful methods to settle the problems with the Yankees.[37]

At Dashkov's suggestion, on May 20, 1812, a four-year agreement with John Jacob Astor's American Fur Company was signed in St. Petersburg by the Russian company. Astor pledged not to engage in trade in the territory belonging to the Russian-American Company. In return, he would exclusively supply the Russian colonies with all the provisions they needed and transport all Russian furs to Canton in his own ships. The American company further pledged not to join with any other American merchants engaged in hunting or trading in the Russian-American colonies.[38]

IV

Dashkov's support for cooperation with Astor's fur company was the result of four years of intensive planning by the American fur magnate. By 1808, Astor had found that a quasimonopoly by the Canadian North West Company forced him to reimport many furs that had been trapped within the boundaries of the United States but had passed through Montreal. Astor believed he could establish a range of trading posts along the route Lewis and Clark had taken from St. Louis to the Pacific Ocean. This, he hoped, would undercut his British competitors. He was convinced the United States government would find it advantageous to aid him, because his company could attach hostile Indians to the American cause by means of commerce. His would be a permanent institution, finding it beneficial, he argued, to deal fairly with the Indians. Astor desired a monopoly for his company and thought that, given the benefits he would extend to the United States, an official monopoly would be a small price for the government to pay.[39]

He enlisted the support of Governor De Witt Clinton of New York,[40] who urged President Jefferson to consider the proposal.[41] Writing to Jefferson on February 27, 1808, Astor represented his proposed company as a great patriotic endeavor.[42] President Jefferson, on April 13, gave his blessing to the project. Jefferson, unlike Astor, envisioned many companies of American nationals engaging in the trade. Nevertheless, he assured Astor that in order to secure the fur trade in "the hands of our citizens and to oust foreign traders . . . every reasonable patronage and facility in the power of the Executive will be afforded."[43] The New York legislature, eager to cooperate, granted Astor a charter on April 6, 1808. The charter, granted to the "American Fur Company," noted the patriotic motives of the organization and stressed that no individual or unincorporated association could carry out the company's purpose. The American Fur Company was incorporated for a twenty-five-year period and allowed to issue a capital stock of one million dollars for two years, after which the total value of the stock could be doubled.[44]

Jefferson's enthusiasm for the project grew. On July 17, 1808, he wrote to Meriwether Lewis, who was now serving as governor of the Missouri Territory, instructing him to give his "particular attention" to Astor and the American Fur Company. Jefferson made it clear to Lewis that Astor's plan to monopolize the commerce of the Indian tribes from St. Louis to the Pacific was essential to further American expansion, for "nothing but the exclusive possession of the Indian commerce can secure us their peace."[45]

While Jefferson may have favored Astor's plans, his other policies retarded the American Fur Company's progress. The embargo, for example, prevented Astor from going any further in 1809 than the planning stages of sending one ship to the Northwest Coast to secure the Indian trade there.[46]

While Astor's plan remained landlocked, Dashkov, the Russian chargé, was on his way to the United States, carrying with him instructions to protest to the American government the practices of American traders who sold arms and ammunition to the Indians of the Northwest Coast. Astor soon learned of Dashkov's mission. Not one to miss an opportunity, Astor suggested to him an agreement between his American Fur Company and the Russian-American Company. Astor's company would supply the Russians with all the articles they needed and would not deal with the Indians near the Russian settlements. The Russians, for their part, would no longer trade with the transient Americans and would promise not to trade with the Indians near the settlement Astor planned to found at the mouth of the Columbia River. Dashkov readily accepted Astor's plan.[47] He believed he had discovered a way out of the dilemma that plagued American–Russian relations in the Pacific Northwest. If the United States government could not control its traders, perhaps, thought Dashkov, Astor could do the job.[48]

On November 7, 1809, Dashkov sent Astor a letter of introduction, which Astor's agent, Captain John Ebbets, could present to Baranov when he arrived in the Russian colony. Dashkov assured Astor: "I cannot tell you how much I wish to see the trade of furs in Canton only in the hands of both you and Mr. Baranoff." He added, "it is a a [sic] matter of no small importance . . . to put the adventurers on these Northwest Coasts out of their [the Russian company's] way."[49] The Russian consul had been instructed to stop Americans from trading freely in the Russian possessions; nothing in his instructions prohibited him from using one American to stop another American.

On November 15, 1809, the *Enterprise,* and Captain John Ebbets, left for New Archangel. Ebbets, who had been trading on the Northwest Coast since 1801, knew Baranov and was chosen by Astor for that reason. The *Enterprise* arrived in New Archangel on November 15, 1810. Two days later, the Russian sloop *Diana,* captained by Vasili Golovnin, rested anchor in the New Archangel harbor. Ebbets soon took the *Enterprise* to Canton to trade furs he acquired from Baranov, and he returned in May 1811.[50] Throughout this period, Golovnin grew more and more suspicious of what he believed to be the United States' plan to seize the Russian-American colony. Golovnin's suspicions were not lessened, even when he learned that Dashkov had given his full support to the Astor enterprise.[51]

Baranov, unlike Golovnin, had no fear that dealing with the Astor company would result in the seizure of the Russian Pacific Northwest colonies. Baranov nevertheless remained unsure that dealing with Astor would be more advantageous than trading contracts with the transient American captains. The Russian governor also desired to retire and was hesitant to make a long-term contract without the approval of the directors. He finally made no decision at all. Writing to Astor, even before the *Enterprise* returned from Canton, Baranov suggested, "Mr. Dashkov should write to the directors of the company at St. Petersbourg [*sic*]."[52]

Prior to receiving Baranov's letter, Astor resolved to move more quickly to effect an alliance with the Russian-American Company. He sent his son-in-law, Adrian B. Bentzon, to Washington, D.C., in the summer of 1810 to win over the newly arrived Russian minister to the United States, Count Frederick Pahlen.[53] Pahlen, like Dashkov, was instructed to express his dissatisfaction over the failure of the American government to take any action with respect to the continuing protests by the Russian government against the conduct of Yankee traders in the Pacific Northwest. Pahlen complained to Bentzon that he had "from the American Government received nothing but vague and general expressions of friendly disposition."[54]

For Bentzon, the minister's concern about the influx of Yankee adventurers was a perfect opener, especially since Pahlen "was convinced of the impossibility of effecting anything with this government [United States]." He assured Pahlen that Astor's plan of exclusive cooperation between the American Fur Company and the Russian-American Company would achieve through commercial dealing what diplomacy had thus far failed to accomplish. Astor's program, Bentzon argued, would put an end to the unwanted American traders along the coasts of Russian-America. Pahlen no doubt realized that if he could settle the one outstanding dispute between the United States and Russia in the first months of his mission, his career would be enhanced. He was, therefore, easily convinced by Bentzon of the feasibility of Astor's enterprise. The Russian envoy told Bentzon that while official arrangements for the contract would have to be made in St. Petersburg with the directors of the Russian-American Company and with the minister of foreign affairs, Count Rumiantsev, he would recommend to the company and the foreign ministry that a contract with the American Fur Company be signed. He gave Bentzon private letters of introduction to persons who might be of aid in influencing the concerned parties at the Russian capital.[55]

Astor wanted to make Bentzon's journey to St. Petersburg seem as official as possible, and, to that end, he requested Secretary of the Treasury Albert Gallatin to permit Bentzon to sail on the United States frigate *John Adams*. The *John Adams* was about to leave for Europe on an official voyage carrying George Erving, a special minister sent to Denmark by President Madison to press United States spoliation claims against that country. In the course of making this request, Astor mentioned to Gallatin "that in case of non-renewal of the charter of the Bank of U.S., all his [Astor's] funds and those of his friends to the amount of two million dollars would be at the command of the Gov't." Gallatin suggested to President Madison that they accept the "offer."[56] Madison, who only four months before had refused to give Astor's projects "official patronage" because "it would be a perplexing precedent, and incur the charge of partiality . . . ,"[57] now reversed himself and agreed to allow Bentzon passage on the *John Adams*.[58]

In March 1811, Bentzon was off to St. Petersburg on the *John*

Adams. Astor instructed him to point out to the Russians that the Russian establishments continued to be "exposed to serious dangers" from hostile Indians who were able to obtain "implements of war from citizens of the United States, who *transiently* trade with them." Since the United States government refused to curb these "transient traders," the solution, proclaimed Astor, was for the Russian-American Company to join in contract with the American Fur Company in order to drive the unwanted traders out.[59]

Bentzon could not have presented his case to Rumiantsev at a better time. After three years of negotiations with the United States government over the Yankee traders in the Pacific Northwest, the Russian government found itself in the same position in which it had begun. Rezanov's and Golovnin's reports, as well as the petitions of the governing board, convinced Rumiantsev that if some action were not taken soon, the Americans would take Russia's colony by force or by attrition. Use of force against the American traders, as Interior Minister Kozodavlev told the board, might lead to a diplomatic break with the United States at a time when Russia needed the United States as a carrier of goods and a makeweight against British sea power. In the first months of 1812, the Russian government, which had tried to end dependence on American traders, signed a twenty-five-year agreement with John Jacob Astor, thereby officially making the Russian colony more dependent on the United States than ever before.[60] Astor would now be the exclusive supplier of provisions and transporter of all furs for the Russian company. By recognizing the legitimacy of the American Fur Company's settlement on the Columbia River, Astoria, the Russians were, moreover, giving de facto recognition to future American territorial claims in the Pacific Northwest.

Astor's scheme was interrupted on June 18, 1812, when the United States declared war on Great Britain. The War of 1812 brought an almost complete halt to the maritime affairs on the Northwest Coast. The North West Company of Canada, the rival that Astor had worked so hard to exclude from the North Pacific trade, actively sought its government's aid in driving the Americans out of the Columbia River region. Late in 1812, the Canadian *Racoon,* a twenty-gun ship, was fitted out in London for a voyage whose purpose was to make Astoria a British possession. But on October 16, 1814, before the *Racoon* arrived, Duncan Mc Dougall (who was in charge of Astoria) sold the rights to Astoria to the North West Company. Mc Dougall knew of the imminent arrival of the British war vessel and decided that a sale was more profitable than a surrender. Astoria had not been supplied by the American Fur Company since early 1812 because of the war, and even if the North West Company and the British navy did not threaten its existence, Mc Dougall and his men would have been forced to abandon the settlement by the end of 1814. Astor's contract with the Russians was a prime victim of the war with Great Britain.[61]

Aside from Astor's vessels, there were many other American ships along the Pacific Northwest Coast when the war broke out. Baranov quickly let it be known that he was in the market to lease or buy the American ships and hire their captains and crews. All would be safe under the Russian-American Company flag. American sea captains quickly responded to Baranov's call. By the end of 1813, the Russian-American Company had leased or bought seven American vessels. Within the next year, it acquired more vessels. The sea otter poaching along the Spanish-American coast continued, but now the flag on the masts of the American ships was that of the Russian-American Company. For the duration of the war, however, the sea otter furs could not be sold at Canton because Russian ships were not allowed to trade there, and no sane captain would fly the American flag while the environs of Canton were patrolled by British warships.[62]

V

By 1812, a firm Yankee commercial interest had been established in the Russian possessions of North America. The valuable sea otter trade of the Northwest Coast that had begun in the 1790s was dominated by Boston firms. The British takeover of Astoria did not change that situation. The North West Company was not interested in supplying the Russians and was proscribed by its charter from trading with China. Astor's contract had never gone into effect anyhow. The Boston firms that Astor planned to supplant in the Pacific Northwest continued to dominate the Russian-American trade. The Russian company depended upon the Yankees not only for the shipment of furs to Canton but also for its very sustenance. This reliance upon United States citizens for Russian-America's survival became a constant source of irritation for the board of the Russian-American Company in St. Petersburg. Try as it might, the Russian government found no way to dislodge the omnipresent Yankee. The frictions of this early period were to continue for the next half century. By the late 1850s, the enterprise of United States citizens in Russian-America had grown to such proportions that the imperial government realized that a viable Russian possession in North America was no longer feasible. Rezanov's and Golovnin's early warnings were to prove prophetic.

2

The Czar's Ukase

When the war ended in 1815, the old Northwest Coast maritime fur trade resumed. After several attempts to reestablish Astoria, John Jacob Astor gave up the project at the end of 1816. Astoria was returned to the United States' sovereignty on October 6, 1818. The trading post, however, remained in the hands of the British North West Company.[1] With the demise of Astoria as an American trading center, the American Fur Company's contract with the Russian-American Company became a worthless piece of paper. Nevertheless, Astor's agents continued to participate in the sea otter trade, and Astor hoped to reenter the competition for landed peltries with the aid, this time, of a federal presence.

Interested only in trapping landed furs along the Columbia, the British North West Company did not interfere with the American maritime fur trade along the Northwest Coast. The British company also made no attempt to sell supplies to the Russian company. Thus, the maritime trade and commerce with Russian-America remained an exclusive Yankee enterprise, while the British retained the landed peltry trade of the area along the Columbia River. The situation in the Pacific Northwest after the War of 1812 returned substantially to what it had been before the war, with the Russians complaining as loudly as ever about Yankee plunderers. A new element, however, seemed to make matters even more threatening to Russian perceptions.

In the United States Congress, discussions and resolutions demanding the protection of American citizens pursuing the fur
trade in the Pacific Northwest were presented. In these debates,
the opinion that Russia ought to be curbed from further expansion
in North America began to crop up, with what seemed to the
Russians to be alarming frequency. This view was especially prev-
alent in the speeches of Congressman John Floyd of Virginia,
who, with his allies, often pointed to the American maritime fur
trade along the Northwest Coast as an interest worth protecting
against Russian monopoly practices. Moreover, Floyd and
Thomas Hart Benton of Missouri urged the United States government to extend protection to future settlers and landed fur
traders in the Pacific Northwest. These men presented the landed
and the maritime peltry trade as complementary parts of the same
interest. For enterprises such as those envisioned by John Jacob
Astor, the landed and maritime trade were one, but, for most of
the Boston traders, this was not the case. Floyd and Benton were
able to bring about an alliance between these two types of traders
on the issue of protection of Americans in the Pacific Northwest.
When the Russian government, already disturbed by the incursions of Yankee traders, discovered that United States congressmen urged protection for American traders in and near
Russian-America, they reacted strongly. In 1821, Czar Alexander
issued a ukase excluding foreigners from Russian-America. This
ukase was as much a response to the sentiments expressed in
Congress as it was to the Yankees trading in North America.

I

In 1815, the Northwest Coast fur trade resumed with vigor. By
the end of that year, ten American vessels had reached Sitka. In
the next six years, ninety-six additional Yankee trading ships
arrived in Russian-America. In 1822, before the ukase was officially delivered to the United States government, eighteen
American vessels, all but one from Boston, traded for furs in
Russian-America.[2]
Boston firms led the postwar trade, but other eastern ports,

such as New York, Philadelphia, and Providence, supplied ships engaged in this trade. The firms that dominated the maritime fur trade were mainly the same ones that had grown rich on it before 1812: Bryant and Sturgis, J. and T. H. Perkins, Boardman and Pope, and Josiah Marshall. John Jacob Astor also owned a considerable number of the vessels participating in this enterprise.[3]

While exact figures are difficult to produce, one can obtain a fair idea of the value of the Northwest Coast trade from the value of the Canton trade. During these years, the amount of nonspecie items Americans traded at Canton averaged $2.5 million.[4] Most of the nonspecie items exchanged for Canton goods were Northwest Coast furs and Hawaiian sandalwood, which the Yankee traders picked up on their way to Canton from Russian-America.[5] In the years preceding the Russian ukase, the number of American vessels trading along the Russian-American coast increased, as did the value of furs traded by United States nationals in Canton.[6] This was significant because, in the years 1819–1821, one might expect a decline in American trade in the Pacific Northwest due to the 1819 depression. While the total United States trade at Canton fell by almost a half in 1820, the decline was the result of a decrease in the specie trade and not a falling off in the volume of Northwest Coast products sold in China. In 1819, American traders spent $7.4 million of specie at Canton. In 1820, the amount of specie exchanged fell to $2.9 million. During the same period, the value of furs and sandalwood fell only $500,000, from $2.8 to $2.3 million.[7] The decline in the value of furs sold at Canton in 1820 was probably due more to the number available in Russian-America than to the national economic situation because more Yankee vessels participated in the Northwest Coast trade in 1820 than in 1819.[8]

While the maritime fur trade had quickly resumed its previous pace at the end of the war, landed peltry trading had been temporarily eclipsed by the closing of Astoria. By 1818, the traders and trappers of the British North West Company were the sole white occupants of the territory between 42° and 55° latitude. On October 20, 1818, the United States and Great Britain signed a convention which provided that the territory west of the Stony

(Rocky) Mountains claimed by either power would remain "free and open to the vessels, citizens, and subjects of both for the space of ten years." To many associated with the Pacific Northwest fur trade, this treaty smacked of a sell-out of American interests in that quarter of the continent. Thomas Hart Benton, then editor and owner of the *St. Louis Enquirer,* bitterly denounced Secretary of State John Quincy Adams for negotiating this treaty. St. Louis, the center of the overland fur trade to the northwest, had been the starting point for Lewis and Clark fourteen years before. John Jacob Astor had planned his land route to Astoria, commencing from St. Louis. Benton saw himself as a spokesman for the overland fur trade. Indeed, he retained close personal and political ties to Astor. Benton's election to the United States Senate in 1820 was due in no small part to Astor's aid.[9] Benton strongly supported the Pacific Northwest peltry business as vital to the growth of the nation and believed the absence of overland fur traders in the Northwest to be a temporary phenomenon. The Monroe administration's policies, he argued, could prevent the inevitable return of this trade. Instead of cooperation with Britain in the Pacific Northwest, Benton urged the national government to set up "an American Fur Company, headed by men of enterprise," in order to "sap at its foundation the solid pillar of British wealth and power [in America]." With the support of the government, he averred, the commerce of the country could be funneled along Lewis and Clark's trail up the Missouri and down the Columbia and then on to China and India via the Pacific.[10]

When Senator-elect Benton arrived in Washington in 1820, he boarded at Brown's Hotel. Two of John Jacob Astor's agents, Ramsey Crooks of New York and Russell Farnham of Massachusetts, also lived at Brown's. Both men had been employed in the Astoria enterprise. Crooks and Farnham now served as a Washington-based lobby for Astor,[11] who, like his friend Benton, feared that measures like the 1818 convention with Great Britain were a step toward surrender of the American landed peltry trade in the Pacific Northwest. Astor, a participant in the revived maritime trade, retained visions of capturing the landed fur trade

in the Pacific Northwest. Having given up the idea of reestablish-
ing Astoria as a private settlement, he and his agents desired that
the federal government take a stronger hand in protecting American fur trading interests in the Pacific Northwest. Astor, Benton,
Crooks, and Farnham hoped to persuade Congress to authorize a
federal occupation of Oregon and thus avoid the problems that
plagued Astoria. With official United States presence in the Columbia River region, the landed and maritime fur traders could
rely upon their government to protect them against the British
and Russian companies if the need arose.[12]

In 1820, Congressman John Floyd of Virginia also moved into
Brown's Hotel. Floyd, elected to Congress from Virginia in 1817,
served in the House for the next twelve years. He led the Virginia
delegation during most of this time and in 1830 became governor
of Virginia. Dr. Floyd had long been aware of the value of the
Pacific Northwest. His friendship with William Clark (of Lewis
and Clark) dated back to his youth.[13] Floyd soon established an
intimate friendship with Benton, Crooks, and Farnham, who had
been searching for someone in the House to argue the Astor line.
Floyd seemed the perfect person. The four reinforced one
another's views on the value of the Northwest Coast trade. Floyd
told Benton that he had read the Missouri Senator's essays on the
subject the year before and fully embraced Benton's position.[14]

Floyd resolved to bring the question of America's position in
the Pacific Northwest to the floor of Congress. On December 19,
1820, a committee of three was appointed, with Floyd as its
chairman to report on the subject. (Thomas Metcalfe of Kentucky
and Thomas V. Swearingen of Virginia were the other two members.) Within six days, Floyd's committee reported a bill "to
authorize the occupation of the Columbia River and to regulate
trade and intercourse with the Indian tribes thereon." The bill
contained a rather elaborate report in support of the measure.
The committee noted that the advantages to such a proposal
would not be limited to aiding the fur trade and the preservation
of American territory but also would support America's "Asiatic
trade." Floyd warned that America must act quickly, for Britain
was not America's only enemy in the Pacific Northwest: "Rus-

sia . . . has long been well informed of the great and increasing value of that [Asiatic] commerce." Russian "forts, magazines, towns, cities, and trade, seem to arise . . . as if by magic." The czar "with an army of a million of men not only . . . menaces the Turk, the Persian, the Japanese, the Chinese, but even the King of Spain's dominions in North America." Floyd warned that Russia's expansion had extended even to the occupation of one of the Sandwich Islands, and soon Russia would "command the whole northern part of the Pacific Ocean." Such action, he noted, formed a direct threat to America's China trade.[15] The House ignored the bill, and nothing more was heard about it during that session. Benton, however, believed that Floyd's bill was "the first blow . . . struck: public attention was awakened, and the geographical, historical, and statistical facts set forth in the report, made a lodgment in the public mind which promised eventual favorable consideration."[16]

On January 26, 1821, Senator Jonathan Eaton of Tennessee sent the *National Intelligencer* a letter from the merchant and adventurer William David Robinson urging the government to establish a settlement along the North Pacific coast to offset the encroachments of the Russians.[17] Within a few days, Commodore David Porter disclosed that in October 1815 he had urged President Madison to send a combined naval and military expedition to the area.[18] Porter's original letter was now signed by over three hundred "concerned" Americans and forwarded to President Monroe as a "memorial."[19]

II

Benton argued that Floyd's report aroused public attention. The report, particularly its anti-Russian tenor, also awakened the Russian government to the possibility of a renewed American thrust in the Pacific Northwest, and this time with possible governmental support. Pierre de Poletica, the Russian minister to the United States since 1818, informed his minister for foreign affairs, Count Karl Nesselrode, that in the past "the curiosity of the Americans about the northwest coast of America and about our settlements in that wild region attained a degree of intensity that truly amazed me." Poletica complained of "private individuals" who often came to his residence demanding information about the Russian activities in Northwest America. Yet, he apologized, he had refrained until now from submitting reports of these "instances of political madness" because he "noticed no disposition on the part of the American government to preoccupy itself seriously" with the Russian settlements. Poletica now warned his government that "all this may radically change, especially now when Congress is preoccupied with those settlements."[20]

Poletica's report added weight to the constant pleas of the governing board of the Russian-American Company that the Russian government to do something about the increasing American penetration of Russian-America. In 1817, the board submitted to the czar a draft of proposed regulations to be imposed upon foreign vessels touching Russian-American shores. The directors, who personally stood to make a large profit if they could supplant United States citizens as the company's supplier of necessities, compared the Russian-American ports with those of the Baltic, noting that they required the same type of protection. The directors raised the old cry against the American traders: United States citizens were procuring animal furs from the natives by selling firearms and gun powder to them, and, to make matters worse, Americans were "teaching them how to use them, to the detriment of our hunters." The directors also complained, perhaps more to the point, that the Yankees set "such low prices" on their goods that the same articles sent from Russia "are much more expensive" to the Russian settlement because of the high cost of transportation through Siberia to Okhotsk.[21]

The situation in the Russian colony was complicated by the fact that the charter granting the Russian-American Company authority in North America was to expire in 1819. The imperial navy desired to replace the company directors as the ruling agency for the American colonies. Captain Vasilli Golovnin, now a member of the state council, charged with advising the governing board on political matters and a strong advocate of naval control of Russian-America, made his second voyage to the colony in

1817–1819. Upon his return to Russia in 1819, he wrote an extensive report on the conditions of the Russian possession. He feared, as he had during his first voyage nine years before, that the United States was about to seize Russian-America. The Yankees, who had complete freedom of movement within the colony, seemed to be everywhere. Despite repeated requests from his imperial majesty's government, the United States government had not restrained the traffic of illegal firearms. Instead of diminishing, this illicit trade continued to grow. Golovnin believed the reason for this refusal was the American intention to make allies of the natives in order to drive the Russians out. Because of the tremendous proportions that trade had assumed in Russian-America, it was necessary to take vigorous and decisive steps to protect the possessions from foreign penetration. The Anglo-American Convention of 1818, allowing joint occupation of Great Britain and the United States from 42° north latitude to 55° north latitude, would only serve to increase the interest of Yankee business circles in the Russian possessions. Golovnin advised the Russian government to act quickly to save Russian-America from imminent peril. He suggested that warships be sent immediately to patrol the waters along the parts of the Northwest Coast that Russia claimed. In the future, he concluded, all foodstuffs should be supplied from Fort Ross and all other commodities by around-the-world shipments from the homeland.[22]

Golovnin's arguments, Poletica's reports, and history convinced the Russian ministry of foreign affairs, as well as the czar, that this was indeed a time for action. From now on, globe-circling expeditions would supply the company. Matvei Muraviev, the new governor of Russian-America, received instructions in 1820 to prepare for a full-scale trade ban with the United States. Golovnin was made a virtual dictator at the company headquarters in St. Petersburg. His first act was to change the southern boundary of the company's charter from 55° to 51° north latitude. The czar's Senate ratified this measure in September 1821. Simultaneously, three Russian war sloops were sent to patrol the Pacific Northwest waters north of 51°.[23]

On September 16, 1821, Czar Alexander I issued an imperial

ukase, which closed the entire area along the Northwest Coast of America. He proclaimed that "from Behring Straits to 51° northern latitude" (including the Aleutian Islands to the eastern coast of Siberia) was "exclusively" Russian territory, and, therefore, "the pursuits of commerce, whaling, and fishery, and all other industry" there were closed to all foreigners. Second, Alexander claimed that the Russian territorial waters in that region extended for a hundred miles. Any foreign vessel that transgressed these waters, the ukase warned, "is subject to confiscation along with the whole cargo." Nine days later, Alexander issued a second ukase renewing the charter of the Russian-American Company for twenty years and reaffirming the southern boundary of the colony as 51° north latitude. This ukase also authorized the company "to annex . . . newly discovered places to Russian dominion" south of the fifty-first parallel, "provided they have not been occupied by any other European nation, or by citizens of the United States."[24]

In his September 16 ukase, Alexander explained that such a measure was necessary "because of secret and illicit traffic" of foreigners along Russia's Northwest Coast. The czar noted his deep concern over "reports submitted to us," meaning, of course, those of Poletica and Golovnin.[25] Although the Russians had often complained about British activities in the Pacific Northwest, the ukase was clearly aimed at United States citizens. A circular Minister of Foreign Affairs Nesselrode sent to all Russian ambassadors and ministers abroad on October 7, 1821, explained that the ukase had to be issued because "foreign adventurers and smugglers" have continually participated in "fraudulent trade in furs and other articles exclusively reserved for the Russian-American Company." Worse than this, Nesselrode pointed out, these traders "appear often to betray a hostile tendency" since they "come and furnish arms and ammunition to the natives in our possessions," exciting them to "resistance and rebellion" against Russian authority.[26]

Along with this circular, the foreign minister sent Poletica a separate letter (sent to none of the other ministers) noting that the provisions of the ukase concerned "new regulations [which] have been principally motivated by the culpable endeavors of several American sailors . . . and it is against these individuals especially that it was judged necessary here to adopt prohibitive measures." Nesselrode also revealed that the Russian government was keenly concerned with Floyd's report calling for American action to offset Russian expansion in the Pacific. Poletica was instructed to pay "particular attention to the report of the committee charged with reporting to the Congress on the existing establishments on the coast of the Pacific Ocean."[27] Sir Charles Bagot, the British ambassador in St. Petersburg, informed his government that Nesselrode assured him the ukase was not aimed in any way at Great Britain. Nesselrode "told me," reported Bagot, "that the object of the measure was to prevent the 'commerce interlope' of the citizens of the United States." American citizens, Nesselrode complained, resorted to Russian-America "for the purpose of interfering in their [Russia's] trade with China in the lucrative article of sea-otter skins."[28]

III

While the United States government was not officially informed of the ukase until February 1822, reports of its promulgation had reached the United States by the time the Seventeenth Congress reconvened in December 1821.[29] As soon as the Congress was underway, Congressman Floyd made a motion requesting that a committee be appointed "to inquire into the expediency" of occupying the Columbia River in order to regulate the trade of the United States along the Northwest Coast of America. A committee was appointed consisting of Floyd (as chairman), Francis Baylies of Massachusetts, and John Scott of Missouri.[30] The choice of Baylies and Scott for this committee showed how careful the House was in balancing the various interest groups concerned with the Pacific Northwest. Baylies, whose constituency included the ports of Nantucket and New Bedford, represented the maritime fur trading interests, which centered in his home state, while Scott represented the landed fur traders. Baylies, wishing to make it clear to the Russians and the British as well that the United States would brook no interference with its commerce in that area, submitted a resolution on December 17, 1821, requesting the Secretary of the Navy to report to the House the cost of "transporting artillery to the mouth of the Columbia River." The measure was unanimously passed.[31]

On January 18, 1822, the committee submitted its report, which was substantially a reiteration of Floyd's report of the year before urging the United States to occupy the Pacific Northwest before the Russians took over the entire area. This time Floyd added, as a preface, the request Baylies had made the month before requiring the Secretary of War to report to the Congress the cost of shipping armaments to the Northwest Coast.[32] The committee's report contained a bill, which returned to the floor for debate in December 1822. Meanwhile, the czar's ukase was officially delivered to the United States government on February 11, 1822.

On February 16, 1822, in an effort to demonstrate to the House the necessity of hastening action on his committee's bill, Floyd resolved that the President be required to submit to the Congress information as to "whether any foreign Government has made a claim on any part of the territory of the United States on the Pacific Ocean." Floyd noted that "the Russian Government laid a claim, it appeared, to a considerable part of the territory on the coast which belonged to the United States." He labeled the claim "erroneous," warning "that the Emperor of Russia had forgotten the cautious policy which had characterized him heretofore." Such a claim, Floyd hastened to add, "would be resisted by any country." The Congress agreed by unanimously endorsing Floyd's resolution.[33]

Secretary of State John Quincy Adams and President James Monroe were slow to respond to the House's call for correspondence on the subject, not wishing to have Congress lose by bluster what Adams might gain by diplomacy. President Monroe's report did not reach the House until April, and by then Adams was well on the way to backing the Russians down.[34] Nothing, however, could convince Floyd that the administration was either willing or capable of securing the Pacific Northwest for American commerce. When the debate on his committee's bill reached the floor of the House of Representatives in December 1822, Floyd's opening salvo was aimed as much at John Quincy Adams as at the Russians.

Speaking first in the debate, Floyd proclaimed that the wealth of the Northwest Coast surpassed "the hopes even of avarice itself." The primary value of the Northwest trade, he noted, "consists principally of things which will purchase the products of China at a better profit than gold and silver." This was an important argument to a nation that had prospered on commerce—especially in the China trade—but could not afford any further specie drain after the 1819 panic. Attacking Secretary of State Adams, Floyd pictured the 1818 convention, which Adams had negotiated, as eventually ceding American claims west of the Rocky Mountains. While the British government aided its traders in the Pacific Northwest, the United States government, he lamented, did nothing. Yet, he pointed out, the United States possessed a better continental route as well as better ports along its East Coast from which to send ships to the Northwest Coast. The recent merger of the British North West Company with the Hudson's Bay Company, warned Floyd, would serve to put American fur traders at an even worse disadvantage.[35]

Floyd argued that a great future for the United States commercial economy rested upon American actions in the Pacific Northwest. Citing customs reports, Floyd demonstrated that the "finest" whaling grounds had shifted from along the coast of South America to the Pacific Northwest. "This trade [whaling]," he averred, "at no distant day, is destined to employ many individuals, and to contribute largely to the wealth of the territory of Oregon." To Nantucket and New Bedford alone, whaling was worth $6 million annually. Floyd pointed out that the United States–China trade (at Canton) in the years 1818–1819 was valued at $10.2 million. While much of that trade was in products of the Northwest Coast, too much of it relied on specie, causing a harmful drain on the American economy. If the United States government were to establish a settlement along the Northwest Coast (especially at the mouth of the Columbia), more United States traders could obtain the valuable peltries of the Northwest Coast to trade at Canton and thus the drain of specie would be lessened. If, on the other hand, nothing were done, American traders would be able to obtain an ever-diminishing number of furs to sell in Canton because Russia and Great Britain would build their outposts along the coasts. The resultant specie loss would do irreparable damage to the American economy. The United States must act soon by making some show of force in the Pacific Northwest. Floyd suggested quickly sending "one hundred and fifty tons of cannon to the mouth" of the Columbia River.[36]

Congressman Robert Wright of Maryland spoke next in favor of the bill. Repeating Floyd's statements about the value of the Northwest Coast to United States commerce and trade, Wright added that this trade would even be more valuable when "the union of the Atlantic with the Pacific, at the Isthmus of Darien," was consummated. Wright was angered by "the preposterous claims of Russia to the vicinage of the Columbia" and hoped this threat "will induce them [the House] to pass the Bill."[37]

Francis Baylies of Massachusetts demonstrated, even more graphically than Floyd, the great value of whale fishery in the Pacific Northwest. He read a letter from the collector of customs at New Bedford, who claimed that the annual profit to New Bedford whalers from the Pacific Northwest fisheries amounted to $500,000. An American settlement along the Northwest Coast would be of immense value to the whaling industry. Baylies presented other correspondence attesting to the great worth of whaling in that area.[38]

Baylies anticipated the arguments of those who would criticize American expansion to the Pacific Northwest as leading to the dismemberment of the nation because the nation then would comprise too large an area. Like Madison in *Federalist* number 10, Baylies noted (giving Madison no credit) that "by multiplying and extending the states of the Union, you will create so many different interests that they will neutralize each other." Besides, he pointed out, now that "the Emperor of Russia had claimed all the Northwest Coast down to the fifty-first degree of North Latitude, and one hundred Italian miles south of that, . . . this measure [Floyd's bill] is one, not of expediency, but of necessity." The Russian claim was "of a character so monstrous that no people in their senses can admit it." Moreover, Baylies noted, "the foundations of some of the most princely fortunes in Boston, were laid in that [Northwest Coast] trade." If colonization increased America's wealth, and Baylies believed it would, then America should colonize the Pacific Northwest.[39]

More interesting in logic were those who spoke against the bill. Starling Tucker of South Carolina objected to the establishment of an American post on the Pacific Northwest because it would draw off population from the other areas of the nation. Besides, Tucker argued, the Pacific Northwest would eventually be United States territory, for "we cannot arrest the progress of our population to the west. . . . It marches on, with the increasing rapidity of a fire, and nothing will stop it until it reaches the shores of the Pacific." The congressman saw no reason to tamper with destiny. While Tucker "was aware of the great advantages of whale fisheries and the fur trade," he did not believe this trade needed protection since "there has been no document laid before the House to show that it is required, or even asked for." He admitted "if protection were required," he would vote for it.[40] Tucker, who opposed the establishment of a permanent American colony and sending of troops and armaments to the Pacific Northwest, was forced to admit, nonetheless, that whaling, fur trading, and the China trade made the area of prime value to the economic growth of the United States.

Floyd's bill was a clear attack on the Monroe administration's policy; it could even be construed as an attempt to usurp the administration's initiative. While many congressmen agreed with Floyd and his allies that something had to be done quickly to guarantee that the Pacific Northwest would not fall into the Russian domain, most favored diplomatic action instead of military threat.[41]

Of paramount importance in the debate was the ever-present political maneuvering for the 1824 presidential contest. Floyd, Benton, and their supporters were backers of Henry Clay for the presidency, and thus all attacks on the administration in general, and John Quincy Adams in particular, had the overtone of presidential politics. Realizing that his bill would not be passed in December, Floyd hoped to mobilize the antiadministration forces and obtained a postponement of further consideration of the bill until the second Monday in January 1823.[42] Floyd's forces and the Monroe administration regrouped, each eager to protect America's interest in the Pacific Northwest and each eager to claim credit for it.

If the Monroe administration would have liked to dismiss Floyd's attacks as partisan politics, it could not ignore other outcries for American action along the Northwest Coast. William Sturgis, of the influential Boston firm of Bryant and Sturgis, had made his fortune in the sea otter trade. In January and February 1822, Sturgis published a series of articles in the *Boston Daily Advertiser* on the importance of the North American Pacific Coast as far as 60° north latitude.[43] He disagreed with Floyd's view that the proper place for an American settlement was the mouth of the Columbia River. He thought a naval and military settlement farther north, perhaps at Port Discovery on the Fuca Strait, would be of more aid to American interests. Port Discovery was a superior harbor to the mouth of the Columbia. Sturgis strongly advocated some sort of American occupation along the Northwest Coast to prevent Russian or British domination of the region.[44]

In October 1822, the *North American Review* carried a long article Sturgis had written, entitled "Examination of Russian Claims to the Northwest Coast of America." In this article, Sturgis labeled the ukase one of "extraordinary character" designed "to monopolize commerce and usurp territory." He traced the history of trading along the Northwest Coast, describing it as predominantly the haunt of United States citizens. The Northwest trade was an integral part of the China trade and "too valuable to be quietly relinquished." He next examined, point by point, the validity of the Russian claims, which, according to Russian Minister Poletica, could be extended even to the forty-ninth parallel. Sturgis concluded the opposite; the Russian claims, he said, "must fall." All that the United States should "concede to Russia" were "the Aleutian Islands and the adjacent coast, including Cook's River, Prince William's Sound, and Behring's Bay." Even this, he argued, would be a "concession." Sturgis warned his readers that Russia's "ostensible object is, evidently, a monopoly of the fur trade." All of the valuable furs were found north of latitude 51°, and "if 'foreign adventurers' can be prevented from approaching that part of the coast, the company [Russian-American Company] would soon be left in undisturbed possession of the whole trade, for south of 51° is not of sufficient value to attract a single vessel in a season." The United States must reject all the Russian regulations: "If these usurpations are submitted to, it is improbable that a further use may be made of 'incontestable rights'?" Rhetorically, Sturgis asked whether the country wanted on its western frontiers "a formidable population, subjects of an ambitious and despotic government." "The Ukase appears," said Sturgis, "a little short of an actual declaration of hostilities." Those very American traders and captains about whom the ukase complained, he pointed out, were "engaged by contract with . . . the Russian Fur Company, in supplying their settlement with necessities and comforts of life. It is a perversion of language to call such a trade 'illicit.'" He concluded by dismissing as preposterous the Russian charges against American captains of selling arms to the Indians and inciting rebellion. Indian rebellions, he noted, were a result of the oppressive way in which the Russians treated the Indians under their control, and those natives who were independent of Russia could not properly be accused of revolution. [45]

Sturgis's article was later to become the document upon which the United States government based much of its case against the ukase. Secretary of State Adams thought Sturgis's position so well argued that he sent a copy of the article to the American minister in Russia, John Middleton, urging him to read it carefully. [46] The Russian consul in Philadelphia, Ivanov, sent Foreign Minister Nesselrode two copies of the article. [47]

The press quickly reacted to reports of the czar's ukase. On December 29, 1821, *Niles' Weekly Register* reprinted the parts of the ukase that claimed Russian territory extended to 51°, excluded all foreign trade, and claimed one-hundred-mile coastal waters for the Russian colony. The *Register* noted that the Russian actions there had precipitated movements in the House of Representatives to transport cannon to the mouth of the Columbia. "It is not impossible," added the journal, "that we may get into a dispute with Russia in regard to our claim to the jurisdiction of the country presumed to have been ceded by the Louisiana purchase, and since adjusted with Spain." Throughout the next year the *Register* continually referred to the Russian claims as usurpations. The journal pointed to "the importance of this subject to the United States, if merely in a commercial view" and "independent of any question of territorial rights which it may be thought to involve." On November 9, 1822, the *Register* reprinted excerpts from Sturgis's article in the *North American Review,* using it as evidence of the commercial importance of the Pacific Northwest to the United States.[48]

The *National Intelligencer,* on the other hand, reflecting the administration's hopes for a negotiated settlement, was more moderate in its initial response. The *Intelligencer* believed the Russian ukase was a response to Floyd's earlier report on the Pacific Northwest. While the newspaper agreed that the United States had a valid claim to the entire coastline up to the fifty-third parallel, it hoped the dispute would be settled amicably. "When Russia and the United States, fall out," concluded the *National Intelligencer,* "it will not be about anything so unimportant, we hope, as the nominal title to a degree or two of almost undiscovered land." By February 16, 1822, however, the *Intelligencer* began to agree with many other journals that the czar's regulations "may be of importance to our mercantile readers, particularly those interested in that trade."[49]

Other newspapers were more belligerent. The *Newburyport* (Rhode Island) *Herald* believed "the contest between that power [Russia] and our government will not be speedily settled." If all negotiation failed, the *Herald* suggested "the last resort would be had to gen. Jackson." The paper had no doubt that the Russians would get Jackson's message about American rights without lengthy negotiations.[50] The *Baltimore Chronicle* published a verse warning that Russian expansion to North America first took the land and now claimed four thousand miles of sea. If Jove does not protect his heavens, warned the poet, "The Russian will bury them all in his belly."[51]

IV

By 1822, the protection of American commercial interests along the Northwest Coast had become an important political issue. While domestic political factions accused each other of laxity in protecting United States' rights in the Pacific Northwest, the arguments centered more on tactics than upon policy goals. More important, the growth of American commerce in the Pacific Northwest emerged as a major point of diplomatic tension between the United States and Russia. The czar's attempt to exclude Yankees from the Northwest Coast, and the Monroe administration's reaction to it, set the bounds for American–Russian diplomatic disputes in the Pacific Northwest for the next forty-five years.

3

John Quincy Adams and the Northwest Coast

John Quincy Adams, Secretary of State in the Monroe administration, made it clear to the Russian government that the United
States government would never accept its ukase excluding
Americans from the Northwest Coast. The foreign ministry in St.
Petersburg soon realized that the American Secretary of State, as
well as the United States Congress and American traders, were
quite serious about their opposition to the ukase. In 1824, the
United States and Russia signed an agreement that, in effect,
abrogated the ukase. The Secretary of State successfully and
forcefully continued to demonstrate the two-decade-old American determination to maintain interests in the Pacific Northwest
and keep the Russian colony open to Yankee traders. More important, Adams prepared the way for the further penetration of
American trade, commerce, and whaling along the Northwest
Coast.

I

Adams had long been subjected to the attacks of westerners
(like Henry Clay and Thomas H. Benton) on his alleged preju-
dice against western needs. After Adams negotiated the 1819
Transcontinental Treaty with Spain, giving the United States a
firm foothold in the Pacific, Benton and Floyd (reputed to have

been Henry Clay's spokesmen on these matters) attacked his work as a sellout of western interests. They argued that this treaty gave up claims to Texas in return for land the United States had already received in the Louisiana purchase. The political undertones of western attacks on the Monroe administration and on John Quincy Adams should not be missed. Adams was convinced that Clay's opposition to Monroe's administration was the result of disappointed ambition.[1] Clay had wanted to be appointed Secretary of State, the stepping-stone to the presidency, and was disappointed at Monroe's selection of Adams.[2] As Speaker of the House, Clay attacked the Secretary of State's handling of foreign policy. He criticized the Adams-Onís treaty and offered a resolution in Congress denying the administration's right to sign away the nation's claims to Texas.[3]

Adams never viewed the attacks by Clay, Benton, and Floyd as anything other than partisan politics. He had long advocated a continental American empire stretching from sea to sea and had worked much of his life until 1821 to bring such an imperium into existence. Unlike many of his western critics, Adams wished to bring the American continental empire into existence without force. He believed such an empire was, in fact, providential and thus saw no need to resort to force to gain what the nation could acquire by patience. Such a view should not preclude the obvious fact that Adams, like his detractors, was also a political man bent on electoral aggrandizement and desirous of attaining the presidency in 1824. John Quincy Adams, however, did not separate his political aspirations from his world view, and one should therefore be careful in discussing Adams not to make such distinctions seem overriding. Simply put, Adams desired to bring to life the inevitable continental American empire, and he believed that in all the nation he was the most qualified to preside at its birth.[4]

In his view that America should extend from sea to sea, Adams had been consistent. As early as 1811, he had written from St. Petersburg that the United States was destined to be "a nation, coextensive with the North American continent."[5] Nevertheless, he saw no need to rush the inevitable. As Secretary of State, he wanted to avoid conflict with the Russians in the Pacific Northwest while maintaining American trading and whale fishing rights in that area.

John Quincy Adams was uniquely qualified to preside over American–Russian relations during this period. He had served as the United States' first minister to Russia from 1809 until 1812 and had been in close personal contact with Czar Alexander, who held Adams in the highest respect.[6] As minister to Russia, Adams had to deal mainly with American policy problems that resulted from the European Napoleonic wars. There was no question in Adams' mind that cooperation with Russia would help offset British predominance on the seas. When war broke out between the United States and Great Britain, the czar and his minister of foreign affairs, Count Nicholas Rumiantsev, offered to mediate. Adams, stretching his powers, indicated the United States would accept their mediation, and Madison and Monroe soon backed their minister.[7] While the British subsequently refused mediation, demanding face-to-face negotiations, the czar had become even more esteemed in Adams's estimate.[8] After Napoleon's defeat, Adams wrote that the only hope for a stable Europe rested "upon the moderation, equity, and humanity of the Emperor Alexander, and I freely confess I have confidence in nothing else."[9]

Regarding Russian interests in North America, John Quincy Adams took a less friendly view. During the first few years of his term as Secretary of State, Adams predicted the Russians would not long remain along the Northwest Coast of North America. Writing to the new American minister in St. Petersburg, George Washington Campbell, in 1818, Adams noted that Alexander had no intention of making Russia a naval power. Indeed, he pointed out, Russia had recently sold a line of battleships and frigates to Spain. "With the neglect of the navy," Adams added, "that of navigation and commercial shipping naturally follows: and without these, however the establishment of distant colonies may be attempted they can never flourish." With that view in mind, Adams therefore concluded that while "it may be proper to observe attentively the movements of Russia with regard to their settlements on the north western coasts . . . they can never form a subject of serious difference, or jarring interest between that Empire and the United States."[10]

Adams believed that the negotiations with Spain leading to the Transcontinental Treaty of 1819, and thus to a firm American boundary on the Pacific Ocean, would be a further suggestion to the Russians and others that North America was to be the sphere of the United States. With the conclusion of this treaty, he hoped that "the world shall be familiarized with the idea of considering our proper domain to be the continent of North America." Adams reaffirmed his belief that "a law of nature" had ordained that North America "should exist permanently contiguous to a great, powerful, enterprising, and rapidly growing nation."[11]

Thus, Adams's strong stand against the czar's ukase was influenced in part by the political pressures of the Floyd, Benton, and Clay westerners, as well as by men such as Sturgis and other Boston traders. Adams's own view of what shape America should take, as a neomercantilist continental and commercial empire, also strongly shaped his response. One should not ignore, however, forces such as the China trade, which also shaped Adams's strong support for American commercial and fishing rights in the Pacific Northwest.

The Northwest Coast trade was intimately tied up with American exploration of the China market. While very lucrative, the China trade was a severe drain on American specie reserves. At a time when America was still feeling the effects of the panic of 1819, caused in some measure by a lack of specie, nothing but harm could come from denying United States traders the commodities of the Northwest Coast that served in place of specie at the Canton marketplace. In the years 1818–1819, for instance, while the Canton trade totaled more than $10 million, $7.4 million of that was specie, the rest being furs from the Northwest and sandalwood. During the depression years of 1820 and 1821, there occurred a specie outflow to Canton of only $677,205 more than furs and other articles. One could have hoped that a general leveling would take place. If, however, the Russian ukase were effected against American traders, almost all of the Canton trade would necessarily have to be in specie. The Monroe administration could not countenance such a development with equanimity.[12]

Given the economic situation, John Quincy Adams was understandably chagrined when, in 1820–1821, Floyd and Benton began to agitate for the use of force in the Pacific Northwest. The Secretary of State saw the anti-Russian tone of Floyd's first report as a direct assault upon his own well-laid plans. Floyd had submitted his report to President Monroe in January 1821 before reading it in the House. The President sent it on to Secretary Adams for his suggestions. Angry at the tenor of the report, Adams would offer no alterations. Instead, he told Monroe that "the paper is a tissue of errors in fact and abortive reasoning, of invidious reflections and rude invectives." Only the "fire" could purify it, he added. Adams was convinced that the language employed in Floyd's report would have the reverse effect of the end intended and force the Russians to move from cooperation to belligerence in the Pacific Northwest. Patience and time, Adams believed, would be America's best weapons to gain this part of its empire from its erstwhile Russian friends.[13]

A few days later, the British minister, Stratford Canning, visited Adams. Canning was angry. He held in his hand the issue of the *National Intelligencer* that reported Floyd's bill calling for the occupation of the Columbia River. Canning, showing an unsophisticated understanding of American politics, suspected that Adams was behind Floyd's maneuvers and wanted to know what would happen if Great Britain undertook to make a settlement on the Northwest Coast. The Secretary of State replied that the United States would object to any such British move. Canning then inquired if the United States also claimed Canada. Adams responded: "We have no disposition to encroach upon it. Keep what is yours, but leave the rest of the continent to us." The British minister protested. Such talk, he said, "affects the rights of Russia and of Spain." The Secretary replied that "Russia and Spain are the guardians of their own rights."[14] Czar Alexander's ukase of 1821 showed, indeed, that the Russians intended to be their own guardians.

With the issuance of the ukase and the increased domestic political pressure upon the administration, Adams was compelled to use diplomacy to insure that the laws of nature would remain in force. The Russian minister, Pierre de Poletica, did not officially inform the Secretary of State of the ukase until February 11, 1822.[15] Adams replied to Poletica that the President saw with "surprise" the claims of the edict. The United States government had expected, said Adams, that, before the Russian government presumed to set any boundaries between the territories of the United States and Russia on the North American continent, a treaty between the parties would first be negotiated. In any event, Adams informed Poletica, "the ordinance affects so deeply the rights of the United States and of their citizens" that Russia must first explain its presumption to such a claim before the American government could even consider it.[16]

Poletica informed Adams that Russia based its claim to the Northwest Coast on first discovery and fifty years of uncontested possession. By claiming to 51° north latitude instead of 49°, he asserted, Russia had "made only moderate use of an incontestable right." The czar, added Poletica, was also moderate in his claim of a hundred-mile coastal limit because Russia possessed the land opposite the Northwest Coast in Asia; this fact "comprehends all the conditions which are ordinarily attached to *shut seas (mers fermées)*." The ukase was not directed at the United States government, claimed Poletica; rather, "it is exclusively directed against the culpable enterprises of foreign adventurers . . . the majority of whom was composed of American citizens." Poletica pointed out that often in the past the imperial government had protested to the American government about this problem. Nevertheless, he noted, "these remonstrances, repeated at different times, remain constantly without effect, and the inconvenience to which they ought to bring a remedy continues to increase."[17]

On March 30, Adams rejected Poletica's historical interpretation of Russian claims to the Northwest Coast and thus refused to accede to the regulations of the ukase. The Secretary of State noted that "from the period of the existence of the United States as an independent nation, their vessels have freely navigated those seas, and the right to navigate them is a part of that independence." For the United States to accept the Russian claim of a hundred-mile territorial water right would be a surrender of the freedom to navigate the seas, and this the United States would never do. Adams ridiculed the Russian attempt to call the seas between North America and Asia closed: "It might suffice to say that the distance from shore to shore on this sea . . . is not less than . . . four thousand miles." Moreover, he argued, the right of the citizens of the United States to trade with the Indians of the Northwest Coast "even in arms and other munitions of war, is as clear and indispensible as that of navigating the seas." Adams admitted that the Russians had made general complaints from time to time against this trade, but he noted that no specific charges had ever been alleged that the United States government was bound, under ordinary usage, to punish. Therefore, Adams expected that American citizens would "remain unmolested in prosecution of their lawful commerce, and that no effect will be given to an interdiction manifestly incompatible with their rights."[18]

Acquiescence to the Russian restrictions for John Quincy Adams would have been a violation of one of his cardinal principles of civilization. He believed "there is no other way by which men can so much contribute to the comfort and well-being of one another as by commerce." For him, commerce was "among the natural rights and duties of men." Nations that restricted the rights of others to commerce failed to meet the prime "duty" of each nation "to hold commercial intercourse with the other." Trade between nations recognized "a joint and moral consideration of the interests of both." He compared it to "the Christian precept to love your neighbor as yourself."[19] The Secretary of State had every intention of making the Russians adhere to this Christian concept along the Northwest Coast.

In answering Adams's note of March 30, Poletica wrote that he was not authorized to continue the discussions on the czar's ukase.[20] Two weeks later (April 16), the Russian envoy, noting the talks about the Russian claims had reached a stalemate, announced to Adams that he was taking a leave of absence to return to Russia.[21] Adams told Poletica that when he reached Russia, he should inform the czar that while the President earnestly desired friendly relations to continue between the two nations, he should also be informed of "the impossibility that the United States should acquiesce either in the interdiction of their lawfully navigating vessels to approach within 100 Italian miles of the shore of an open sea, or in the disturbance of their citizens in the prosecution of their intercourse with the natives of this continent beyond the degree of 51 north latitude."[22]

At the same time, Adams wrote to the American minister in Russia, Henry Middleton, instructing him to "insist upon the revocation of any orders" that "infringe upon the unquestionable rights of our navigators." The Secretary of State told Middleton that American trading vessels would continue to trade along the Northwest Coast, and he warned that if American ships "should be molested, the excitement in the country will be very great." At this point, Adams set the minister's course by concluding: "You will . . . make it most distinctly to be understood that the United States cannot for a moment acquiesce in those regulations, and that they will never admit [that those regulations] can in any manner impair their rights, or those of their citizens."[23]

Even before receiving Adams's instructions of May 13, Middleton informed Russian officials, albeit unofficially, that the United States government would never submit to the Russian regulations of September 1821.[24] As soon as Middleton received the Secretary of State's instructions, on July 24, he called upon Count Capodistrias, the assistant minister of foreign affairs. He told Capodistrias that he intended to seek a formal interview with Foreign Affairs Minister Nesselrode in order to present the case of his government concerning the ukase. Middleton read Capodistrias the note he had prepared to present formally to Nesselrode: "public opinion" in the United States was "greatly opposed to these regulations," and the President "is fully convinced that it is quite impossible for the United States Government to acquiesce in them." Furthermore, Middleton pointed out, with obvious hyperbole, that a careful perusal of the correspondence between the two governments on this subject "cannot fail to show that a state of war between the two powers exists already, owing to the principles that have been avowed on both sides." Nothing was needed now, he said, but "a declaration or acts of violence, which latter cannot be long in coming." The only way to avoid war, Middleton concluded, was if "the Russian Government should abstain from putting into execution the measures ordered by the Ukase of September 4, 1821."[25]

The Russians retreated slightly. Capodistrias requested Middleton not to present his note to Nesselrode. He informed the American minister that "the Emperor has had the good sense to see that this affair should not be pushed too far."[26] But he was stalling: Russian warships were already on their way to the Northwest Coast with orders to enforce the decree. Although the ministry of finance had prepared a memorandum six days earlier ordering Russian ships not to enforce the ukase against American shipping within the hundred-mile limit until the new Russian minister to the United States, Baron Hendrik de Tuyll, met with the United States government,[27] no final decision was made to put such an order into effect until seven days after Middleton's conversation with Capodistrias.[28] Adams's May 1822 instructions to Middleton, however, were known to the Russian government before the ministry of finance prepared its memorandum, for Adams had asked Poletica, who was returning to Russia, to deliver these instructions personally to Middleton. The Secretary of State made the contents of his instructions known to Poletica, and one suspects that Adams's views were sufficient impetus, without Middleton's allusions to war, to convince the Russian government to review its policy.

If the Russians were still weighing the consequences of enforcing the ukase, Middleton's conversation with Capodistrias left no doubt that enforcement would mean war with the United States. On August 12, the board of the Russian-American Company, in a secret document, approved Finance Minister Guriev's memorandum and sent it on to the colony. The board noted that the new minister to the United States, Baron Hendrik de Tuyll, had been instructed "to agree with that Government upon the measures necessary to be adopted in order to prevent any further disputes."[29] The Russian government then hastily sent Tuyll to Washington to reach an agreement on the subject of the jurisdiction of both nations along the Northwest Coast. Until Baron Tuyll completed his mission, the Russian company and warships in the Northwest were instructed not to enforce the hundred-mile limit, although the company was told to exercise "control over such an extent of water as is by common custom considered to be under the jurisdiction of any power which has the possession of the seaboard." Furthermore, the board and ministry of finance instructed the company to introduce on the coast "such a system of surveillance as may be found necessary for the protection of our territory from attack and for the prevention of illicit trading."[30] Thus, the Russian government backed down only from those issues which could lead to a *casus belli*, but many substantial disputes remained to be negotiated.[31]

Tuyll arrived in Washington, D.C., in April 1823. He informed Secretary of State Adams of the czar's desire to settle by friendly negotiations all the conflicts that arose from the issuance of the ukase. The Russian minister told Adams that the czar had persuaded the British government to give its minister in St. Petersburg full power to negotiate these issues, and the czar hoped that Middleton, the American minister, would be given similar powers.[32] Adams did not immediately reply to Tuyll's note; instead, he informed the British minister, Stratford Canning, of Tuyll's request, suggesting that the British and American ministers in St. Petersburg "act in the proposed negotiations on a common understanding," because both nations protested Russia's claims to the Northwest Coast.[33] Although Adams certainly had no desire to support future British expansion in the Western Hemisphere, he made this request as a tactical maneuver. Four days after his meeting with Canning, Adams informed Baron Tuyll that the President would accept the Russian proposal to move the negotiations to St. Petersburg. He added the condition, however, that during the negotiations, the United States government expected that the Russian government would take no steps to try to effect the ukase.[34]

The British government, whose claims in the Pacific Northwest dated back to Cook's voyages in the late 1770s, hesitated to make any decision about cooperating with the United States in negotiating with the Russians. The British feared binding themselves to negotiations that might have the result of excluding them from all claims to the Pacific Northwest. While Canning assured his government that the United States would make no territorial claims north of 51° latitude,[35] Sir Charles Bagot in St. Petersburg warned the British foreign secretary that the United States government would make a pretention to the "whole coast as high as the sixty-first degree."[36]

Meanwhile, Monroe's cabinet met on June 28, 1823, to discuss the instructions that were to be sent to Middleton. Adams argued that the United States should admit "no territorial right . . . on this continent" to Russia. The cabinet concurred that Middleton should be instructed to propose a convention (similar to the 1818 convention with Great Britain) "agreeing that the whole coast should be open for the navigation of all parties for a definite term of years." If the Russians would not agree to this, Middleton was authorized to offer a boundary line for Russia at 55° latitude "on the condition that the coast might be frequented for trade with the natives, as it has been heretofore." In essence, the cabinet members ratified John Quincy Adams's earlier actions. They would accept nothing less than a total repudiation by the Russian government of its czar's ukase.[37]

II

During this period, John Quincy Adams came to his final formulation of what has become known as the "no future colonization principle," which Monroe enunciated in his December 1823 annual message. In a letter to Senator James Lloyd of Massachusetts on July 15, 1823, Adams denied that Russia had the right to any territory in North America:

> But what right has Russia to *any* colonial footing on the *continent* of North America? Has she any that we are bound to recognize? And is it not time for the American *Nations* to inform the sovereigns of Europe, that the American continents are no longer open to the settlement of new European colonies?[38]

Lloyd, who had been Adams' Federalist successor in 1808 and

now had been returned to the Senate, appealed to President Monroe for protection of American rights on the Northwest Coast. Having written to Monroe on May 16, 1823, Lloyd emphasized the value of the fur trade from Russian-America to China. The sea and whale fisheries, he said, were also of great commercial value. Lloyd told the President that American traders used the natives of the area to catch sea otters and fur seals. The region between 51° and 60° north latitude were the most valuable. If the Russians succeeded in enforcing their ukase, fur trading from the Northwest Coast to China would be terminated, and whaling vessels, which required landing places for refreshment, could no longer hunt in the North Pacific. Lloyd relied heavily upon Sturgis's 1822 article in the *North American Review* and enclosed a letter from Sturgis that affirmed Lloyd's statements.[39]

While Adams was certainly no political ally of Lloyd, he agreed with him on the value of the Northwest trade. In his July 15 letter to Lloyd, Adams acknowledged that he had "come to the conclusion that we ought to have without any delay, a permanently established post" at the mouth of the Columbia River. Lloyd replied that he was less interested in establishing a post on the Columbia than in ending trade restrictions against Americans there. He believed it would be much better "to await the certain, and not tardy march of our pioneer settlers, to find its own way" to the Pacific Ocean.[40] Adams, as events proved, agreed with this point of view.

On July 17, Secretary of State Adams informed Russian Minister Tuyll that the United States would "contest the right of Russia to *any* territorial establishment on this continent, and that we should assume distinctly the principle that the American continents are no longer subjects for any new European colonial establishments."[41]

By the fall of 1823, the issue of Russian–American relations along the Northwest Coast had become inextricably tied to the growing problem of the threat of European intervention to restore Spain's lost colonies in Latin America. At the Conference of Verona in November 1822, the Russian government emphasized that it was unwilling to recognize the aspirations of revolutionary peoples. The czar declared his willingness to send troops to South America to restore legitimate rule. To John Quincy Adams, this had seemed like so much talk; he was sure that the allied monarchs would not intervene in South America.[42] On November 15, 1823, Adams received a note from the Russian minister that led him to reassess these optimistic views. Tuyll, as instructed,[43] presented the Secretary of State with the czar's views on revolution in both Europe and South America. Alexander noted that both he and his monarchical allies (Austria and France) would continue in their full support of legitimate regimes and extend their utmost efforts to crushing revolutions against authority as they had in the cases of Spain and Portugal. He added that if Spain or Portugal now desired aid in solidifying its "external politics," the emperors would not hesitate to offer every help. As for Russia, it would receive no representatives from the late Spanish colonies.[44]

When the cabinet met on November 21 to discuss the czar's statement, it agreed with Adams that the United States government should tell the Russian government that, since the United States had no intention of interfering in the "political affairs of Europe," it expected "that the European powers will equally abstain from the attempt to spread their principles in the American hemisphere, or to subjugate by force any part of these continents by their will."[45] The draft that Adams presented to the cabinet four days later was much stronger in both tone and content than the message to which the cabinet had agreed. Adams' draft noted that so long as it was possible for Spain to restore itself to control of its colonies, the United States had remained neutral. A reassertion of Spanish domination was now no longer remotely possible. The Secretary of State, while acknowledging the long friendship between the United States and Russia, was shocked by the czar's most recent communications relating to South America. The President, said Adams, hoped that these communications "are not intended *either* to mark either a change, in the friendly dispositions of the Emperor towards the United States or of hostility to the principles upon which their Governments are founded." The Holy Alliance, Adams averred, "was not intended to embrace the United States of America, nor any portion of the American Hemisphere." He concluded on an ominous note:

> Deeply desirous as the United States are of preserving the general peace . . . especially . . . with the Imperial Government of Russia, it is due as well to their own unalterable sentiments, as well as explicit avowals of them . . . that the United States of America . . . could not see with indifference the forcible interposition of any European Power, other than Spain, either to restore the dominion of Spain over her emancipated colonies in America, or to establish Monarchical Government in those countries, or to transfer any of the possessions . . . in the Western Hemisphere to any other European power."[46]

When Adams presented this note to the cabinet, the President, Secretary of War John Calhoun, and Attorney General William Wirt, while agreeing with its sentiments, thought the wording too harsh. Calhoun suggested the best way to answer Russia would be in a presidential message. Adams vigorously protested: "The Communications from the Russian Minister," he said, "required a direct and explicit answer. A communication of a paragraph of the President's message would be no answer, and if given as an answer would certainly be very inconsistent with the position that foreigners have no right to notice it, because it was said among ourselves." Adams prevailed, and on November 27, 1823, he sent his draft to Tuyll.[47]

Before Monroe delivered his message of December 2, 1823, the Russians had been informed of both its basic parts. Adams' July 17 note to Tuyll had announced that the United States would contest any Russian territorial establishment in North America and that the Western Hemisphere was no longer subject to new European colonial establishments. His November 27 note stated the "nonintervention" principle and implied the United States would meet force with force if the Russians dared to intervene in South America. Equally interesting is that the language and tenor of both these notes to the Russians were much stronger than the Monroe Doctrine itself. Monroe's message of December 1823 was superfluous to Russian–American relations. It was also gratuitous as a statement to the other continental powers, since the czar's November 15 note was written in his role as spokesman for the continental powers. Adams's answer to the czar was aimed at the entire Holy Alliance. Furthermore, Adams had argued, and Monroe's cabinet eventually agreed, that if the Russians were answered in a presidential message to Congress,

> This would be precisely as if a stranger should come to me with a formal and insulting display of his principles in the management of his family and his conduct toward his neighbors, knowing them to be the opposite of mine, and as if I, instead of turning upon him and answering him face to face, should turn to my own family and discourse to them upon my principles and conduct, with sharp innuendoes upon those of the stranger, and then say to him "There! take that for your answer. And yet you have no right to take notice of it: for it was only said to my own family and behind your back."[48]

According to Adams, such a pronouncement as the Monroe Doctrine would be a dubious way to deal with an intended threat. Before the doctrine was announced, there was no question in the Russian mind about the American attitude. If we are to take Adams at his word, Monroe's message could be construed only as something other than a warning to the continental powers. The President's announcement was not aimed at Russian movements in the Pacific Northwest. Indeed, it seems that one intended recipient was Great Britain. On November 26, Adams suggested that "the answer to be given to the Russian communications should be used as a means of answering also the proposals of Mr. George Canning."[49] In that context, the message is not superfluous; rather, it is apparent, as a noted American historian suggested, that "Adams . . . was at least as concerned with establishing American commercial supremacy as he was with blocking further colonial experiments by European nations."[50] The only other nation that could and did rival the United States in Latin America was Great Britain.

Second, as Adams had taken pains to point out, presidential messages to the Congress were designed for domestic consumption. In this case, the intended recipients were the Clay, Benton, and Floyd forces. The Monroe Doctrine announced to that faction that the administration had succeeded in ending European encroachments in the Pacific Northwest and in South America. It also announced to the nation that the end had been achieved without resort to arms as the Clay forces had demanded.

The Monroe Doctrine had an effect on the negotiations then taking place in St. Petersburg. The British government, which had been hesitant to cooperate with Middleton in joint negotiations with the Russians, used Monroe's message as an excuse to instruct Bagot to proceed independently in the negotiations.[51] The administration actually was happy that the British had made this move first, since continued joint negotiations were no longer feasible. Two months earlier, Middleton had written Adams that great differences of opinion between him and Sir Charles Bagot "upon all points relative to the Northwest question must render fruitless" all attempts at coming to an understanding "with the British."[52]

Unlike the British, the Russians did not break off talks with the United States because of Adams' strong messages. Aside from the clear avowal of the United States government that it would not accept the ukase, the Russian government found itself pressured from within to rescind its previous pronouncements.

III

The effect of the ukase on the Russian-American colony by 1824 was nothing short of a disaster. In 1818 and 1819, the Russian-American Company paid a dividend of 155 rubles per share. While this dividend had dropped by 1820 and 1821 to 82 rubles, the return was still handsome in relation to the original investment. But from 1822 until the abrogation of the ukase, the company was unable to pay any dividends. The exclusion of Boston traders, instead of allowing the colony to prosper, had caused a loss of at least 300,000 rubles annually. The around-the-world expeditions sent out by the directors proved ruinous to the stockholders, although some of the directors made themselves quite wealthy in the process.[53] The scheme to provide the colony with food grown at Fort Ross proved another dismal failure. The governor of Russian-America, Matevi Muraviev, angrily wrote to the board in St. Petersburg in 1823 that if they did not lay aside his orders not to trade with the Yankees, he would do so himself. Finally, in desperation, Muraviev, ignoring his instructions, sent to Hawaii and California for food and purchased an American vessel for the voyage. Meanwhile the assembly of stockholders adopted a resolution petitioning the government to reopen Sitka to foreign vessels.[54]

Formal negotiations between the United States and Russia on the question of the future of the Northwest Coast began in February 1824. In December 1823, Middleton had submitted to the Russian foreign ministry a "confidential Memorial," which he had prepared and which Adams had approved. The czar, Nesselrode, and other important Russian officials read the "Memorial," which restated the American position: Spain had a prior claim as high as 61° north latitude, but that entire claim had been ceded to the United States in 1819. Russia, on the other hand, had no valid claim to the Pacific Northwest, except in the areas it had settled. Aside from that, American merchants had been trading along the Northwest Coast for years, obtaining furs to sell to China. To stop them now and to interfere with free navigation in time of peace would be a violation of American rights.

During the first week of negotiations, Middleton reported that while he and his Russian counterparts expressed "very opposing attitudes," he was optimistic about the outcome. The American minister believed that his government's late "frank and constant conduct [toward Russia] inspires respect." Most of all, he noted, the Russians knew that if hostilities broke out with the United States over the Northwest Coast, "our *maritime force* and the consequent *impossibility* of *dictation* towards us must also be taken into the account."[55]

Middleton signed a treaty with the Russian government on April 17, 1824, "relative to navigation, fishing, and trading in the Pacific Ocean and to Establishments on the Northwest Coast." The treaty provided:

1. Citizens of both nations could navigate or fish without restraint along the Northwest Coast at points not already

occupied. They also could trade freely with the Indians of the area at unsettled points.

2. In order to end illicit trade, citizens of the United States should not resort to any point along the coast where there was a Russian establishment without permission of the governor or commander. Russian citizens suffered the same restrictions in American ports.

3. The Russian government agreed to form no new establishments south of 54° 40′ north latitude and the United States none north of that parallel.

4. For a ten-year period, the ships and citizens of both powers could "frequent, without any hindrance whatever, the interior seas, gulfs, harbors, and creeks, upon the coast . . . for the purpose of fishing and trading with the natives of the country." Thus, for ten years both the occupied settlements and the unoccupied areas would remain open to United States citizens.

5. All spirituous liquors, firearms, and powder were exempted from the commerce of this area. This stipulation, however, "shall never afford a pretext . . . to authorize search or detention of vehicles, seizure of merchandise, or . . . any measure of constraint whatever towards the merchants or crews who may carry on this commerce."[56]

The treaty was a complete victory for John Quincy Adams. The Russians, by signing this treaty, agreed to retract the czar's ukase; they dropped their pretension to Russian dominion as far south as 51° north latitude and to their hundred-mile coastal water claim. Americans were free to trade in all of Russian-America for a ten-year period. While the treaty outlawed the sale of liquor and firearms to the Indians, it also stipulated that such a rule could not be enforced. The United States, while agreeing not to build any establishments north of 54° 40′, did not by so agreeing recognize that area as Russian territory. The treaty met Adams's specifications exactly. He had desired to keep the Northwest Coast open to American commerce, and he expected that American pioneers, following their manifest destiny, would soon settle the area, making it clearly American. The ten-year clause of the fourth article was especially written with that end in view. Both Adams and

Middleton hoped that during this ten-year period, the Russian settlements would become so dependent on United States trade that the continuance of this clause would become indispensable to them.[57]

During the previous summer, John Quincy Adams had informed Richard Rush, the American minister in Great Britain, that the questions under discussion in St. Petersburg relating to the Northwest Coast were of vital importance to the United States. "That the United States should form establishments there [Northwest Coast], with views of absolute territorial right and inland communication, is not only to be expected, but is pointed out by the finger of nature." The consequence of such inevitability, noted the Secretary, "will be that the American continents henceforth will no longer be subjects of colonization." But, Adams added, the most important present aspects of the Northwest Coast to the United States (before actual settlement) "are the fisheries on its adjoining seas and trade with the aboriginal inhabitants of the country." This commercial aspect had deep implications because it inevitably involved America's "commerce with the Sandwich Islands, China, and the American boundary with Mexico."[58] Thus, Adams reiterated his long-range plan for a continental empire that stretched from coast to coast and a commercial empire that would some day girdle the earth from Boston to China and beyond. (Adams's Transcontinental Treaty of 1819 had been the first step.) In forcing the czar to recall his ukase and in obtaining the Treaty of 1824 with Russia, he had helped the "finger of nature" point in the direction of his own plan.

Russian Foreign Minister Nesselrode had another interpretation of the 1824 treaty. He viewed the pact as the only way to stop American penetration of the Russian possession, because "by signing this agreement, the Americans have just as solemnly admitted that, at the expiration of a few stipulated years, we shall have the legal power to forbid them absolutely to trade or fish in that whole area."[59] Clearly, both sides read the same treaty in very different ways.

The events of 1821–1825, however, displayed Russia's weakness in defending its Pacific Northwest colony. Lacking a strong navy, it was in no position to beat back American maritime power should hostilities break out. Moreover, after more than forty years, Russian-America had yet to prove a viable economic or political asset to the Russian empire. These realities could lead many Russian policy makers to question whether the retention of Russian-America was an overextension of Russian interests. Clashes with United States citizens and the United States government certainly made such questioning seem more urgent. While the American leaders in Washington proved to be split over the best methods of protecting and expanding American interests in the Pacific Northwest, Russian leaders would increasingly question whether Russian-America was worth protecting. This difference would prove crucial in the years to come.

4

A Tenuous Coexistence, 1825–1838

Instead of clearly defining the rights of Yankees and Russians in the Pacific Northwest, the Treaty of 1824 opened up new issues and tensions in American–Russian relations. The virtual freedom of trade allowed to United States nationals in Russian-America created a situation whereby the Russian colony depended upon them for sustenance while Russian-American Company officials in St. Petersburg feared the ruin of their investments due to Yankee depletions of resources in Russian-America. Although the Americans supplied the czar's colony with necessities, they also traded with the natives and removed valuable furs. The Russian company, however, was supposed to be a profit-making venture. If the very sources of Russian income—trade with the Indians and procurement of peltries—were depleted by foreigners, the company's ability to pay dividends to its stockholders would be severely hampered. As early as 1831, the Russian-American Company's supply of furs was so low that it was forced to pay for supplies with letters of credit instead of peltries.[1]

During the ten-year period when Americans were permitted freedom of trade in the Russian possession—per the 1824 agreement—their trade in the area increased. In 1834, when the Russian government attempted to enforce the ten-year provision of the treaty, the United States government protested, and traders ignored the czar's new rules. The Russian-American Company in St. Petersburg had the dubious satisfaction of reminding its government that its officials had predicted such a course of events as early as 1824.

I

The results of Russian diplomacy were a source of much complaint in the St. Petersburg offices of the Russian-American Company. While the Treaty of 1824 was being negotiated with the United States, influential stockholders urged the Russian ministry of foreign affairs not to make commercial concessions to Americans. One of them, Count N. S. Mordvinov, warned Foreign Minister Nesselrode that by allowing continued American penetration into this seemingly "desert land," the Russian government would be making a serious mistake. Mordvinov had hoped his government would not sign any treaty giving the United States rights that would cause "great losses" to the Russian-American Company.[2] As soon as the convention was signed, Konrad Ryleyev, manager of the company's St. Petersburg office, wrote to the minister of finance, Egor Kankrin, in an attempt to convince the government not to ratify the treaty. Ryleyev feared that once the Americans "received the legal right to enter into competition with the Company . . . not only would those who used to frequent our shores and sail our waters flock there but also so would those who have never given a thought to such an enterprise." If the convention is ratified, concluded Ryleyev, "the Company has every reason to fear that not alone within ten years but within a much shorter period the foreigners . . . will bring the Company to a state of complete destruction."[3]

Kankrin transmitted Mordvinov's protest along with others, but to no avail.[4] The czar, Kankrin was informed, favored ratification of the convention with the United States.[5] The czar's approval, however, did not put an end to the company's protests. D. I. Zavalishin, a company official, submitted a memorandum to the governing board of the Russian-American Company entitled "Concerning the Ban on American Citizens to Visit the Northwest Coast of America.'' He predicted that if the government did not rescind the permission granted to American citizens giving them free access to Russian-America, the end of Russian rule in the Pacific Northwest would soon follow. "Only one thing could assure the security of Sitka," he argued, "the complete removal of the citizens of the United States from its shores." If the Russian government found itself unable to effect such a result, Zavalishin suggested that Russia "abandon" the Northwest Coast outposts altogether.[6]

While the Russians did not abandon Sitka, American activities to the south made the retention of Fort Ross a hardly worthwhile venture. The company's manager, Ryleyev, believed "the agreement with the North American Union" spelled the end of Ross as "a strong base" for future Russian expansion as well as a supplier of grain for the Russian colonies to the north.[7]

If the Russians had any illusions about further expansion after John Quincy Adams' notes to Tuyll in 1823, increased American activity along the Columbia River during the subsequent ten years proved to Russian planners that Ross was finished as a base for future operations. The Russian-American Company first settled the colony at Ross, ninety-five miles north of San Francisco, in 1812. It had hoped that the colony would serve a twofold purpose of granary for the Russian settlements farther to the north and as a jumping-off point for further expansion to the south. Adams' notes of 1823 and the Treaty of 1824 implicitly forbade new Russian colonies south of 54° 40'. In the 1830s, some Russian-American Company officials nevertheless retained the hope that the Ross settlement could serve as the food supplier for the rest of the Russian-American colonies.[8]

The sea otter trade was no longer the chief American operation along the Northwest Coast. Yankee ingenuity had all but exterminated that mammal. While Bryant and Sturgis, as well as Josiah Marshall's firm, were still able to squeeze a handy profit at the otter's expense, the days of the sea otter as an important medium for the China trade were over by 1834.[9]

Bostonian traders continued to be the chief supplier of foodstuffs and other articles for the Russian colonies.[10] Until

1829, the Russians paid these traders mainly with fur seal skins, which the Americans then sold at the Canton market. After 1829, due to the diminishing number of seals, these traders were paid with letters of credit from the general administration of the company.[11]

During this period of diplomatic respite, American interest in the Pacific Northwest grew. This increased attention was tied together with what was to become the great American push for Oregon territory. The name "Oregon" during these years often coincided with the entire coastline north of California. That American interests during this period set no latitudinal boundaries should be kept in mind when reexamining this era. One thing was certain: the Russian government continued to see the growing American interest in the Northwest as a threat to its colony's survival.

The 1824 treaty opened Russian-America to virtually unrestrained trading privileges for American citizens. Although the treaty forbade the sale of firearms and spirituous liquors to the natives, such illicit trade continued.[12] Boston firms were in the vanguard of those supplying the Russian colonies with goods. By the early 1830s, William H. Boardman and Company and Perkins and Company became the major suppliers of the Russian colony.[13] Boardman had found trade with the Russians in the Pacific Northwest so profitable that in 1835 he petitioned the Russian government for permission to extend his trade to Kamchatka on the Asian continent.[14] His request was granted. In 1838, his contract to supply the colonies under the jurisdiction of the Russian-American Company was renewed and extended. He supplied the company with tobacco, rum, sugar, molasses, hardtack, cotton, dry goods, and other sundries—and he even sold the company a steam engine in 1834.[15] Adding to this increased American activity, the British Hudson's Bay Company quickly used its privileges gained from the 1825 Anglo-Russian Treaty to divert much of the traditional Russian fur acquisitions to British use.[16]

As aggressive as American trading groups in Russian-America during this period were American politicians who posed as the protectors of those interests. While many issues divided the supporters of John Quincy Adams and Andrew Jackson, the American government's official position on American rights along the Northwest Coast remained constant. President Adams, in his first annual message in December 1825, noted that the Northwest Coast region was frequented by American navigators, but "barely touched by our public ships," even though the Columbia River had been discovered by an American sea captain. He reported that the Northwest Coast supported "a flourishing commerce and fishery to the islands of the Pacific and to China." This situation required "that the protecting power of the Union should be displayed under its flag as well upon the ocean as upon the land." To this end, Adams suggested "the establishment of a military post there, or at some other point on that coast." He further recommended sending a naval expedition to explore the whole Northwest Coast of the continent.[17] The latter was done. President Andrew Jackson's first annual message reaffirmed his administration's support of strong American governmental action in the Pacific Northwest: "The policy for keeping adequate force will be preserved . . . for the protection of our commerce and fisheries in the Pacific."[18]

The alleged importance of the Pacific Northwest to the American economy was also kept constantly before the attention of the Congress. The only action that the Congress could agree to take related to the sending of a naval expedition to explore the Pacific Coast of North America "and also [inquire] whether it would be practicable to transport more of the munitions of war in such vessels."[19] The debates in Congress, nevertheless, provided a forum to educate the nation on the value of the Northwest Coast.

Soon after the Treaty of 1824 with Russia was signed, Congressman John Floyd of Virginia again raised the question of the need for a stronger American presence along the Northwest Coast. He urged American occupation of the mouth of the Columbia River lest it fall into British or Russian hands and repeated arguments that must have seemed tiresome to everyone but himself. The Canton trade, he proclaimed, was "the most valuable commerce known to the United States, as it created its own capi-

tal, and enriched by its labor.'' The continued success of this
trade, he repeated, depended upon American control of the
Northwest Coast. Floyd reminded his colleagues of the growing
importance of this area to whale fishing and warned that the only
way to insure that a monarchy would not control the Pacific was
for Americans to settle this area. Only settlement by United
States citizens would "give this vast country the blessings of free
government . . . as to the Russians . . . the thing was simply impossible.''[20]

Floyd's bill for the occupation of the mouth of the Columbia
River passed the House only to be tabled in the Senate.[21] In the
Senate, the proposal found strong western support, with only two
western Senators supporting the motion to table. Both Massa-
chusetts Senators favored Floyd's act, while the rest of the New
England Senators opposed it. Clearly, the issue of the Northwest
Coast appealed to special interest groups and not to political factions. Senator Andrew Jackson of Tennessee favored Floyd's
bill, while Senator Martin Van Buren of New York did not.[22]
In both the House and the Senate, Floyd's bill received some
support from every section. One western Congressman, David
Trimble of Kentucky, summed up the case of those who saw the
need for a stronger American presence in the Pacific Northwest.
He argued that in order to "command the trade of China, Japan,
the East Indies, and the North Pacific," the United States must
establish "military posts" along the Northwest Coast. The use of
naval force to control this trade is important, he noted, because
"for the last 3000 years, the nation that has held the control of the
East India and China trade, has had the supremacy of naval
strength and power.''[23]

In December 1828, Floyd opened the Oregon question again.
This time he asked for an act authorizing the President to erect
and garrison forts along the Northwest Coast from 42° to 54° 40'.
The House, by a vote of 99 to 75, rejected the bill. Opposition to
it ranged from arguments about its impracticability to the distance
separating the Northwest Coast from the rest of the nation.
Perhaps the most significant objection was raised by James

K. Polk of Tennessee. He believed that the provision for military occupation would provoke collision with Great Britain. The 1818 joint occupation treaty had either to be renewed or abrogated first. Polk and others argued that no step should be taken until further negotiation had been undertaken with Britain. The dissatisfaction with Floyd's bill seemed to rest more upon its particular provisions than upon its intention of strengthening the United States position in the Pacific Northwest. Even so, the debate on Floyd's proposal was long and intricate; and the importance of the Northwest Coast to the United States was kept alive in the Congress.[24]

The sporadic rhetorical attacks by members of the United States Congress upon the Russian government did not disturb American–Russian relations in the late 1820s and early 1830s. In December 1832, the American minister to Russia, James Buchanan, negotiated a most-favored nation treaty with the Russian government. While the American press assailed the policy of Czar Nicholas in his suppression of the Polish revolution, the American government moved coolly toward commercial amity with the Russians.[25] This amity was strained when the Russian chargé to the United States, Baron Dimitri von der Osten-Sacken, accused President Jackson of duplicity because Osten-Sacken believed that the denunciations of the czar's Polish policy which appeared in the proadministration *Washington Globe* had the President's sanction.[26] The administration, however, delayed its rebuke to the Russian representative in order not to interfere with the negotiations then going on in St. Petersburg dealing with the commercial treaty.[27] The Jackson government was willing to accept Russian monarchical policies and insults so long as they did not threaten the commerce of the United States.

But when the Russians again attempted to close their Pacific Northwest ports to American traders and whalers in 1834, the response from Washington was strong. American interests in the Pacific Northwest had grown to such an extent that no American administration could ignore such action without incurring the wrath of special interest groups. In April 1834, the ten-year period of free access by United States citizens to Russian-America, allowed by article IV of the 1824 treaty, expired. The Russian government immediately closed its colonies to all American traders. Unfortunately, from the Russian point of view, American traders and whalers had no respect for the Russian construction of the treaty. Within a year the Russian government began to lodge vigorous complaints to the American government claiming that "since the expiration of the said ten years, . . . navigators of the United States . . . have frequented the Russian possessions on the northwest coast of North America." The Russians invited "the Government of the United States to take the most suitable measures" to end these violations by its citizens.[28]

The Jackson government responded quickly. Secretary of State John Forsyth ordered the American minister to Russia, William Wilkins, to renegotiate article IV of the 1824 treaty "for an indefinite period; or if this cannot be had, for a term of years." If, however, the Russians refused to grant this concession, the President asked Wilkins to obtain precise information about Russian intentions "in relation to the admission of American vessels into the ports, harbors, bays and rivers of the Russian settlements." Wilkins was to imply to the Russians that they must either allow American ships into Russian-America or find "that corresponding regulations . . . may be made by this Government" against Russian shipping.[29]

It is easy to understand the reasons for the Jackson administration's quick reaction and its strong protest. American interests in the Pacific Northwest, especially near the area of the Russian settlements, had increased during the previous ten-year period. John Quincy Adams had hoped that this period of open trading would lead to such a dependence upon American trade that the Russians would never again consider excluding American commerce from their possessions. Again the Yankee trader outdid himself. The Russian government, instead of welcoming Yankee trade, feared it. Once more in St. Petersburg, the specter of an American takeover of Russia's North American possessions was exposed, exaggerated, and, no doubt, believed.

II

The Russian-American Company's fear of United States encroachment had been reinforced by events related to the settlement at Fort Ross, near San Francisco. Until the mid-1820s, Ross had been successful in its attempts to supply the Spanish, and later the Mexican, Californians with the limited productions of the Russians there.[30] Growing American enterprise in California after 1824 put an end to Ross's usefulness to the Russian-American Company. In 1833, Baron Ferdinand Wrangell, the governor of Russian-America, visited the colony. His report to the company directors in St. Petersburg was most pessimistic. Farming, he noted, was a complete failure at Ross; the settlement produced barely enough grain to feed itself. Cattle breeding had not succeeded, and fur hunting was on a decline. In 1832, he lamented, only one sea otter had been captured. As if all those things were not cause enough for despair, Wrangell had to report that while the settlement had once derived a certain income from orders of the California Spaniards for wheels, barges, and dishes, by 1830 this income was lost. The reason, he wrote, was the Yankees, "who have captured the California trade, have brought in all kinds of things that people need and have been supplying them at such low prices that we simply cannot compete with them." Because of these factors, the report went on, the maintenance of Fort Ross cost the company 10,000 rubles.[31]

Wrangell saw only two possible ways to save the California colony. The company could liquidate the colony and transfer it to a new and better located site. But he rejected this alternative, for "such an undertaking would arouse the envy of the foreigners [U. S. citizens] living in California who would shrewdly set the government of Mexico against us." The second alternative—recognition of the Mexican government in return for a fifty-year lease to Bodega Bay near Ross—would obtain Mexican cooperation against the encroachments of the United States and Britain. This alternative, Wrangell believed, was the last hope to save Fort Ross.[32]

The Russian government, however, refused to go along with

Wrangell's plan. Recognition of Mexico by Nicholas I's regime would contradict the czar's policy of unconditional support of legitimism. More important, the foreign ministry in St. Petersburg, which found it could not deter American enterprise north of 54° 40′ where a treaty clearly excluded American citizens, realized the futility of attempting to exclude them in California, where the Russian colony could not even claim color of treaty. Nicholas' decision not to follow Wrangell's advice was the first, and perhaps most important, step in the Russian withdrawal from California. After 1834, the Russian government never again considered the Ross colony a viable possession. The only question that remained was how to dispose of Fort Ross in the least embarrassing manner.[33]

In 1866, Dimitry Zavalishin, an official of the Russian-American Company, submitted a final, retrospective report on the liquidation of the Ross colony, which had taken place twenty-five years before. "Our principle error concerning the colony of Ross," he observed, was "that we sought the consent and permission to do what we had a full right to do . . . as other nations constantly acted, asking nobody." The Americans, Zavalishin explained, "not asking permission," settled wherever they wanted. "The Americans indeed would not give up places occupied by them and this unavoidably would lead to those encounters with the U.S." which Russia sought to avoid. "To such a position," the report concluded, "there was nothing left, either direct . . . encounter, . . . having in view endless . . . troubles and losses, or to abandon the colony. The latter was chosen."[34]

The results of American competition at Ross had provided the Russian government with additional evidence of the necessity of excluding American traders and whalers from all contact with Russian-America. John Forsyth, a nationalist and unionist from Georgia who was then serving as Secretary of State, lacked the depth of intellect of a John Quincy Adams or the vision of a William H. Seward. He owed his retention of high office more to party loyalty and opportunism than to brilliance. While in the Senate, he had been a leading spokesman in support of Martin

Van Buren's ill-fated nomination as minister to England in 1831. Forsyth had also deserted the majority of his state in 1832 to vote for the "force bill,"[35] an act only one other southern Senator had the face to duplicate. While Forsyth had opposed the 1816, 1824, and 1828 tariff bills, he followed the promise of high office and voted for both the 1832 and 1833 tariffs, while most other Senators from his region did not. Certainly his diplomatic experience hardly recommended him as a future Secretary of State. Serving as minister to Spain from 1819 to 1822, Forsyth so insulted the procrastinating Spanish government that it refused to ratify the 1819 Transcontinental Treaty until after Adams recalled the blundering minister. Forsyth's other experience in foreign affairs—he was chairman of the House Committee on Foreign Affairs—added little to his reputation in that area.[36]

Even though party loyalty seems to have been the greatest stimulus to Forsyth's advancement, this fact in no way precluded his following a strong policy with regard to American interests in the Pacific Northwest. As a strong supporter of the Monroe administration, Forsyth had vigorously supported John Quincy Adams's continentalism. Forsyth's impatience with the Spanish government during his mission to Spain proved that he was alive to the importance and significance of the Transcontinental Treaty and its relation to American interests in the Pacific. Secretary of State Forsyth's actions in the dispute with Russia demonstrate that, however unqualified he may have been to serve at the highest level of statesmanship, he immediately realized what was at stake and acted quickly to protect American interests on the Northwest Coast.

Forsyth and William Wilkins, American minister to Russia, were not sure, at first, how the Russians intended to construe the termination of the fourth article of the 1824 treaty.[37] They could interpret its expiration to mean that American ships were excluded from all areas north of 54° 40′ north latitude or that American vessels were denied access only to settled areas in the Russian possession. The American government, of course, chose the latter interpretation. On July 22, 1835, Forsyth published a notice in the *Washington Globe*:

Those interested in trade will not fail to observe that, under the second article of the convention, it is necessary for all American vessels, resorting to any point on the coast *where there is a Russian establishment,* to obtain permission of the governor or commander.[38]

The Russian government did not choose to accept the Secretary of State's definition. All of Russian-America was closed to American ships, according to Count Nesselrode, the Russian foreign minister. Nesselrode explained to Wilkins that the United States should not complain about this restriction since it had so little commerce in the area anyhow.[39] Nesselrode, of course, knew better, as subsequent events and conversations revealed. Wilkins was quick to correct the foreign minister's "erroneous idea . . . by informing him that our ships were annually upon that coast" selling supplies to Russians there as well as participating in other enterprises.[40] He tried to persuade Nesselrode to renegotiate the terminated clause of the 1824 treaty and threatened to discriminate against Russian shipping if Russian-America were closed to United States traders. In the wilds of North America, for either government to expect American citizens or Russian subjects "to render restraint and proper responsibility to the law," Wilkins argued, was "well-nigh out of the question." Neither the American government nor the Russian could keep American traders and fishermen out of the Russian possessions; therefore, argued Wilkins, the renewal of American rights to trade freely in this area was the only way "to avoid . . . collision between the inhabitants, traders, and fishermen upon that wild coast." He added that such an agreement was not without precedent since British citizens already enjoyed these privileges. By including the United States, Russia, England, and the United States would be placed "upon the same fair footing and upon the same equality in the enjoyment of a community of privileges."[41]

The board of directors of the Russian-American Company exerted additional pressure upon the Russian foreign ministry in late November, complaining of American captains who "would stop at nothing for the sake of gain," including attempts in "converting the natives to Christianity, to bind them by means of religious ties." It urged the government not to accept new conventions from the United States because of "the ill-will of the American captains, who take advantage of the rights of trade, enjoyed during the ten year term of the convention, but since prohibited by the same." To continue "to allow their captains to freely navigate our waters for the purpose of trading in our possessions," the report concluded, "will be decidedly prejudicial to the Russian-American Company."[42]

Secretary of State Forsyth and Minister Wilkins were nonetheless insistent on preserving present, as well as future, American commercial and political rights in this area. Writing to Secretary Forsyth on December 11, 1835, Wilkins related his representations to the Russian government: "I took the ground that it was not a mere interested and selfish question of gain in the traffic of the northwest coast, but one of a higher character, involving political and national considerations." Nevertheless, he freely admitted that America would have an advantage over the Russian-American Company due to a "more active commercial enterprise and superior shipping of the citizens of the United States." Wilkins, however, wanted the Russians to avoid judging the issue solely in terms of commercial competition and let it rather "turn upon the consideration of our national good-will and our amicable and disinterested reciprocal intercourse." Wilkins was, of course, more candid with Forsyth when he added:

> The Russian-American Fur Company are not likely to be governed by high political considerations or disinterested national views. The objects which alone exercise an influence over their proceedings are exclusive privileges.

Wilkins offered a suggestion to resolve the conflict once and for all. He believed that the Russian government considered its possessions in North America unimportant from "a *political* point of view" and predicted that "the only way in which you can avert collision and difficulties there, will be to throw the entire coast open to the fair competition of the three powers—the United States, England, and Russia." By this method, Wilkins assured his government, all problems would be avoided: "Each strives for the trade; each is jealous of each other. Let the most enterprising and intelligent carry off the profits.'' William Wilkins was confident who the victor would be in a Pacific Northwestern open door: ''The Russians are not at all liked by the native Indians— the Americans are greatly preferred.''[43]

Nesselrode and his government found themselves in a quandary: to agree to allow American ships to continue to frequent Russian-America could result in the destruction of the Russian-American Fur Company; yet to refuse to accept the American demands could lead to increased tensions and possibly destroy the Russian hope to use Russian-American diplomatic amity to offset British commercial and political power. As Czar Nicholas was later to point out to George M. Dallas, Wilkins' successor in St. Petersburg, Russia and America could maintain an atmosphere of friendship because ''not only are our interests alike, but *our enemies are the same*.''[44] Nesselrode met this dilemma in the classic diplomatic manner: he stalled. He told Wilkins that he could not answer the United States' request until he heard from the Russian-American Company, which, he added, might take some time.[45] Meanwhile, American traders and fishermen continued to interpret the diplomatic ambiguity in their own favor.

Martin Van Buren, inaugurated President in March 1837, retained John Forsyth as Secretary of State and sent Senator George M. Dallas[46] of Pennsylvania to St. Petersburg to replace Wilkins. Forsyth's instructions to Dallas in April 1837, as the latter took leave of Washington, emphasized the need to ''remind the Count de Nesselrode that no definite answer has yet been given to the communication of Mr. Wilkins on the subject of the renewal of the fourth article of the Convention of 1824.'' The United States, he added, ''anxiously looked for'' a favorable reply.[47]

Before Dallas could reopen his nation's case for renewal of article IV, Forsyth informed him of a new development in the Russian territories that gave the matter a more serious dimension. On August 22, 1836, the American brig *Loriot*, captained by Richard D. Blinn, sailed from Hawaii bound for the Northwest Coast of America to procure provisions and Indians for hunting sea otter. On September 14, the *Loriot* anchored in the harbor of

Tuckesson. The area was not settled or inhabited and lay in the latitude 54° 55' north and longitude 132° 31' west. Before a party could land on an area called Forrester's Island, a ship belonging to the Russian-American Company forced Blinn and his brig to depart. Captain Blinn and the *Loriot*'s owner, alleging a great financial loss, filed a complaint against the Russian company and asked indemnification. Clearly the American government could no longer ignore the issue of American trading rights in uninhabited areas of Russian-America, as well as the renegotiation of article IV. As soon as Forsyth heard about Blinn's case, he ordered Dallas to protest the Russian action, pointing out that the ship was rightfully in the area, since Forrester's Island was not part of Russian settlement as described in article IV of the 1824 treaty.[48]

Despite Forsyth's and Dallas's protests, Nesselrode continued stalling. This time the Americans would have no more of such tactics. Dallas remained adamant, proclaiming to Forsyth, "I shall never acquiesce, until instructed to do so by you."[49] Forsyth issued no instruction to acquiesce; he instead denied that the Treaty of 1824 gave up the entire territory north of 54° 40' to Russian possession. "The United States can only be considered," argued Forsyth, "as acknowledging the right of Russia to acquire by actual occupation a just claim to the unoccupied lands above the latitude of 54° 40' north." "Even this," he observed, "is a mere matter of inference, as the convention of 1824 contains nothing more than a negation of the right of the United States to occupy points within that limit." Forsyth firmly concluded that the United States never intended to abandon the "right . . . to frequent any part of the unoccupied coast of North America for the purpose of fishing or trading with the natives."[50] Dallas, accurately predicting his chief's views, bluntly protested to Nesselrode that the treatment of Blinn was "not merely . . . unfriendly, but as so obviously inconsistent with our national rights, as to render it impossible for me to suppose it warranted or sanctioned by the [Russian] Government."[51]

Nesselrode rejected the American argument. Captain Blinn, he explained, had violated the 1824 treaty, and the Russian-

American Company was within its rights in ousting him from the territory.[52] Dallas angrily suggested to Forsyth that "a refusal to revise their decision definitely communicated, would seem to invite the United States to the protection of their lawful commerce by forceable means:—an invitation which will, I presume, however unwelcome, need not to be twice repeated." The czar, Dallas reported, was under the impression that the United States Treasury was bankrupt; that wars—with Great Britain, over the Maine boundary, and with Mexico, over Texas—were imminent; and that an American civil war lurked just over the horizon. He suggested that a show of force in the Pacific Northwest would serve to correct the czar's opinions.[53] In turn, he warned Nesselrode that "armed opposition to American trade" would bring results that he could not "venture to foresee." The United States would not accept the Russian demand to keep its citizens out of the unoccupied parts of Russian North America.[54]

The Russians would not back down.On March 9, 1838, Nesselrode told Dallas that continued American competition would ruin the Russian-American Company. The imperial government, he wrote, was under an "obligation . . . to protect the commerce and navigation of the Russian colonies."[55] At this point, Dallas believed that reason could not overcome "the grasping policy of the Fur Company." He urged the United States government to tell the Russians that American traders would not be shut out of the benefits of commerce, fur, and fish in the unoccupied area north of latitude 54° 40'. He suggested sending one or two vessels of war to make a thorough examination of the area, as well as to assert the right of the United States to trade freely upon the unoccupied coast.[56]

The Van Buren administration was willing neither to risk a war with Russia nor to capitulate. Van Buren knew that the Russians did not have the armed resources in North America to prevent American traders and fishermen from plying their vocations along the unsettled Russian-American coast, and he was as aware as Czar Nicholas of the common commercial enemy, Great Britain. Van Buren and Forsyth were also reasonably sure that the Russian government, which was having strained relations with Britain over the Russians' tacit support of the Canadian rebels, would not dare to add to their troubles by putting the United States on the side of the British. The Russian government would not risk American enmity toward larger Russian policy designs solely for the sake of the yet unproven Russian-American Fur Company.[57]

In case the Russian foreign ministry considered inaction to be acquiescence, President Van Buren, in his annual message in December 1838, made it clear that his government maintained "that the citizens of the United States have, independent of the provisions of the Convention of 1824, a right to trade with the natives upon the coast in question at unoccupied points." He added that while "the capital and tonnage employed by our citizens in their trade with the northwest coast" may *seem* to be "too inconsiderable to attract much attention, yet the subject may in other respects deserve the careful consideration of the Congress."[58] Van Buren, Forsyth, Dallas, the American whaling captains, and the fur traders of the Northwest Coast clearly were not going to forfeit a promising commercial future in the Russian-American colonies of North America.

III

Aside from troubles with Americans, the Russians were being pressured by the British Hudson's Bay Company. In 1836, several employees of the Russian-American Company crossed the Stikine River into the British sphere in violation of the 1825 Anglo-Russian Convention. The resultant conflict led to a 250,000-ruble claim by the Hudson's Bay Company against the Russian company. Wrangell was now in St. Petersburg serving as director of the board of the company. Both he and Nesselrode found in this incident a way to deal with the pressures coming from American traders and whalers, as well as from the Van Buren government. Nesselrode devised a method by which he believed he could play off the British against the Yankees. The Russian government offered the Hudson's Bay Company a ten-year lease of a lisiere running from Cape Spencer south to 54° 40' in lieu of the 250,000 rubles the British company demanded. The temporary lease, Nesselrode believed, would halt American penetration. After a ten-year period, during which the Yankees would hopefully find other areas in which to exert their energies, the Russians could remain in North America in peace. Nesselrode explained to the minister of finance, Egor Kankrin, that by adopting this course, "we should gain the advantage of doing away with all rivalry in the fur trade and of putting an end to the frequent occasions of friction with England and with the citizens of the United States of America which have already often led to unpleasant correspondence with those Governments."[59]

Russian minister to the United States, Alexander Bodisco, warned his government that if the Russian-American Company granted the Hudson's Bay Company privileges to exploit the Russian possessions, it would produce "a bad impression" in the United States. The American government, he predicted, would say "that we turned out the Americans to let in the English." The United States, he concluded, "attach great importance to the Northwest." Nevertheless, the lease was granted to Great Britain. When Secretary of State Forsyth learned of the grant, he told Bodisco that he hoped what he had heard was not true and suggested that if the Russians had indeed signed a contract with the Hudson's Bay Company, "such lease means renunciation of possession."[60]

Nesselrode's plan to use the Hudson's Bay Company to exclude Yankees from the Northwest Coast failed.[61] Individual American whalers and traders were not deterred by the British company's lease to this area.

5

Yankee Whaling Along the Coasts of Russian-America 1835–1852

Herman Melville's classic account of Yankee whalers in *Moby Dick* has led most Americans to picture the leviathan hunters sailing the warm South Pacific in search of their prey. In his earlier and less well-known romance, *Mardi* (1849), Melville presented another impression of the climate under which Yankee whalers labored:

> To the uninitiated in the business of whaling . . . let me say: that right whaling on the Nor'West Coast in chill and fogs, the sullen, inert monsters rafting the sea all around like Hartz forest logs on the Rhine and submitting to the harpoon like half-stunned bullocks to the knife—this horrid and indecent right whaling, I say, compared to a spirited hunt for the gentlemanly cachalot in southern and more genial seas is as the butchery of white bears upon blank Greenland icebergs is to zebra hunting in Caffraria, where the lively quarry bounds before you through leafy glades.[1]

This drearier scene more accurately describes American whaling during its golden age from 1835 to 1845 and the decade following, when Yankee whalers made their greatest profits along the Northwest coasts of Russian-America. Despite its great profit, the Northwest Coast whaling interest had little influence upon federal legislation or national policy during this period. On the other hand, the activity of Yankee whalers in Russian-America made a strong impact upon the management of the Russian-American Company and led some Russian policy makers to conclude that their colony should, sooner or later, be ceded to the United States.

I

Commercial opportunities for Americans in whaling continued to grow along the coastline of Russian-America from 1837 to 1845. While Yankee whalers had visited these coasts since the 1790s, not until the late 1830s did the North Pacific whaling grounds assume great importance. Soon after the Kodiak, or Coast Right Whaling, grounds were discovered by Captain Bazillar T. Folger of the ship *Ganges* of Nantucket in 1835,[2] the grounds became the most important in the North Pacific. In 1843, two New Bedford captains, Ricketson and Turner, found the valuable bowhead whale swimming in Russian-American waters.[3] From 1835 until after the Alaska purchase, these Northwest Coast whaling grounds produced 60 percent of all the oil secured by the American whaling fleet. More than 55 percent of this fleet fished in these waters from 1840 to 1845. In 1845, for instance, of the 257 vessels sent out from American ports, 200 went to the North Pacific waters and 139 of these to the Russian coast. Moreover, in that year, 263 of the estimated 690 vessels that made up the Yankee whaling fleet were fishing exclusively in seas under the jurisdiction of the Russian-American Company.[4]

By the end of 1845, the whaling fleet of the United States numbered 736 vessels, totaling 233,262 tons. The value of the fleet exceeded $21 million; all investment connected with the industry was valued at more than $70 million. American whale fishery was responsible for directly or indirectly supporting 70,000 people.[5] During the late 1830s and early 1840s, the prices for whale products rose. Sperm oil, which sold at 84 cents per gallon when the Russian-American waters first assumed their great importance in 1835, was selling at 90½ cents by 1845. Whale oil, which sold for 32 cents a gallon when the depression began in 1837, sold for 36½ cents in 1845. Whalebone rose from 19 cents to 40 cents per pound during the same period.[6] The profits to owners of whaling vessels were high. An average successful voyage to the Pacific Northwest brought a return of almost 100 percent profit.[7]

In the late 1830s and early 1840s, whaling was less affected by financial stress than other segments of the economy. In 1837, the United States experienced a severe economic panic. While the economy seemed to begin a recovery in 1838, a downturn in 1839 resulted in a general deflation that lasted until 1843.

That a boom in whaling occurred in the midst of a severe economic recession was not surprising. Most scholars agree that the panic was set off by the Bank of England's desire to stem the outflow of specie and credit to the United States in 1836 and 1837. That decision had a disastrous effect upon the export of cotton to England, and the fall in the price of cotton had an equally harmful effect upon the American economy as a whole.[8] Nonagricultural pursuits, aside from cotton, were the hardest hit in this panic and the deflation that followed. The whaling industry, however, suffered less from this situation than other industries. Whaling was a unique industry; its system of procurement of labor and investment capital was a holdover from the postrevolutionary economy. It depended less upon the cotton-based economic structure than most other nonagricultural pursuits of the late 1830s.[9] The home of the whaling industry, New England, was also the base for a growing cotton-textiles industry. In the late 1830s, most reports of unemployment came from New England cotton-textile centers,[10] while many of the investors in the textile industry also were large investors in whaling enterprises.[11] A sizable number of those who had previously invested in cotton-textiles and cotton shipping, in which British credits were essential, probably turned instead to whaling[12] where neither cotton prices nor British discounts played a significant role.

For the duration of this recession, additional investments in the whaling fleet increased its tonnage from 124,860 tons in the beginning of 1835 to 199,192 tons in 1843, a gain of 59.7 percent. New Bedford, whaling's most important port, increased its whaling fleet during this period from 66 to 179 vessels—a 270 percent increase.[13] During the same years, cotton-textile profits in Massachusetts fell 12 percent.[14]

Massachusetts was the main beneficiary of the huge profits from whaling. In the 1840s, the manufacture and sale of the by-products of whaling ranked after shoes and cotton products in that state. As early as 1830, the port of New Bedford boasted a whaling fleet twice as large as that of Nantucket, its nearest rival. New Bedford with its oil refineries, cooper's shops, tool works, and many other industries subsidiary to whaling, was the fifth largest shipping port in the United States; by 1850, it was actively competing with Baltimore for fourth place. Almost all of New Bedford's ships fished in grounds over which the Russian-American Company claimed jurisdiction. In 1845, for instance, New Bedford and its sister port, Fairhaven, sent 86.5 percent of their entire whaling fleet to these Russian-American waters.[15] Massachusetts ports were not alone in pursuit of the whales that swam adjacent to the Russian-American Company territory. New London, Connecticut, with a fleet of seventy whaling vessels, sent 72 percent of them to these North Pacific grounds in 1845. Sag Harbor, New York, with a fleet of sixty vessels, followed the trend set by New Bedford and New London.[16]

While the New England states were the most rewarded by the opening of the North Pacific whaling grounds, the whaling industry also benefited the rest of the national economy. Unlike many other American enterprises of the 1840s, whaling was an industry almost entirely of native products and production. The men, ships, and most of the equipment were American. Because whaling voyages accounted for the consumption of almost a half-million barrels of flour and over a half-million barrels of pork and beef, countless bolts of duck, millions of staves, and millions of tons of cordage,[17] the farmer, merchant, and mechanic all received their share of the business. More importantly, the cotton and woolens industries used a great deal of the whale's spermaceti oil. Depending upon the year, one-third to one-fourth of all the spermaceti oil produced by the American whale fishery was used in the cotton and woolens industries.[18] By 1845, the export of common whale oil and bone constituted 3.6 percent of all United States merchandise exports. The demand for spermaceti oil was so great that virtually none of it was exported except during times of decreased production in American cotton textiles. That whaling produce accounted for 3.6 percent of all national merchandise exports is significant in light of the direct correlation from 1837 to 1845 of the balance of all United States trade to the balance of merchandise trade.[19] While the whaling industry was in no sense the most important American enterprise, it was a substantial and growing part of the economy of the United States by 1845. For New Bedford, Nantucket, New London, and Sag Harbor, whaling was the barometer of prosperity.

In the 1840s, whaling was not an industry in which men made their fortunes; rather, it was an enterprise in which men of substance invested their wealth. The cost of a single whaling voyage was so expensive and the results so unpredictable that generally several investors held shares in a single whaling expedition. Only men of capital could invest in whaling because it was often necessary to suffer long periods of severe losses.[20]

The peculiar nature of the investment precluded the creation of a group of men with cohesive economic and specific political interests. Some investors had made their money in shipping, some in maritime insurance, some in textiles, some in all three, and some in other enterprises. Nevertheless, some generalizations can be made about the whaling industry, its leaders, and their relation to American politics and diplomacy. By the mid-1840s, whaling enterprises were dominated by the financial elite of New Bedford, Nantucket, New London, and Sag Harbor, as well as Boston and New York City. Most, though by no means all, who heavily invested in whaling had made their money in other branches of maritime enterprise.[21]

Some, like United States Congressman Joseph Grinnell, left their native New Bedford to make their fortunes in New York City as agents for New Bedford whale-oil merchants.[22] Others, like Grinnell's uncle, Gardiner Howland, had worldwide commercial interests. Howland established primacy in New York City mercantile circles after 1816, and by 1845 the Howland family dominated New Bedford whaling.[23] Charles Morgan, who owed his affluence to maritime shipping, heavily invested in whaling enterprises.[24] In fact, like Jonathan Bourne and the Perkins family, most heavy investors in whaling voyages had made their fortunes in New York and Boston commercial centers.[25]

The men who dominated the whaling industry were Whigs.

Most had been Federalists or had come from Federalist families, and virtually all came from the Northeast. As a group, they favored high tariffs, development of domestic manufactures, and support for federally sponsored internal improvements.[26] In 1843, they heartily supported Daniel Webster's settlement of the Maine boundary dispute with Great Britain.[27]

Those concerned with Northwest Coast whaling, nevertheless, made no concerted effort to influence the legislation of the United States Congress. There seem to be two reasons for this. First, aside from the program dealing with federal aid for internal improvements, the whalers appeared to have no special requirements that demanded congressional action. Second, the very nature of Northwest Coast whaling and investment in it meant that this interest group was too factionalized to agree upon specific proposals that would benefit all participants.

An analysis of the voting records of the Congressmen elected from whaling districts from 1840 to 1845 demonstrates that the whaling interest did not or could not assert much influence over Congress. The four whaling ports most concerned with Northwest Coast whaling were New Bedford, Nantucket, New London, and Sag Harbor. These ports generally voted for candidates from the Whig party.[28] The Tenth Massachusetts Congressional District, which included New Bedford and Nantucket, consistently elected Whigs to Congress in the 1840s. New London, Connecticut, in its state's Third Congressional District, was represented by Whigs except in the Twenty-eighth Congress.[29] This district was highly competitive, although the New London voters regularly cast their ballots for Whig candidates on the congressional and national level. From 1839 until 1843, Thomas W. Williams, a dominant figure in the whaling industry at New London, represented this district in Congress.[30] While Sag Harbor was a predominantly Whig area, its congressional district, the New York First, elected only Democrats until 1846.[31]

An analysis of congressional voting from these three districts from 1841 to 1845 demonstrates that the representatives generally voted along party lines.[32] One important exception was the strongly antiexpansionist voting of Democrat George H. Catlin of the Third District of Connecticut (New London). Catlin, unlike the other three Connecticut Democratic Congressmen in the Twenty-eighth Congress, voted the same antiexpansionist line then supported by those Whigs from other whaling districts.[33] He also supported and introduced legislation for internal improvements,[34] a position that deviated from the national Democratic party view and that was consistent with that of the New Bedford and Nantucket Whigs. Catlin's position, however, had more to do with the fact that he represented a constituency which had consistently supported Whig party policies than that he came from a whaling port.

When the Twenty-eighth Congress assembled in March 1843, Joseph Grinnell of New Bedford served as spokesman for the whaling industry. He was uniquely qualified for this role. His mother was a Howland, and the Howland family by the 1820s controlled the largest mercantile firm in New York City. In 1809, at the age of twenty-one, Joseph moved to New York City to work in the shipping firm of his uncle, John Howland. By 1815, Grinnell had, albeit with family aid, established his own firm with another relative, Preserved Fish. The firm of Fish and Grinnell soon became one of the largest agents for New Bedford whale-oil merchants. By 1825, Joseph Grinnell had made enough money to retire at the age of thirty-seven. Returning to New Bedford in 1832, he was elected president of the newly chartered Marine Bank, and in 1841 he became a director of the Boston and Providence Railroad, eventually attaining the office of president. Grinnell won election to Congress in 1843 as a Whig, where he served continuously until March 3, 1851, when he retired.[35]

When Congress reopened the discussion on lowering the tariff in 1844, Grinnell argued that a lower tariff would harm the whaling industry. From the House floor and in a widely circulated pamphlet, *Speech on the Tariff with Statistical Tables of the Whale Fishery,* parts of which were reprinted in Hunt's *Merchant's Magazine,* the New Bedford Congressman argued his case. Grinnell observed that even though no direct harm would befall his district in lowering the tariff, the whaling industry was related to other manufacturing industries that needed protection against foreign competition. The manufacturing and maritime industries, he explained, were interdependent and, in turn, stimulated the entire economic growth of the United States.[36]

Grinnell nevertheless introduced no specific legislation aimed at aiding the whaling industry. While he may have cited whaling as an enterprise that would be indirectly harmed by a low tariff, Grinnell was only using the whale fishery as another example in the Whig party's arsenal of arguments against such measures. From 1835 to 1845, no single piece of legislation dealing solely with whaling in the Pacific Northwest was offered or discussed in the United States Congress.

While the whaling industry had little influence upon United States policy, it had a marked effect upon the attitudes of some Russian policy makers toward Russian-America. The Russian-American Company feared the Yankees. In 1842, it transmitted a report to the government in St. Petersburg from Captain Kadlikoff, commander of the company's ship, *Nasledvik Alexander*. Kadlikoff reported that at least thirty American whalers were seen fishing in the Bering Sea alone, and the previous year fifty other American vessels had been sighted in the same waters.[37] The minister of finance told Nesselrode that the company complained that "American whalers are injuring its commerce."[38] The company requested the imperial government to send armed cruisers for the preservation of the Bering Sea as a *mare clausum*. The government replied that the cost of keeping cruisers in the Bering Sea and along the coast of Russian-America was too high and implied that the possible results were too risky. "Whalers can be kept from landing," replied the minister of foreign affairs, "but not from whaling."[39]

In 1843, Adolf Etolin, manager of the company in Sitka, requested that the directors supply him with more definite instructions as to what to do about "whaling vessels which threatened to ruin the fur trade by scaring the sea otters away and what to do about whaling captains, who despite the Convention and Russian orders, continue to enter harbors, etc., in the Russian possession."[40] While awaiting instructions, Etolin grew impatient and ordered two cruisers to patrol the areas frequented by the Yankee fleets.[41]

Etolin's complaints coincided with the beginnings of a debate in St. Petersburg over the limits of eastward Russian expansion. This discussion, which included the future of the Russian possessions in North America, continued well into the 1850s and 1860s. As early as February 1843, the *St. Petersburg Journal* presented a case favorable to United States claims in Oregon and in opposition to the claims of Great Britain. The *Journal* implied that Russia was wasting its time and resources in North America and should concentrate its energies in Asia. In that sphere, observed the article, Great Britain endangered Russia's well-being, especially since the British successes in the Opium War.[42]

In May 1844, the Russian-American Company issued a long report, which seemed to support the *St. Petersburg Journal*'s earlier conclusions. The report admitted that dividends were down but predicted a swift upturn since the company intended to concentrate its future efforts in its Asian holdings. To that end, the directors decided to order a search of "the Bay of Ayan on the coast of the Okhotsk Sea in the hope of finding there a port more secure and whose entrance presents less difficulties" than the present harbor at Okhotsk.[43]

Although the Russian-American Company retained its possessions in North America for another twenty-three years, the Russian government began to explore alternatives to constant disagreements with Yankees along the Northwest Coast. Cooperation with the United States on both sides of the Pacific against the British was one solution. This alternative would be returned to again and again in the internal policy debates each time Yankee encroachments seemed to threaten the czar's sovereignty in North America. In the early 1840s, however, the alternative suggested by the *St. Petersburg Journal* and the 1844 Russian company report remained a matter for conversation rather than policy.

The problem of Yankee encroachments had not improved, in the view of the Russian-American Company, by 1845. Referring to the American whaling vessels as "hell-ships," company officials complained that the Yankees stole oil, as well as food and women, from the Aleuts and Eskimos, leaving in return bad liquor and syphilis. The Russian company again asserted that American whalers were ruining its trade. The Russian foreign ministry explained to company officials that whenever the imperial government requested that the United States restrict its whalers, the American government always replied that it "did not have enough power . . . to restrict its citizens from arbitrary actions."[44] This time, however, the St. Petersburg government agreed to threaten to send armed cruisers to keep Yankee vessels out of the Russian dominion.[45] As Yankee whaling along the Russian–American coast and Bering Sea continued to prosper after 1845, it seemed that nothing short of force could stop American captains from pursuing their prey. The cruisers St. Petersburg sent to Russian-America were needed to protect populated areas and never interfered with the whalers. By 1845, 263 Yankee whaling vessels were hunting in Russian waters.[46] The foreign ministry, while agreeing to send cruisers to Russian-America, explicitly instructed their captains to "be very careful in their actions and so far as possible avoid occurrences that can lead to complaints."[47]

II

While the whaling industry as a whole began to decline after 1845, Northwest Coast whaling reached its greatest heights between 1846 and 1852. The reason for the substantial growth in whaling in the late 1830s and early 1840s had been the discovery of the coast-right whales in the Kodiak grounds in 1835. This find stimulated increased investment in whaling in the early 1840s, which led, in turn, to the opening of new grounds for bowhead whales in the Sea of Okhotsk and along Kamchatka in 1848.[48]

These new whaling grounds pushed profits to their highest levels in the history of the industry. While sperm oil sold at 88 cents per gallon in 1845, by 1851 the price had risen to $1.27¼ per gallon. During the same period, whale oil rose from 33 cents per gallon to 45.8 cents. Only whalebone remained about the same, its price rising only ¼ cent in those six years to 34¼ cents (although in 1852 the price jumped to 50.8 cents per pound).[49] In 1845, 77.8 percent of the whaling vessels sent out fished in North Pacific waters; by 1851, 85.3 percent fished there.[50] The total value of importation of whale oil and bone rose to over $10 million in 1851.[51]

Officials in Russian-America and in St. Petersburg grew increasingly alarmed over the penetration of Yankee whalers in Russian waters. Nikolai Muraviev, governor of eastern Siberia, complained in September 1849 that 250 United States whaleships were hunting in the Sea of Okhotsk. "The figure given me as to the number of ships," noted Muraviev, "is very conservative. I heard higher figures from the whalers themselves."[52] The following year, the Russian-American Company petitioned its government to declare "a complete prohibition to hunt whales in the Okhotsk sea." If the government could not declare the area a closed sea, "at least" it could provide "efficient protection by naval cruisers of some of the places where the whalers abound."[53]

The Russian government was either unable or unwilling to use force to drive away the unwelcome Yankees. Certainly the threat of force had proved no detriment, but one course of action still remained open to the Russians. Since 1847, certain officials in the Russian-American Company had been urging the creation of a Russian-operated whaling company to compete with the Yankees. These officials did not fail to point out that the company would not only be able to deal effectively with the Americans by competing with them, but it could join in on the profits of the whaling boom.[54] In 1849, the ministry of finance granted permission to the Russian-American Company to engage in whale fishery. The Russo-Finland Whaling Company, the official subsidiary of the Russian company, finally began operations in August 1851, but the less experienced Russians quickly proved incapable of competing with the Yankees and folded in 1854.[55]

III

Yankee whaling enterprises in Russian-America seemed to demonstrate the actual weakness of the Russian-American Company to maintain its sovereignty in North America. After 1850, the debates within the inner circles of the Russian government generally concluded that Russia's colony in the new world could not survive sustained Yankee curiosity. By 1853, Nikolai Muraviev, a staunch advocate of his country's expansion into Asia and the conqueror, as well as governor, of the Amur region, urged Czar Nicholas to cede the Russian-American possessions to the United States. "The ultimate rule of the United States over the whole of North America is so natural," Muraviev wrote, "that we must sooner or later recede."[56] The growth of Yankee whaling along the coasts of Russian-America from 1835 to 1852 was an important factor in the formulation of official Russian attitudes and policy toward its North American possession.

6

The Oregon Question and Russian-America

By the mid-1840s protection of Northwest Coast whaling was an important aspect of northeastern Whig opposition to those who demanded the United States take all of the Oregon territory. To many concerned with the whaling and maritime commerce of the Pacific Northwest, the Polk administration's initial policy in Oregon seemed to be leading toward a clash with Great Britain. The leaders of the whaling industry and their representatives in Congress feared the potential of British sea power and wished to avoid any incidents that might provoke war with Britain. Some northeastern Whigs probably overreacted to Polk's Oregon policy. Nevertheless, many of these Whigs believed that Polk and his Secretary of State, James Buchanan, might lead the United States into war with England, which would destroy American commerce and whaling in the Pacific Northwest. Because Yankee whalers came into constant contact with Russia's North American colony, those concerned with whaling not only worried about the Oregon issue and its effect upon Anglo-American relations, but they also feared its consequences upon American-Russian relations in the Pacific Northwest. An Anglophobic posture in the Pacific Northwest could lead the Polk administration toward a more reconciliatory policy with the Russians, whose colony's southern border formed the northern border of the disputed Oregon territory. The Russian government during the previous ten

93

years had repeatedly protested against Yankee traders and whalers who landed and hunted along the Russian–American coasts. The Russians, moreover, had requested the United States government to restrain United States nationals from landing, trading, or hunting along the Russian–American coast or within its territorial waters. The northeastern Whigs thus feared that Polk's call for all of Oregon could cut two ways. First, British control of the sea could drive the whalers and traders out of the Northwest Coast in event of war. Second, the Russian price for cooperation in the Pacific Northwest might be the exclusion of Yankee traders and whalers from Russian-America and its coasts.

This chapter will concentrate primarily upon the perceptions of those who sought to protect and extend whaling and maritime interests along the Northwest Coast. Upon these perceptions, as parochial as they might have been, the foundations of the Taylor–Fillmore administration's policy toward Russian–America was laid; it was a policy that attempted to reverse what the Whigs had viewed as Polk's sell-out of Yankee commercial interests in the Pacific Northwest. The success of the Taylor–Fillmore Whig policy laid the groundwork for another Whig, William Henry Seward, who fifteen years later would settle the problem of Russian-America once and for all.

I

After the financial downturn of 1837–1843, migration to Oregon surged. By 1845, almost five thousand Americans had settled in Oregon; all but eight resided south of the Columbia River in the fertile Willamette Valley.[1] While the earlier immigrants to the territory had come from New England, those who arrived in 1843 and after were generally from the Midwest, particularly Missouri. More often than not, these new settlers were destitute, bringing with them only their strong anti-British bias.[2] The British living in the Hudson's Bay Company's settlements north of the Columbia River began to grow increasingly frightened of these new settlers. Threats on British persons and property grew to such an extent that by 1844 the Hudson's Bay Company strengthened its defenses at Fort Vancouver and appealed to the British government for additional naval protection.[3] In Washington, exaggerated charges of British brutality presented in Congress served only to inflame expansionist segments of the American people.[4]

In summer 1844, Secretary of State John C. Calhoun attempted—unsuccessfully—to negotiate a settlement of the Oregon boundary at the forty-ninth parallel with British Minister Pakenham.[5] The advent of James K. Polk to the presidency seemed to signal a stiffening of the American position. Prior to the Democratic convention of May 1844, Polk had pledged to support United States' claims to all of Oregon.[6] Once nominated, he committed himself to his party's platform, which declared that the United States' "title to the whole territory of Oregon is clear and unquestionable; that no portion of the same ought to be ceded to England or any other power."[7] His inaugural message proclaimed once again that the American claim to all of Oregon was "clear and unquestionable."[8]

It has been argued most convincingly that President Polk's public positions and subsequent actions were a calculated show of belligerence, which he hoped would persuade the British to come to terms on an Oregon boundary of 49°.[9] But even if Polk was attempting compromise through confrontation diplomacy, those concerned with commerce and whaling along the Northwest Coast were uneasy. Some, no doubt, believed Polk's rhetoric and feared he would drag the United States into war with Great Britain. Others, used to the hyperbole of American politics, worried that the British might take Polk at his word, which could be as dangerous as if the President intended to go to war over 54° 40′. The rhetoric, as we shall see, was not one-sided. Those concerned with protecting whaling and commercial interests in the Pacific Northwest often exaggerated the dangers of the Polk administration's public pronouncements.

Polk's choice of James Buchanan as Secretary of State did not calm the northeastern Whigs' apprehensions. Buchanan, a Democrat from western Pennsylvania, was hardly a friend of the whaling and Northwest Coast commercial concerns. He had been one of the earliest proponents of the "whole of Oregon" movement. As a United States Senator, he had lashed out at the Massachusetts Whigs who, he claimed, urged peace at any price. These Whigs, Buchanan had observed, did not want to protect American rights in Oregon because they feared war with England would destroy their whaling and commerce in the Pacific Northwest. He averred that this was a selfish view, because the fur traders and trappers, unlike the maritime interests on the Northwest coast, had to contend with the Hudson's Bay Company. Our citizens, Buchanan proclaimed, could not compete with the Hudson's Bay Company because the British government had extended to that company a monopoly of the landed fur trade in the Northwest. The only way to protect the American traders from British monopoly practice was to drive out the British. He argued that he was merely advocating a policy that had been urged by John Floyd since 1821. Buchanan made it clear, moreover, that his vision of the nation would relegate exports to a minor role:

> The extension of our nation thus far has not weakened its strength; on the contrary, this very extension had bound us together by still stronger bonds of mutual interest and mutual dependence. Our internal commerce has grown to be worth ten times our foreign trade.[10]

Senator Buchanan's words of March 1844 displeased those interested in Northwest Coast whaling and trading. Later that year, when Polk announced his intention to appoint Buchanan to head the Department of State, Buchanan's views became a cause for concern on the part of many Whigs. Among the first to speak out was William Sturgis, who owed his prosperity to the Pacific Northwest trade. He quickly aimed his sights on the Democrats' rhetoric. His influence in convincing the Monroe administration and John Quincy Adams of the need for protecting American rights against the czar's 1821 ukase had been significant.[11] In January 1845, Sturgis delivered a lecture before the Mercantile Library Association, which was subsequently published in pamphlet form and extensively circulated by opponents of the drive for all of Oregon. Taking the incoming administration at its word, he warned of the "danger of collision" with Britain. Sturgis believed that the retention of the entire Oregon territory would "not . . . add to the power or promote the prosperity of the United States." Rather, he observed, it could have the reverse effect. The real value of the Pacific Northwest, he argued, had always been maritime in nature; a war with Great Britain over this area could only serve to destroy the worth of the Northwest Coast to the United States.[12]

By February 1845, the maritime establishments in New York and Boston were so worried over the possibility that Polk would lead the nation into war over Oregon and/or bring the United States to economic disaster that they recalled Daniel Webster from private life.[13] Senator Webster did not disappoint his sponsors. Before leaving for Washington, he spoke out against those who talked about the need for war against Great Britain to obtain the whole of Oregon. Constant speculation about war, he explained, harmed the nation, for "it confounds and confuses men in regard to their own business plans."[14] In the Senate, Webster decried the current talk of war: "All know what an immense amount of property is afloat upon the ocean, carried there by our citizens in the prosecution of their maritime pursuits." Did not the administration and the Senate understand, he queried, that "the breath of a rumor of war will affect the value of that property"?[15]

Spokesmen for northwestern commercial and whaling interests in the House of Representatives demonstrated an almost paranoid attitude toward suggestions that the United States battle Britain for the possession of all of Oregon. On March 18, 1844, Robert Winthrop[16] of Massachusetts reacted to the position Buchanan had put forward. Winthrop denied that Oregon was a "western question." The territory had been discovered and exploited by Boston men long before "westerners" heard of it. "The great present value of this territory," he observed, "has relation to the commerce and navigation of the Pacific Ocean." Those who had actual commercial concerns, Winthrop added, were whale fishermen. "The single town of New Bedford . . . sends out 92,000, out of a little more than 130,000 tons of American shipping employed in this business; and those other towns in the same district employ 31,170 tons of the remainder." He suggested that "so far, then, as the whaling interest is to be regarded, the Oregon question is emphatically a Massachusetts question." Winthrop, nevertheless, felt obliged to add "that the whole coast of Oregon can hardly furnish one really good harbor." He agreed with those who proposed a compromise with Great Britain at the forty-ninth parallel.[17]

After President Polk broke off negotiations with Britain, those from whaling districts in Congress intensified their prophesies of doom. John Rockwell of Connecticut, who represented New London, presented to the House a peace petition from his constituents. He reminded those who would talk of taking all Oregon that his own district sent out a large number of vessels to the North Pacific and had "vast amounts of capital invested in shipping at the ports of New London and Stonington, all of which was, in case of war, to be exposed to entire destruction."[18]

Joseph Grinnell of New Bedford, generally regarded as the congressional spokesman for the whaling industry, repeatedly brought the value of whale fishery to the Congress's attention. Grinnell, along with his northeastern Whig colleagues, feared that a war with Great Britain would destroy American commerce in the Pacific Northwest. Yankee interests there, he argued, were commercial and not territorial in nature.[19]

Washington Hunt[20] of New York combined the arguments of the whaling interests with those of the maritime community as a whole by carrying his confreres' arguments one step further. Hunt noted that in the commercial view all that the United States required in Oregon was a foothold on the Pacific. This, he explained, it had. For the good of the nation and its commerce, he suggested, Congress should think "not only of avoiding war, but the apprehensions of war, whose influence was so disastrous to all the interests of the country."[21]

The worst fears of the whaling interests seemed to be confirmed in September 1845 when Secretary of State Buchanan agreed to cooperate with the Russian demands that the United States government help keep Yankee traders and whalers from hunting or trading along the Russian–American coasts. Buchanan, who served as United States minister to Russia from 1832 to

1833, was well aware of the Russian displeasure over Yankee penetration of the czar's North American possession.[22] In July 1845, while the debate over Oregon raged in Congress, the Russian minister to the United States, Alexander Bodisco, complained about the great number of Yankee whalers and traders who violated Russian sovereignty along the coasts of Russian-America. Bodisco informed Buchanan that under the provisions of the 1824 treaty, all vessels owned by citizens of the United States were excluded from fishing within the territorial waters of the Russian possession or landing anywhere along its coasts.[23] "To tolerate longer such a state of things," observed the Russian minister, "would be to aid in the ruin of the Russian establishments, to contribute to the demoralization of the native population, and to provoke painful and inevitable collisions." He informed Secretary of State Buchanan that, in light of these circumstances, the Russian government "has resolved to establish a system of cruisers, along the Russian shores, for the purpose of enforcing respect for the stipulations of our treaty with the United States, of putting an end to the encroachments of whalers, and above all to maintain the prohibition against American vessels."[24]

Buchanan, no doubt eager to obtain Russian amity during this period of Anglo-American enmity, agreed to tender administration support to Bodisco's demands. On September 26, 1845, the Secretary of State published a caveat in the *Washington Union* to all American vessels sailing in Pacific Northwest waters. Buchanan had even submitted this notice, in its entirety, to Bodisco for approval before publication. The official United States government position was a warning to Yankee ships "not to violate the existing treaty . . . by resorting to any point on the Russian coast where there is a Russian settlement . . . *nor to frequent the interior seas, gulfs, harbors and creeks* upon that coast at any point north of the latitude of 54° 40'."[25]

By admitting that United States vessels should not be permitted to land on the unoccupied shores of Russian-America, Buchanan conceded more than any of his predecessors. The Secretary of State told Bodisco that the sending of Russian cruisers to the Northwest Coast "cannot but contribute to keep up the excellent relations between the two countries."[26] Perhaps Buchanan realized that the Russian fleet was incapable of patrolling Russian-American waters against 260 Yankee whalers. He naturally feared that if a war broke out with Britain over the Oregon issue, Russian neutrality would be more valuable than latent hostility. No doubt both he and Bodisco were aware that the warning to American sea captains would have little effect. Nevertheless, the failure of the Polk administration to assert United States' maritime rights along the unoccupied coasts of Russian-America did demonstrate that those who had advocated the protection of whaling and trading from the perils of war had some justification for their fear that Polk's policies could lead to the destruction of the maritime commerce of the Pacific Northwest.[27]

When the smoke cleared from the war of words, all sides readily supported the compromise settlement submitted to the Senate by President Polk in June 1846.[28] This did not mean, however, that northeastern Whigs either perceived the Oregon compromise as the intention of the President or that they believed their interests secure under Polk's leadership.

Norman Graebner has argued that Polk's desires for California were the same as those of the commercially oriented Whigs.[29] Yet, as Charles Sellers has since pointed out, Polk's expansion was basically continental in 1845.[30] Furthermore, even if one agrees that Polk's general policies coincided with those interested in Northwest Coast whaling and commerce, the differences in tactics seemed extreme enough to create a general mistrust of the President by northeastern Whigs. The maritime community was most careful to avoid collision with the British from fear that altercation would bring down the British fleet on Yankee commerce. These same northeasterners were willing to suffer the sustained belligerence of the Russians, realizing that the latter were powerless to exclude Yankee commerce. Polk, on the other hand, seemed to invite Great Britain's hostility both in Oregon and Texas, while attempting to secure Russia's friendship as a makeweight against Great Britain. The differences between the commercial Whigs and Polk, even if only tactical, were extreme.

II

When the Whigs regained the presidency in 1849, they set out to reverse Polk's policies toward Russian-America. Daniel Webster and many other northeastern Whigs were unhappy with their party's choice in 1848 of Zachary Taylor for the presidency.[31] Most Whigs agreed, however, that anyone was better than Polk or Lewis Cass, the Democratic nominee.[32] Taylor chose as his Secretary of State John M. Clayton of Delaware, who had been a strong and loyal supporter of both John Quincy Adams' policies and his presidential candidacies. While a United States Senator, Clayton had opposed war with Mexico and favored a compromise with Great Britain at the forty-ninth parallel. Like Adams and Webster, Clayton strongly promoted commercial, rather than unlimited territorial, expansion. The new Secretary of State proved receptive to those who urged both expansion and protection of American enterprise in the Pacific Northwest.[33]

Moreover, the Taylor administration desired to demonstrate to the doubting northeastern Whigs that it would support policies beneficial to those with commercial interests in the Pacific Northwest. As a first act of good faith, Secretary of State Clayton ordered John Folsom, assistant quartermaster of the United States Army in San Francisco, to prepare a report about "American interests on the Pacific Coasts."[34]

Folsom had arrived in San Francisco in 1847 serving as a captain in the army. That year, he was appointed senior officer of the Quartermaster's Department on the North Pacific Coast. Folsom had purchased large amounts of real estate before the discovery of gold, and by 1849 his property holdings in San Francisco had made him a very wealthy man.[35]

Folsom delivered his report in October 1849. He informed Secretary of State Clayton that the Russian-American Company was consolidating its interests and "fast diverting their capital and labour from the fur to the lumber and coal trades and the fisheries. The change," noted Folsom, "is now becoming injurious in various points of view" to American commerce. He pointed out the existence of a large trade between Russian-America and San Francisco. Due to the Treaty of 1824 and the lease the Hudson's Bay Company obtained in 1840, much of the carrying trade unfortunately would go in British ships.[36] "American vessels . . . are prohibited from taking them [goods] to the point of consumption. But," he added, "the rivalry of the Russian and English shipping fostered into importance by a consortium so detrimental to our agriculture, manufacturing, and commercial interests is not . . . the most serious aspect which this question assumes." Folsom explained: "Steam navigation is undoubtedly destined to be the most efficient agent in building up our supremacy in the Pacific, and to place its success upon a secure basis it is necessary that coals should be supplied at the cheapest possible rate." He observed that "the Russians have an abundance of coals at the Island of Kodiak and at other points on the coast." If the Russians did not agree to give Americans free access to this coal, Congress merely had to "pass a law" to discriminate against Russian imports and place port charges on all Russian ships. Such action, Folsom assured Clayton, would convince the czar's government to allow Yankee traders to enter the harbors of Russian-America.[37]

In January 1850, Samuel Thurston, a delegate from the Oregon Territory, requested the Secretary of State to attempt to secure for those on the Pacific the privileges to trade "in provisions with the Russian possessions" held exclusively by the Hudson's Bay Company. "It is very desirable," said Thurston, "that this trade be laid open to our commerce in the Pacific."[38] Clayton sent Thurston's request along with Folsom's report to the Russian chargé d'affaires, Edward de Stoeckl. Secretary Clayton claimed that the Russians were illegally preventing American trade from entering Russian-America. The 1832 Treaty of Commerce with Russia, he argued, superseded the Treaty of 1824. According to the 1832 treaty, Clayton observed, the intercourse of the two nations fell under the category of "most-favored-nation." Yet he was dismayed to learn that "restrictions exist in Russian ports on this trade, as you will perceive from the accompanying copies of letters relating to this subject." Clayton noted that his object in writing to Stoeckl was "to inquire if you can give me any certain information whether, under existing regulations, our commerce and navigation are freely admitted into the ports and places of Russia on the Northwest coast of America, as in other ports of his Imperial Majesty; and if not what are the restrictions to which United States vessels and their cargoes are subjected?'' Because of Folsom's report, Clayton knew the answer to the first part of his question: American vessels were not given most-favored-nation treatment. The second part of the question, which dealt with restrictions on American trade, was intended to point out to the Russians that if they did not lift restrictions on Yankee vessels in North America, they might find similar restrictions placed on Russian ships arriving in American ports.[39]

Stoeckl replied on the following day that he would refer the matter to his government in St. Petersburg.[40] On May 27, 1850 Nesselrode informed the secretary of the Russian legation to the United States, Waldemar Bodisco, that the Russian government would not accede to the American request to permit its vessels to visit Russian-America.[41] Before this message could be relayed to Clayton, President Taylor died (July 1850), and Clayton was replaced by Daniel Webster.

Given Daniel Webster's earlier strong defense of American maritime interests in the Pacific Northwest, it seemed likely that he would take an even more belligerent attitude toward Russian policy in North America than his predecessor. Moreover, Webster had assumed a hostile stand toward the Russian government in November 1849. The then Senator had called the Russian czar ''a criminal and a malefactor'' for his part in suppressing the Hungarian revolution. The czar's actions, he proclaimed, were ''an offense against the rights of the civilized world.''[42] Webster, however, knew the difference between rhetorical flourish and public policy. To the Hungarians he offered only his indignation. When he returned to the Department of State in 1850, he moved away from Clayton's more belligerent policy and offered cooperation instead of conflict.

Webster quickly perceived that Clayton's veiled threats were not persuading the Russians to open their North American colony to United States enterprise. The new Secretary of State decided that a policy of conciliation, rather than reprisal, could gain the desired results. In June 1851 Webster instructed United States commercial and consular agents in the Sandwich Islands and China "to extend assistance to the subjects of Russia." Russian nationals would have use of United States diplomatic "good offices" in areas where the Russian government lacked official agents. He sent copies of these instructions to Russian Minister Bodisco.[43] By implication, Webster attempted to persuade the Russian government that cooperation with the United States in Asia was worth the price of increased Yankee enterprise in Russian-America.

Webster's policy worked. In February 1852, the Russian-American Company signed a contract allowing a San Francisco firm to import coal and ice from the Russian possession.[44] In December of that year, Czar Nicholas gave his permission for an American squadron, which was making a survey of whaling grounds in the North Pacific and Bering Strait, to land in Russian-America.[45]

III

By the end of the 1850s, the United States possessed the entire Pacific Coast from lower California to the Straits of Juan de Fuca. The discovery of gold in California increased the momentum of American settlement there. One of the results of the rapid growth of population on the Pacific Coast was the growth of curiosity about Russian-America. While the idea of acquiring the Russian possession did not gain political support until the middle of the 1850s, the first traces of such a movement were evident by the end of the 1840s.

In February 1849, the Whig *Niles' National Register* reprinted in full an article from the Democratic Newark, New Jersey, *Sentinel,* "Russian-America—Our Pacific Settlements." The Russian settlements in North America, reported the *Sentinel,* had scarcely been known to most United States citizens; but, since Oregon and California had been added to the republic, "the West Coast of America is destined to witness mighty things." New Archangel (Sitka) was described as a port which "speaks of life,

of energy, and of the spread of civilization." The mercantile fleet
there, added the *Sentinel,* "would do credit to many a proud port
in Europe or the United States." The Russian possessions were
described as an attractive place to settle since "the climate of
Russian-America is mild for its latitude, like Western Europe."
The area, predicted the author, was "destined to support a considerable population." Unfortunately, observed the *Sentinel,*
"the Russian-American Company, who have the entire government of this country, do not encourage migration, as it tends to
destroy their monopoly of fur." Nevertheless, forecast the writer, "change must come with the general increase of the population." Indeed, a Yankee technician was already employed by the
Russian-American Company to instruct the Russians on the
building of steam vessels. The *Sentinel* concluded, he soon "will
have many companions speaking his own language."[46]

The events of the period from 1845 to 1852 are pivotal for any
understanding of the meaning of the purchase of Alaska in 1867.
Buchanan's 1845 policy of submitting to Russian demands had no
effect in the long run upon American enterprise along the Northwest Coast. With the annexation of Oregon and California to the
republic, United States predominance on the North American
Pacific coast was assured. By 1852, those Americans with concerns in Russian-America came not only from Boston, but also
from San Francisco and the Puget Sound settlement. The addition
of the San Francisco interests was to prove a decisive factor in
the Russian decision to cede Alaska. Northeastern Whig resistance to the all-Oregon movement in the 1840s is one more example of the commercial value that some Americans placed upon the
Northwest Coast long before Alaska's purchase. The emphasis
that the Taylor–Fillmore administration placed upon American
commerce in the Pacific Northwest moved the United States one
step closer to the annexation of Russian-America.

7

Visions of the Northwest Coast
Gwin and Seward in the 1850s

The domestic portrait of the 1850s has been distorted because of scholars' commitments to a Civil War synthesis that proclaims the nation spent that decade in sectional conflict awaiting a general national disintegration.[1] This sectional bias has precluded a fair picture of American attitudes toward expansionism in the 1850s. Many historians have assumed, along with Frederick Merk, that expansionism virtually disappeared from American thought after 1848.[2] Others have argued that while such sentiment existed in this prewar period for the annexation of both Cuba and Mexico, the refusal of northern Whigs and northern Democrats to support such acquisitions because they could result in the extension of slavery doomed expansionist plans.[3] Both these views, however, neglect the attempt by important elements of the leadership of both parties to expand commercially and territorially into the Pacific Northwest. These schemes suffered from neither sectional bias nor from political party opposition. Only the outbreak of war prevented these plans from being carried out very early in the 1860s.

I

An examination of the relationship between William Henry Seward and William McKendree Gwin during the 1850s demonstrates this proposition. Both men were active and public

106

advocates of expansionism[4] in the Pacific Northwest during this decade. These were not obscure men. Senator Gwin of California was a native of Mississippi and a resident of that state until 1849. He served as leader of the Democratic forces in the Senate under both Presidents Pierce and Buchanan. When the Civil War broke out, Gwin was incarcerated by the Union government for his alleged southern sympathies.[5] William Henry Seward, on the other hand, was the acknowledged leader of the Whig and, later, of the Republican party. Not only was Seward regarded as the man most likely to receive the Republican presidential nomination in 1856 and in 1860, but also he earned the distinction in the Senate as the chief spokesman for abolition. That two such diverse politicians could agree on important schemes for American expansionism in the 1850s is a significant comment on the nature of American expansionism both before and after the war.

While Gwin and Seward centered their plans on the Pacific Northwest, and particularly upon Russian-America, the wider implications of their visions are evident. Gwin, like Seward, envisioned a worldwide commercial empire of which the United States would be the center. To secure such an empire, the United States would have to link the Atlantic with the Pacific across Panama, Nicaragua, and Tehuantepec; build overland mail routes, transcontinental railroads, and telegraphs to cement the union; and use the islands of the Pacific as bases for expansion in all directions. Gwin suggested the American government encourage friendly relations with Russia to gain needed cooperation in opening the Far East. He feared Great Britain as a rival and urged the Senate to speed plans for the construction of the Pacific railroad before British schemes for a transcontinental railway from Halifax to the west coast could establish British supremacy. American control of all North America was essential to Gwin's vision, and the Russian-American possession would have to fall into the American domain before a then-sandwiched British Pacific possession could do likewise.[6]

Seward, even more than Gwin, combined in his own worldview all those various forces that, since 1790, had contributed to American interest in the Russian possession. He brought together the traditional maritime interest with the landed expansionist

view in a manner which the nation had not seen since John
Quincy Adams had served as Secretary of State. Unlike Webster,
who warred with the manifest destinarians, Seward brought the
maritime interests into a new alliance with the landed expansionists. He proposed a new integrated American empire with
room, he hoped, for all factions.

Seward and Gwin shared similar visions for the future of the
American empire even though they came from distinctly dissimi-
lar backgrounds. William McKendree Gwin was born on October
9, 1805, in Sumner County, northeast of Nashville, Tennessee.
His father, James Gwin, formed a close friendship with his
neighbor Andrew Jackson. William read law in Gallatin, Tennessee, and was admitted to the bar by his twenty-first birthday.
Tennessee in 1826 was glutted with lawyers, and Gwin decided on
a medical career. Two years later, he received his medical degree
and moved to Clinton, Mississippi, where he practiced medicine
for the next six years. Gwin's close connections with President
Jackson soon moved him toward politics. Serving first as
Jackson's personal secretary and then in 1833 as United States
Marshall for the Southern District of Mississippi, Gwin abandoned his medical practice. He became a close friend and business associate of Robert J. Walker, who was elected to the
United States Senate from Mississippi in 1836. Elected to Congress in 1841, Gwin refused to run for a second term and returned
to Vicksburg to pursue various business schemes, including
Texas land speculation.[7]

Born into a wealthy upstate New York family, Seward was
Gwin's senior by four years. Harry (as he was then called) at-
tended Union College in Schenectady and was admitted to the
New York bar in 1822. While Gwin was an ardent Jackson man,
Seward supported John Quincy Adams for President in 1824 and
1828. When Adams died in 1848, Seward proclaimed, "I have lost
a patron, a guide, a consellor and a friend—one whom I . . . ven-
erated above all that was mortal among men."[8] By 1828, Seward,
along with Thurlow Weed, led the Anti-Masons against Van Buren's Regency. Seward and Weed joined the Whig coalition in
1834, and in 1838 Seward was elected governor of New York.

After two terms as governor, he temporarily retired from politics, returning to law in order to refurbish his money supply. By the mid-1840s, Governor Seward was regarded as one of the major antislavery spokesmen in the nation. The Liberty party offered him the presidential nomination in 1844, which he declined. Four years later, he was elected to the United States Senate, where he would remain until 1861.[9]

In March 1849, Gwin, attending the inauguration of Zachary Taylor, informed Senator Stephen A. Douglas of Illinois of his intention to leave for California and return within a year as that state's first United States Senator. "Within a year," Gwin prophesied, he would ask Douglas "to present his [Gwin's] credentials as a Senator from the State of Calif."[10] Within eleven months, Gwin returned to Washington as one of the two elected United States Senators from California. California's admission to the union, however, had not won Senate approval. The state constitution specifically outlawed slavery, and Gwin, though a slaveholder, had strongly supported this clause.[11]

One of the most vocal supporters of the admission of California was Senator Seward, a Whig from New York. Gwin and Seward became fast friends and allies on bills that urged the need for commercial transportation expansion in order to tie the West to the East of the nation and link Asia to the whole. This partnership lasted until the outbreak of the Civil War. Gwin's views on the West complemented Seward's, and this relationship helped educate Seward in the advantages of making Russian-America a possession of the United States.[12]

Seward tied his interest in the Pacific Northwest to his larger view of the necessity for expanded commerce in a continental and integrated American empire. He especially envisioned the Northwest Coast as a key to the American capture and control of Asian commerce. Like William Sturgis, John Quincy Adams, Daniel Webster, and William McKendree Gwin, Seward saw a unique relation between the Northwest Coast and American commercial enterprise in Asia. Unlike Sturgis and Webster, Seward had discounted the possibility of war with Britain over Oregon in 1845, believing the Democrats would never risk their political power on such an issue. The Oregon dispute, as all American preoccupation in the Pacific Northwest, he told Thurlow Weed, was part of the larger "battle . . . *for Asia.*" [13]

When the Russians sent an armed corvette to patrol the Russian-American coast against Yankee intruders, Gwin introduced an amendment to the Naval Appropriations Bill of 1852 for the building or purchase of suitable vessels "for prosecuting a survey and a reconnaissance for naval and commercial purposes, of such parts of Behring's Straits, of the North Pacific Ocean . . . frequented by American whale ships, and by trading vessels." The bill, when passed, provided for the sum of $125,000 for the vessels; additional sums, however, could be spent on "armaments." [14]

As a United States Senator, Seward's advocacy of protection of American rights in the Pacific Northwest never flagged. In the early 1850s, the New Yorker introduced a resolution in the Senate for a survey of the Arctic and Pacific oceans in order to aid the whaling industry as well as the expansion of American trade in the Far East. [15] In a Senate speech on Kansas and Nebraska in February 1854, Seward alluded to the possibility of the purchase or conquest of Russian-America by the United States. [16] In the 1850s, he often described future boundaries of the United States, which included the area of the Russian possessions in North America. [17] American involvement in Russian-America converged upon Seward in a way that uniquely qualified him to strike the last blows at Russian sovereignty in North America.

As a Whig and strong supporter of the maritime interests, Seward spoke out in July 1852 on the importance of the whaling industry to his section, his party, and the nation. He explained the value of whaling to the economy as a whole. Seward looked upon "the whale fishery as a source of national wealth, and an element of national force and strength." Tracing the history of this industry, Seward pointed out that whaling now centered "in the seas of Okhotsk, and Anadir, South of Behring Straits, and in that part of the Arctic Ocean lying north of them." The annual value of whale fishing in the area of Russian-America "was equal to $9,000,000, and thus exceeded by nearly $2,000,000, the highest annual import from China." Yet, he was sorry to find the "want of accurate topographical knowledge" to guide Yankee whaling fleets in that area. Since whaling was a vocation that had become an enterprise composed virtually of only United States citizens, the United States government was the appropriate agency to conduct the needed "exploration and reconnaissance" of these seas. Seward introduced a bill to that end, and Gwin served as cosponsor of the bill in the Senate. As Seward pointed out, California's "enterprising citizens are already engaged in this pursuit [whaling]."[18]

Many of these Yankee whalers used the Sandwich Islands as a base for their Pacific operations. By the early 1850s, Hawaiian sugar plantations were coming increasingly under the ownership of United States citizens. At this time, however, French and British citizens, in competition with the Americans, attempted to persuade their governments to take a more active role in the Sandwich Islands. In this context, both Seward and Gwin sought the annexation of the Hawaiian Islands to the United States. In 1852, Seward tried, unsuccessfully, to convince President Millard Fillmore to consider such a scheme.[19] Similarly, in April 1855, Gwin urged Secretary of State William Marcy to push for a reciprocity treaty between the islands and the United States. An earlier attempt by Marcy to annex the archipelago aborted in 1854 when the Hawaiians demanded that immediate statehood accompany annexation. Senator Gwin, in pressing for a Hawaiian reciprocity treaty in 1855, told the Secretary of State that such a treaty would "produce an identity of feeling and interest" that would not only benefit the West Coast economically but would also lead to the eventual annexation of the Sandwich Islands.[20] The reciprocity treaty, successfully opposed by the Louisiana sugar interests whose spokesmen in the Senate were John Slidell and Judah Benjamin, was tabled in the Senate. In July 1867, Seward, now Secretary of State, again submitted to the Senate a reciprocity treaty with the Sandwich Islands, which, like Gwin's earlier attempt, never came to a full Senate vote.[21]

In 1854, Gwin approached Russian Minister Edward de Stoeckl with an offer to buy Russian-America.[22] Stoeckl tried to defer any answer, and Gwin soon realized that too much pressure on the Russians could work to American disadvantage. The reports of Perry M. Collins, United States commercial agent to the Amur River region, had convinced Gwin (as well as Buchanan, Secretary of State Cass, and others) that American cooperation with Russia in the Amur region could bring untold benefits to the American republic.[23] The Buchanan administration was anxious to persuade reluctant Congressmen to extend financial remuneration to Collins's earlier efforts. In this effort, Secretary of State Cass obtained the aid of Gwin and California Congressman Charles L. Scott. Gwin and Scott wrote a letter to Cass (at the latter's solicitation) attesting that they were "fully convinced" of the value and commercial importance of the Amur region: "As a new field for commercial enterprise, we can hardly conceive of one more important to our varied interests." They believed the commercial value of the Amur region to the United States was unlimited. The Amur would open Siberia, with a large European population, as well as Mongolia, Manchuria, and northern China, to American commerce. "The Amoor River," claimed Gwin and Scott, "affords a ready and facile access to the very center of Northern Asia, where by that mighty agent steam, we can come in contact and competitions, in a very few days, with an annual commerce of $50,000,000, capable under the elasticity of American enterprise to be increased indefinitely." With American-made steamboats, which the Russians were already sailing down the Amur, United States commerce, they proclaimed, would be "pushed into the very heart of so vast and populous a country, [and] what we ask, may, or rather may not be accomplished within a very few years?" Gwin and Scott pointed to American history as their precedent for such optimism: "Steam has worked wonders on our own Mississippi . . . may not the Amoor, 'the Mississippi of Northern Asia,' find in the life-giving principle of steam the same advancement in commerce and industry?"[24]

From its inception in the 1850s, Seward advocated governmental aid for the construction of the Collins overland telegraph line to link Asia and Europe to the United States via Russian-

America. When Seward became Secretary of State, in 1861, he vigorously supported the scheme. He was later to claim that Collins's success in obtaining a charter from the Russian government had been effected "under the instruction and with the approbation" of his Department of State. He thought this venture so important that even during the worst moments of the Civil War, he kept a close surveillance on this project. He extended every possible aid to Collins and the Western Union chairman, Hiram Sibley, when the two men visited Russia in 1864.[25]

Gwin, Seward, and others who favored an American takeover of Russian-America found themselves walking a tightrope. They had to use enough force to persuade the Russians that the maintenance of Russian-America would be unprofitable; but if too much pressure was employed, the Russian government might fear that future cooperation with the United States in Asia, especially along the Amur, would lead to American expansion into that area as well. In 1859, Gwin, with the blessing of the Buchanan administration, again suggested to Russian Minister Stoeckl that Russia consider selling its North American possession to the United States. While Stoeckl urged his government to accept the offer,[26] American domestic disruptions intervened before negotiations could begin.

II

To the Buchanan administration, the Russian possession seemed to have political as well as economic value. Faced with the divisive nature of the domestic problems, President James Buchanan hoped to divert the nation's attention by a series of foreign adventures, of which the acquisition of Russian-America was but one. In 1857, when the bitter national debate over the Lecompton constitution reached its highest pitch, the nation also discovered it was in the midst of a severe financial panic. Added to these problems was the continuing war with the Mormons in Utah. As a true disciple of Polk's policy, Buchanan resolved to move the nation's attention away from domestic problems by foreign adventures. The President's second annual message spoke to that point. He claimed that the nation had recovered from the effects of the Kansas dispute, the financial panic, and the Mormon war. Only a few small details, implied Buchanan, remained, and soon the union would be healthier than ever. The real issues upon which the nation would be called to expend its energies were external in nature. "Cuba," he proclaimed, "is a constant source of injury and annoyance to the American people." Moreover, to encourage the rapid expansion of the economy, the navy must be increased, and authority to protect transit routes through Panama, Nicaragua, and Mexico must be granted. The construction of a transcontinental railroad, predicted the President, could not only tie America's East and West, but would also guarantee to the United States commerce the "rich and populous Empires" of China and Japan. "The history of the world proves," he said, "that the nation which has gained possession of the trade with Eastern Asia has always become wealthy and powerful."[27] Buchanan's message did not contain a specific plan but a method. While the President did not mention Russian-America in his message, nonetheless when his good friend and leader of the administration forces in the Senate, William McKendree Gwin, brought to the President's attention the availability of Russian-America for purchase, Buchanan reacted enthusiastically.[28]

By the end of 1859, however, the Buchanan administration found the nation no longer receptive to Polk's policies. It abandoned not only the purchase of Russian-America,[29] but also the acquisition of Cuba, a treaty establishing a virtual protectorate over Mexico, and many other projects in the realm of foreign affairs, which fifteen years before would have gained the support of a wide cross-section of the nation. Most of Buchanan's plans would be revived by a later American empire; some, like the proposed purchase of Russian-America, would quietly receive the attention of the incoming administration, especially of its Secretary of State, William Henry Seward.

Seward's close friendship with Senator Gwin is an important comment upon American expansionism. While the two men differed on party politics, they closely cooperated in securing governmental support for the Pacific railway, the China trade, and Pacific Coast whaling and trading projects. In 1856, when it appeared Gwin might not be returned to the Senate, he wrote Seward that while "we are as far apart as the North and South pole on these [political] questions, we could as Senators . . . work shoulder to shoulder as we have heretofore done in favor of those measures so vital to the prosperity . . . of the whole union." If Gwin were not returned to the Senate, he begged Seward to "stand by" those measures which the two had worked for in the past.[30] Perhaps Gwin's attempts to purchase Alaska in 1854 gave rise to Seward's suggestion in a speech that same year that the United States ought to purchase or conquer Russian-America.[31] Certainly the corresponding interest and friendship of Seward and Gwin added to the future Secretary of State's awareness of the value and availability of Russian-America. Given the cooperation of the two on projects and bills dealing with the Pacific Northwest, it would have been highly unlikely that Seward remained unaware of Gwin's and Assistant Secretary of State John Appleton's 1859 attempt to buy the Russian possession.

As a Senator in the 1850s urging statehood for California, Seward proclaimed that America "may reasonably hope for greatness . . . excelling any hitherto attained by any nation, if standing firmly on the continent, we loose [sic] not our grasp on the shore of either ocean." What was true of California in 1850, given Seward's logic, could be no less true of Russian-America in the 1860s: "Commerce is the god of boundaries, and no man now living can foretell his ultimate decree."[32] In 1852, Seward had proclaimed: "Commerce is the great agent of movement. Whatever nation shall put that commerce into full employment, and shall conduct it steadily with *adequate expansion,* will become necessarily the greatest of existing states." While Seward predicted in 1852 that the Pacific Ocean would become the "chief theater in the events of the world's great hereafter,"[33] in the 1860s he consciously set out to make that prediction a reality. In 1860, he reaffirmed his earlier assertion about the acquisition of Alaska, telling a St. Paul, Minnesota, audience that they should join him in saying to the Russians: "Go on and build your outposts all along the coast, even to the Arctic Ocean—they will yet become the outposts of my own country—monuments to the civilization of the United States in the northwest."[34] He then went forth to make his prophecy a reality.

While the nation would split over slavery, men of each persuasion could agree, like Gwin and Seward, that expansion in the Pacific Northwest was a worthy national goal. They were not alone either. The growth of American commercial interest in Russian-America during the 1850s proved to be the decisive blow to Russian sovereignty in North America.

8

American Commerce in Russian-America
1852–1867

The period from 1852 until the end of the Civil War saw old interests in Russian-America sustained and new interests born. The whaling industry continued to reap huge profits from hunting in the waters that fell under the nominal jurisdiction of the Russian-American Company. The incorporation of Oregon and California into the United States provided a new and more solid base for American penetration of the Russian possession. In the San Francisco of the 1850s, where enterprising schemes grew with a multiplicity born of the hysteria and hope of instant fortune, increased interest in Russian-America was merely one result. The settlers who resided along the West Coast understood their debt to landed expansionists of the past and had few doubts that expansion would continue in North America. Given the continental expansion of the past fifty years, there were probably few in America in 1850 who did not accept as an article of faith the proposition that all North America would eventually become part of the United States. The Russian and British possessions to the north could not avoid the fate of the former Spanish and French holdings in North America. Indeed, by 1850, as uneasy as some had become about relations within the union itself, most Americans probably looked to the future in terms of expansion and not with an eye toward disunion.[1]

I

The United States economy in 1852 was growing rapidly. While a rather sharp recession in 1857 seemed to slow this pace, the economic turndown was much less serious than the 1837 panic. The growth of industrialization accelerated over its record of the past decade. By the middle 1850s, the Northeast was a distinctive manufacturing region. Cotton, losing its grip on the national economy since the 1840s, was no longer dominant. As the 1840s heralded the beginning of the end of eastern dependence on the southern cash crop, the 1850s saw a new and firm economic interdependence of the Northeast and the West. Railroad construction in the 1850s was greater than all previous decades combined. This great railway expansion served to connect more securely the highly populated East with the West than ever before. The facility of East–West transport when combined with steadily increasing agricultural prices, proved that the new alliance was indeed worthwhile.[2]

The cementing of the East–West economic alliance had political effects as well. The ancient antagonism between the landed expansionists of the West and the commercial expansionists of the East began to disappear. Political leaders like William Henry Seward of New York believed that certain landed expansion could bring immense benefit to the maritime East. As the East and West moved closer economically and politically, new-found far-western interests in Russian-America combined with more traditional interests, so that by 1859 Californians and Oregonians, as well as northeasterners, were calling for the annexation of Russian-America to the United States.

The Northeast was in its last decade of shipping prosperity. Stimulated by the addition of California and the European troubles in the Crimea, New England ship construction boomed. Manufacturing exports showed substantial increases in the 1850s, and the total volume of all exports increased dramatically. Nevertheless, the Northeast, and the United States export trade in general, remained closely tied to European prosperity. The specie drain on England and France that resulted from the Crimean War had a crisis effect on American specie reserves by 1857. From October to December, New York bankers were forced to suspend all specie payments.[3] As always during times of financial setbacks, many Americans looked outward. Interest in Russian-America grew to surprising heights from 1857 to 1861.

In the 1850s, the whaling boom in the Pacific Northwest continued. While the profits for all whaling began to decline after 1857, the Northwest Coast whale fishery continued to maintain high profits for another decade. The main stimulus for this continued profitability of whale fishery was the bowhead whales captured in the Okhotsk Sea, along the Kamchatka Coast, and in the Bering Strait.[4] The Russians in the area of Okhotsk reported that from 1850 to 1860 more than a hundred Yankee vessels fished there annually. Some Russian reports estimated that the total number of vessels annually fishing in the three areas ranged somewhere between 500 and 600 vessels. Depending upon which report one selects, the year 1857 found between 300 and 366 Yankee whalers in these waters.[5] The total value of the importation of whale oil and whalebone reached its highest levels in the history of whale fishery in 1857. In the ten-year period ending in 1860, $89.3 million of whale products were imported by United States whalers, an increase of $18.7 million over the previous decade.[6] That increase is quite impressive in view of the economic downturn from 1857 to 1860, which resulted in a decreased investment in whaling and thus a decreased number of whaling vessels sent out.

The 1850s were a time of renewed interest in other enterprises in Russian-America. During this decade, concern of United States citizens about the Russian possessions surpassed even that of the days of the lucrative sea otter trade. The failure of the Hudson's Bay Company to keep the Russian colony supplied with food, as required by the 1840 agreement between British and Russian companies, aided Yankee commercial penetration. In 1848, the Russian-American Company refused to renew the Hudson's Bay Company's right to be the prime supplier of foodstuffs and supplies for the Russian colonies in North America.[7] While California gold-rush prices in the late 1840s made it less profitable for San Franciscans to supply the Russians than to feed and clothe the newly arrived fortune seekers, by 1851 the inflated prices of the gold rush were gone. Supplying the Russian possessions seemed to many Americans a new chance to strike it rich.

One such group to step into the Hudson's Bay Company's shoes was the American-Russian Commercial Company, founded in 1851 by San Francisco's most prominent attorneys and businessmen. The company's list of stockholders reads like a social directory of San Francisco in the early 1850s. Its president, Beverley C. Sanders, a lifetime Whig who had married Daniel Webster's niece, was appointed collector of the port of San Francisco by President Fillmore in 1852.[8] Sanders' banking partner, Charles J. Brenham, a large stockholder in the Commercial Company, was mayor of San Francisco from 1851 to 1853.[9] William Burling, who served as the company's secretary, joined with William McPherson Hill, another stockholder, to form the brokerage firm of Burling and Hill in 1849.[10] Samuel J. Hensley, a holder of a substantial number of shares in the American-Russian Commercial Company, had arrived in California in 1843 to work as a clerk for Captain John Sutter. By 1850, Hensley was one of the richest men in California.[11] Abel Guy, the owner of the largest block of Commercial Company stock, was a wealthy attorney in San Francisco.[12] Archibald C. Peachy, a renowned California attorney, held a large number of shares. Brenham and Peachy often joined in real estate ventures with John L. Folsom, who had written an official government report at Secretary of State Clayton's request in 1849, urging the opening of Russian-America to Yankee commerce.[13]

The Commercial Company made its first contract with the agent of the Russian-American Company in San Francisco for 250 tons of ice to be shipped from Sitka at $75 per ton (or $18,750). In February 1852, the American ship *Bacchus* arrived in San Francisco loaded with the ice. In October, the Commercial Company succeeded in persuading the Russians to agree to reduce the price of future shipments of ice to $35 a ton, with the stipulation that the American company would take at least a thousand tons per year.[14]

During the Crimean War, the Russian-American Company was hard-pressed for general supplies as well as for articles of daily necessity. It requested the American-Russian Commercial Company to supply these articles, which the San Franciscans were happy to do for the price of a new and more favorable contract. In order to negotiate this contract, Beverley Sanders traveled to St. Petersburg. In March 1854, before his departure for Russia, Sanders journeyed to Washington to obtain letters of recommendation from President Franklin Pierce and the Russian chargé, Stoeckl.[15] Once in St. Petersburg, he persuaded the Russian-American Company directors to sign a twenty-year contract with his company, which would extend the company's trading privileges to coal and fish as well as ice. Under this new charter, the San Francisco company would be the sole foreign firm permitted to trade for the ice, timber, coal, and fish from the Russian possessions in North America and from the Russian islands in the North Pacific Ocean. The American-Russian company was also to be the chief supplier of foodstuffs and other necessities for the colony.[16] The Russian company, wishing to guarantee its supply of necessities during the Crimean War, had little choice but to agree to Sanders' terms. Since the proposed contract had a life of twenty years, a longer time than the Russian-American Company's charter had left to run, the czar had to give his special permission. Much to his displeasure, the czar acquiesced.[17]

From 1852 to 1859, the American company took 13,960 tons of ice from Sitka and 7,403 tons from Kodiak, for an average of about three thousand tons per year. During the Crimean War, the Commercial Company was the largest single supplier of goods to the Russian possession. In 1860, it signed a new contract with the Russian company under which the Russians agreed to furnish three thousand tons of ice annually at $7 per ton; it also agreed not to sell ice to any other firm for less than $25 per ton.[18]

The American-Russian Commercial Company sold most of its ice in San Francisco, but considerable amounts were exported to Mexican and Central and South American ports. The company even made serious attempts to expand its sales to Asia. In 1858 an agent of the Commercial Company wrote to Messrs. Augustine Heard and Company of Hong Kong, inquiring "if it would not be profitable and possible to send cargoes of ice to your port or any other in China."[19]

About the same time that the American-Russian company was enlarging its designs upon the resources of Russian-America, Perry M. Collins of California arrived in Washington, D.C., with the intention of presenting an elaborate plan to President Franklin Pierce. Collins informed the President that the recent Russian acquisition of the Amur River region could be of great value to American merchants. For years, Collins reminded Pierce, Americans had been trading in the Russian possessions in Asia. If United States traders were to utilize the Amur, they could not only capture the interior trade of Russian Asia, which Collins alleged was worth $50 million a year, but they could also tap the markets of China and Japan, which navigation of the Amur would more fully open.[20]

Collins was correct about the movement of American traders. Since these traders and whalers had first penetrated the Russian-American possessions, they had slowly moved up the coast and across the ocean to the Russian possessions of Kamchatka and Okhotsk in Asia. The Russian-American company, which administered these areas, had tried unsuccessfully to exclude them. No doubt Collins first learned about the wonders of the Amur from these traders, many of whom had stopped in California.[21]

Collins's proposal included the President's sending him to the Amur River region "to look at it in a commercial point of view and open it up to commerce by way of this river; present to the knowledge of our people the nature and extent of this country." The Amur region, he argued, was "so important" to the growth and commerce of California, Oregon, and Washington. "In California," he noted, "our productions (aside from gold) are already seeking a market in exchange for such commodities as she does not produce."[22] Collins's letter and the urgings of the California delegation to Congress coincided with Pierce's and Secretary of State Marcy's own inclination. On March 24, 1856, Perry M. Collins was appointed United States commercial agent to the Amur River.[23]

Arriving in St. Petersburg, Collins received the instant attention of the United States minister to Russia, Thomas Seymour. Marcy had instructed the minister to extend all possible assistance to Collins. Seymour took his job seriously.[24] Through the United States legation's influence and hard work, Collins was able to leave for the Amur River region with full Russian governmental approval by December 1856. The American agent, moreover, was to travel to the Amur in the company of the governor-general of eastern Siberia, Nicholai Muraviev. During the next year, Collins explored the Amur region and wrote to Marcy and his successor, Lewis Cass, of the many possibilities which this region held for American commerce. He referred to the Amur as the "Mississippi" of Siberia, noting that the increasing Yankee trade at Kamchatka could expand from that area down the Amur and tap the immense trade of northern Asia. This trade, Collins predicted, "will not be confined alone to the Russian possessions, but will extend into the Tartaries, Bukaria, Northern China, and Thibet, so as to take in the whole range of trade." He suggested that the Amur could be penetrated easily from the American West Coast on a line with Kamchatka, or from Hawaii via the same route.[25]

Collins returned to the United States by way of San Francisco in December 1857. When he left the Amur, Collins decided to retain a "vice commercial agent" in charge of his mission. He picked George S. Cushing, a resident agent of W. A. Boardman and Company of Boston, which had been active in the Russian–American trade for over a quarter of a century. Now Boardman was extending its operations from Kamchatka to the Amur. Cushing was only too happy to tend shop for the United States commercial agent on leave.[26]

Collins's return to Washington in 1858 brought his venture a deluge of publicity. His reports were published and utilized by some Congressmen as another reason for the need for speedy construction of a transcontinental railway.[27] More important, Collins's adventure caught the attention of Hiram Sibley, the president of Western Union Telegraph Company. Collins had suggested the construction of an overland telegraph system that would link Asia and Europe to the United States via Russian-

America. The commerce the Amur tapped would then flow eastward to the American West as would the communication system of Europe and Asia. Sibley seemed just the man to back the flamboyant project.[28]

In 1859, Collins set out once again for the Amur. For the next two years, he worked to gain a charter from the Russian government. While he would not be successful until 1863, by 1861 Collins and Sibley had won the support of the Lincoln administration for their project. Not even the Civil War would hamper their grand design.[29]

Other schemes involving Yankee enterprise in Russian-America cropped up time and again before 1861. Like the Collins overland line, most of these projects were filled with grandiose visions. Some brought their originators profits, like that of the American-Russian Commercial Company; others, like that of Joseph Lane McDonald, ended less happily. McDonald's interest in Russian-America began in the 1840s when he worked in the fishing trade at New Bedford. New Bedford during this period sent almost all of its whaling fleet to the Northwest Coast, and McDonald heard many tales from the returning whalemen about the valuable waters along the Russian-American coast. He arrived in San Francisco in 1858. Unlike many others, he had journeyed to California not to find gold but to find fishing grounds. In 1859, McDonald explored the coastline from Oregon to the Arctic, reporting that what he saw along the Russian-American coastline was a fishing treasure that surpassed all his expectations. Returning to San Francisco in the late fall, McDonald formed a commercial company, including in its membership the Russian consul at San Francisco. McDonald desired a lease from the Russian-American Company for the privilege of exploiting the salt fisheries along the Russian-American coast. When the Russian consul failed in his attempts to persuade the Russian governor to grant the privilege, McDonald wrote to Secretary of State Cass requesting aid. Cass replied that national troubles precluded any action at that time and that McDonald should "wait for a more convenient season." McDonald then wrote to Senator William McKendree Gwin, who was more receptive. No doubt some of the impetus behind Gwin's proposal to Stoeckl in late 1859 for the purchase of the Russian possession came from McDonald's request. Nevertheless, the imminence of the Civil War dampened McDonald's efforts to obtain fishing rights along the Russian-American coast in the same way it stalled Gwin's and Appleton's later attempt to purchase it.[30]

II

The Civil War was more of an annoyance than a stumbling block to continued Yankee enterprise in Russian-America. Most firms dealing in the Russian colony experienced little hindrance due to the war. While Northwest Coast whalers were subjected to attacks from the Confederate navy, the American-Russian Commercial Company and the Collins Overland Line Company expanded their plans and operations despite the war. Similarly, Joseph Lane McDonald's schemes took on new dimensions during the war. Other firms wishing to join in the Russian-American trade were formed as the last battles in the South were being fought. Politically and diplomatically, however, the war between the states made acquisition of the czar's colony untenable. As early as December 1863, nevertheless, Secretary of State William H. Seward began to make plans for the purchase of Russian-America. On March 29, 1867, he signed the Treaty of Cession with Baron de Stoeckl.

Even with the effects of the 1857 to 1861 economic recession and the resultant decreased investment in whaling, the Pacific Northwest whaling grounds continued to be the mainstay of the whaling industry. While many whaling ports ceased their operations, from 1857 to 1867 the ports of New Bedford and New London continued to make substantial profits from Northwest Coast whale fishery.[31] After 1857, this industry would never again attain its former primacy in New England. Investors who had speculated in whaling turned to investment in cotton mills, which suddenly sprang up in the old northeastern whaling ports during the middle 1850s.[32] Cotton mills were a safer and, as it turned out, more lucrative investment than bowhead whales. The first cotton mill in New Bedford was founded by Joseph Grinnell, the whaling industry's spokesman in Congress.[33] The discovery of oil in Pennsylvania in 1859, however, signaled the real end of whaling as a profitable investment. With the widespread use of kerosene, whale oil lamps began to go out all over America.[34] Even so, whaling continued in the North Pacific waters during the American Civil War. The southerners believed these whalers so important to the northern economy that Confederate privateers continually harassed them in the Pacific Northwest, destroying more than fifty vessels and requisitioning many more.[35] At the time of the sale of Russian-America to the United States, some ninety to one hundred American-owned whaling vessels were hunting in the waters near Russian-America, Okhotsk, Kamchatka, and the Bering Strait.[36]

During the period of American civil strife, the American-Russian Commercial Company continued its enterprises in the Russian possession. By 1863, it was purchasing more than three thousand tons of ice per year from Russian-America.[37] Frederick Whymper, the English explorer and author, traveling in Alaska shortly after the purchase, regarded the ice industry important enough to justify the purchase.[38] George Davidson, who was sent by Seward to make a survey and report on Alaska in November 1867, wrote that the Commercial Company sold 3,200 tons of ice annually to San Francisco alone.[39] In November 1867, the *Alta California* reported that the ice company was "enlarging operations" and next year will "transport 20,000 tons of ice."[40]

Like the ice company, the Collins scheme continued during the war. Collins had returned to the Amur in 1859, where he spent the next several years working to obtain a charter for his telegraph company from the Russian government. He received powerful support from Secretary of State Cass[41] and Cass's Republican successor, William Henry Seward,[42] as well as the constant attention of Hiram Sibley.[43] At Seward's direction, the imperial government was advised that if it granted a charter to Collins, the United States government would subsidize the building of the line.[44] Finally, in May 1863, the Russian government agreed to grant Collins his charter.[45]

Collins's success in Russia brought him quick rewards in the United States. Sibley readily persuaded the board of directors of Western Union to purchase the rights that Collins had obtained by the charter for $100,000 and 10 percent of the stock issued for the company created to construct the line. Collins was also appointed to the board of directors of Western Union and made manager of the Collins Overland Line Company, which was charged with stringing the telegraphic line.[46] By the end of 1864, Collins was off again to Russia. This time his traveling companion was Hiram Sibley.[47]

Collins and Sibley met with the czar and Foreign Minister Gorchakov. For the next several months, the American visitors haggled with the Russian government over the percentage of rebate the Russians would receive from the telegraphic operations. While the imperial government desired a 40 percent rebate, Sibley thought that 20 percent was a fair compromise. Grudgingly, Sibley acquiesced to the 40 percent figure and hoped that United States Minister Cassius M. Clay would later be able to negotiate a reduction.[48]

During his conversations with Gorchakov, Sibley indicated that if the British government had not agreed to allow the telegraphic line to pass through British Columbia, he would have purchased the Hudson's Bay Company, which retained a charter from the British crown in that area. Sibley named a sum of money which he would have offered for the Hudson's Bay Company. Gorchakov replied that for a few dollars more, the Russian government would sell its possessions in North America. Sibley rapidly pursued the line of conversation. He asked the foreign minister for permission to inform the United States government of Russia's willingness to part with Russian-America.[49] Gorchakov had no objection, and Seward was quickly informed.[50]

Seward immediately instructed the American minister to Russia to invite the czar's brother, the Grand Duke Constantine, to the United States. Seward learned from the dispatches of his ministers in Russia that Constantine had been an early and consistent advocate of the cession of Russian-America to the United States. "I think it [a visit by Constantine] would be beneficial to the United States," the Secretary of State wrote to Clay on December 26, 1864, "and by no means unprofitable to Russia." Seward added, "I forbear from specifying my reasons. They will readily occur to you, as they would to his Imperial Highness, if his thoughts were turned in that direction."[51] There can be no doubt that Seward was speaking of the acquisition of Russian-America, since the Secretary of State sent this letter, along with other documents relating to the purchase of Alaska, to the House of Representatives in 1868 in an attempt to persuade the House to pay for what the administration had bought. Constantine declined the invitation, but Seward later obtained from Minister Stoeckl what he desired from Constantine.[52]

The Collins line was never completed, although construction had begun before the project was abandoned.[53] Perry Collins had excited American interest in the Russian-held areas of Asia, helping to extend American commerce from the possession of the Russian-American Company in Kamchatka and Okhotsk to Siberia. This increased American presence in Russian-Asia was to become a prime consideration in the decision of the Russian government to sell Russian-America to the United States. Moreover, Collins and Sibley kept the door open during the American Civil War for the eventual resurgence of American governmental interest in the acquisition of Russian-America.

Like Collins, Joseph Land McDonald redoubled his efforts during the Civil War period, gaining additional supporters for his fishing schemes. He moved to Puget Sound in the Washington Territory, and, in 1863, he was appointed chief clerk of the lower legislative house of the territory. When the war ended, McDonald recommenced his activities to obtain fishing rights in Russian-America. This time, his plans were more grandiose: he proposed the formation of an "Oriental and Occidental Railroad and Steamship Company," which would transport goods from Europe to Asia via the United States and Russian-America. This corporation would, in turn, be a parent to many subsidiary concerns such as cod packets, whaling, and manufacturing of fishery products.[54]

McDonald decided that it might be more productive to begin

his ventures with a smaller, but still ambitious, undertaking, called the "Puget Sound Steam Navigation Company," which would aim at controlling commerce and fishing along the Pacific Northwest Coast from Puget Sound to the Arctic Ocean. On October 4, 1864, the company, with a capital stock amounting to $50,000, issued its prospectus. The resume claimed that "the convenience of safe harbors and the prospective travel and commerce on Puget Sound, renders the immediate organization and incorporation of a Steam Navigation Company indispensible." The Puget Sound Company, alleged the prospectus, had "been in correspondence with steamship owners 'beyond the seas.'" Success and profits, according to this analysis, were "just around the corner." The incorporation bill easily passed through the Washington legislature.[55]

More difficult was the securing of the right from the Russian-American Company to trade and fish along the coast of Russian-America. McDonald, in January 1866, used his influential position as chief clerk of the legislature to prevail upon the territorial lawmakers to send a memorial to President Johnson and Secretary of State Seward requesting the United States government "to obtain such *rights and privileges* of the Government of Russia, as will enable our fishing vessels to visit the harbors of its possessions." The memorial noted "that vast quantities of cod, halibut, and salmon of excellent quality are found along the shores of Russian-America." But for Americans to reap the benefits of this fishing trade, they must be allowed to obtain "fuel, water and provisions"; the right to have sick and disabled fishermen receive sanitary assistance; and the "privilege of taking and curing fish and repairing vessels." McDonald's memorial concluded by requesting that the government "employ such ships as may be spared from the Pacific Naval Fleet in surveying the fishing banks."[56]

McDonald's schemes soon collapsed. The Puget Sound Steam Navigation Company did buy one ship, but it soon went bankrupt.[57] The pressures McDonald tried to exert on the federal government were nonetheless useful to the eager Seward. The Secretary of State later argued that "the memorial of the legislature of Washington Territory" was used to persuade Stoeckl of "the importance of some early and comprehensive arrangement between the two countries to prevent the growth of difficulties arising out of the fisheries in the Russian possessions."[58] Both Seward and Stoeckl realized that American desires for fishing rights in Russian-America were no chimera; past history had demonstrated that.

With the end of the Civil War, a fur trading issue once again demonstrated to the Russians that American entrepreneurs could not be restrained for long by national boundaries. As with the McDonald schemes, the Yankee fur traders had influential and governmental support in pursuing their aims. In 1865, Lewis Goldstone, an American fur dealer in Victoria, British Columbia, developed a plan to obtain for a San Francisco-based company the soon-to-expire sublease to the fur trade of the Russian-American mainland, which was held by the Hudson's Bay Company. Goldstone succeeded in inducing a number of influential persons to join him in this venture, including John F. Miller, collector of the port of San Francisco; Eugene Sullivan, Miller's successor; Samuel Brannan, one of the wealthiest men in California; Louis Sloss, a San Francisco businessman; and Judge E. Burke, brother-in-law of California's Senator Cornelius Cole.[59]

At first Goldstone planned to obtain only a sublease. Soon, however, he and his colleagues decided that if they were successful in obtaining the sublease, they would make a bid for a lease to the fur and trading rights for all the territory under the domain of the Russian-American Company. This area included (besides the mainland) the Pribilof, Aleutian, Kurile, and Commander islands; the latter two were part of Kamchatka in Asia. Goldstone purchased two schooners, the *Lord Raglan* and the *Native,* and sent them out "to make a thorough exploration" of the Russian-American coasts. During the next twelve months, he launched three consecutive expeditions "to explore the 'jurisdiction' of the Russian-American Fur Company." The total cost Goldstone and his associates expended for these explorations was $183,700. The San Francisco group prepared several maps of Russian-America and a long report on the resources of that area. They forwarded the maps and report to Senator Cole.[60]

Cornelius Cole, who had read law in William H. Seward's Auburn, New York, office, was instructed to speak to Russian Minister Stoeckl in Washington. Cole's aim was to obtain Stoeckl's aid in persuading the Russian government "to invest us [Goldstone and Co.] with the right in trading in all the country between the British American line and the Russian archipelago." The San Franciscans thought these rights so valuable that they were willing to top the price the Hudson's Bay Company had been paying and, in addition, offered to aid in "ameliorating the conditions of the Indians by employing missionaries."[61]

Senator Cole soon developed a strong interest in the venture. By the end of 1866, he took charge of the scheme.[62] After Stoeckl left for Russia in October 1866, Seward persuaded Cole to work through the United States minister to Russia, Cassius M. Clay, to obtain the lease.[63] After receiving a letter from Clay in late December, Cole instructed his California colleagues "*to have a company incorporated under the general corporation laws of California and . . . let the company send our Minister in St. Petersburg a full power of attorney, and instructions how to act in purchasing this right of the Russian American Company.*" Cole suggested that the San Francisco company could also obtain "really valuable" mining privileges if they would "give the *Directors* of the Russian Company . . . *blanc [sic] dollars* (some limited amount) *for the privileges asked. That is the only way to do the thing.*" The California Senator also suggested that the company issue some stock to Clay "*for* his *troubles* and *services,* which are *outside of* his *diplomatic duties.*"[64]

Clay wrote to Cole on February 1, 1867, that the Russian government had informed him that the Hudson's Bay Company lease was up for renewal and the government "could not enter into negotiations with us or your California Company" until the discussions with the Hudson's Bay Company were completed. Clay, however, assured Cole that if the Russians "can get off with the Hudson's Bay Company . . . we can make some arrangements with the Russian-American Company."[65] Later that month, Cole informed his associates that the minister's latest letter "is a new and not more encouraging phase of this affair, but I think you had better organize as if you expected to succeed."[66]

Neither Clay nor Cole realized that Stoeckl had been called back to St. Petersburg in order to complete plans to cede the Russian possessions in North America to the United States. Stoeckl returned to the United States in early February 1867. Cole went to see Stoeckl twice in March.[67] He was somewhat shocked on April 1 when Stoeckl informed him of the treaty of cession. The California senator lamented: "It would have been better if we could have obtained the privilege we desired—but if the treaty is ratified that scheme (of exclusiveness) will all be up."[68] Writing to his brother-in-law Judge Burke, after the treaty had won Senate confirmation, Cole sensed an irony in his role: the cession of Russian-America, he observed, "sprang out of our negotiations for trading in fur. Baron Stoeckl said so. But we did not anticipate this result. . . . Our negotiations related *not* to acquisition *but* to exclusive privilege in the territory."[69]

Stoeckl, of course, exaggerated the importance of the Cole and Goldstone negotiations. The decision to sell had been made over a period of years after 1853, and the final decision was made by Gorchakov before Stoeckl returned to the United States.[70] Nevertheless, schemes like Cole's and Goldstone's were among the prime contributors in helping the Russian government reach this decision.

9

The Russian Reaction to American Commercial Expansion in the Pacific Northwest 1852–1867

The ever-increasing American preoccupation with Russian-America from 1852 to 1867 had a profound impact on the decisions of Russian policy makers. A growing number of czarist officials came to believe that so long as a viable American republic existed, Russian possessions in North America could not be safe. The continued failure to keep United States citizens out of Russian-America led some influential policy makers in St. Petersburg to urge the cession of the Russian possession to the United States before the United States took it. Nikolai Muraviev, a staunch advocate of his country's expansion in Asia and conqueror of the Amur region for the imperial government, urged Czar Nicholas in 1853 to give the Russian-American colonies to the United States. Muraviev wrote:

> The ultimate rule of the United States over the whole of North America is so natural . . . that we must ourselves sooner or later recede—but we must recede *peacefully,* in return for which we might receive other advantages from the Americans. Due to its present amazing development of railroads, the United States will soon spread over all North America. We must face the fact that we will have to cede our North American possessions to them.

Moreover, he believed other advantages would accrue to his nation in "yielding peacefully" to the United States in North America. Muraviev argued that Russia's destiny was, "if not to control the whole of Eastern Asia, at least to hold sway over the whole Asiatic Coast of the Pacific." The Russian-American Company, he suggested, should be relocated and established "on Sakhalin whence its trade with Japan and Korea will develop." Muraviev was convinced that, with the cession of Russian-America to the United States, the Americans would be sated and the Russians could concentrate on Asia and their enemy there, the British. The governor-general hoped that in Asia "a close alliance between us and the United States" could be effected.[1]

I

In 1854, at the beginning of the Crimean War, the Russian-American Company considered a fictitious sale of Russian-America to the American-Russian Commercial Company in order to avoid seizure by the British. The idea was quickly dismissed because the Russian government realized the British might see through the maneuver and seize the colony anyway. They also feared that if the United States held Russian-America, they might keep it. An Anglo-Russian agreement in 1855 declaring North America a sanctuary from the war neatly avoided a most unpleasant dilemma for the Russians.

Rumors nevertheless appeared in the press alleging that Russia was willing to sell its North American possession to the United States.[2] Senator William M. Gwin of California and Secretary of State Marcy informed the Russian chargé, Stoeckl, in March 1854 that if Russia were willing to sell, the United States was willing to buy, but Stoeckl told them that there was no truth to such rumors. The chargé wrote to his government about the conversation with the Secretary of State and the Senator. Once such ideas were planted in the American mind, he noted, they were not easily uprooted. "They are dangerous neighbors," he warned, "and we must avoid giving them the least quarrel."[3]

In January 1856, Stoeckl wrote of his exasperation in trying to protect the interests of the Russian-American Company. Each year, he explained, because more and more Americans were settling in the Oregon Territory "in the neighborhood of our Northwest possessions it will put these extremes in actual danger and will be a growing source of worries between the two governments."[4]

Czar Alexander II's brother, the Grand Duke Constantine Nikolaevich, read over Stoeckl's correspondence regarding American-Russian relations in North America. Constantine had been trained for a career in the Imperial Russian Navy, and his tours of inspection had taken him to all corners of the empire. In 1855, he became minister of marine and at once set out on the task of modernization and naval development. Constantine was determined to create for himself an independent sphere of action. To that end, he used his position as director of naval affairs to direct Russian expansion and commerce away from Europe and, instead, toward the Far East, Central Asia, and the Mediterranean. As the Crimean War drew to a close, Constantine's power and influence were considerable.[5]

In order to redirect Russian expansion, as well as to recover from the Crimean War, Constantine urged his brother's government to consolidate its widespread holdings. Like Muraviev, the grand duke desired the Russian empire's eastern border to end at the Pacific coast of Asia. Russian-America, he argued, was expendable. In December 1857, Constantine prepared a long memorandum for Russian Foreign Minister Gorchakov. He noted "that the Company could not proceed with its present system without involving our Government in . . . controversies with the Americans." If the company and the government continued to resist letting American ships trade with Russian-America, Constantine feared "the Americans will harm not only the Company's trade, but all Russian trade in America." He added his powerful voice to the others urging the Russian government to give up its North American possession to the United States:

> Having in view the future development of Russia and the United
> States of America in accordance with their particular nature and in
> accordance with the historical significance of both states, Russia
> must endeavor to become stronger in her center in order to be able
> to hold those extremities which bring her real benefit. The United
> States of America following the natural order of things is bound to

aim at the possession of the whole of North America and therefore there will be a time when we shall meet there. No doubt they shall take possession of our colonies without much effort and we shall never be in a position to regain them.[6]

Foreign Minister Gorchakov was unenthusiastic about giving up Russia's American possession to the United States, especially under the threat of force. He suggested to Constantine that if Russia must cede its American possession to the United States, it might be politic at least to let the American government take the first step.[7]

Other memorandums the foreign ministry received advised taking the course Constantine suggested. In one, "Concerning the Cession of Our American Colonies to the Government of the United States," Baron Wrangell, who had served as governor of Russian-America in the 1830s, urged the Russian government to turn its colony over to the Americans. Wrangell noted that the possessions were valuable for their rich coal deposits, ice, construction timber, fish, and excellent seaports. He agreed that "if it were not for the *fears of the future,* there could be no doubt that even twenty million silver rubles could not be regarded as complete remuneration for the loss of possessions which promise important results in the development of industrial activity." But, concluded Wrangel, "*anticipatory prudence*" dictated a cession to the United States.[8]

As a result of Baron Wrangell's April 9 advice, Czar Alexander reluctantly approved a "Highly Confidential Memorandum Concerning the Cession to the United States of Our Possessions in North America" in which he noted that the "contract between our Company and San Francisco [American-Russian Commercial Company] . . . exceedingly reduce[s] the value of our possessions in North America." This memorandum, which embodied Wrangell's earlier suggestion, proposed that the negotiations with the United States should be carried out in secret and that a sale should take place in 1861 when the Russian-American Company's charter expired.[9]

In case the government in St. Petersburg needed any further urging to sell, its minister in Washington provided some additional reasons. On November 13, 1857, Stoeckl warned that if the Russian government continued its monopoly practices in North America, it would create "continual embarrassments provoking serious discussions between the two governments and injuring its own interests." The American government, Stoeckl feared, would retaliate by closing all its ports to Russians.[10] Stoeckl wrote on December 2 that Brigham Young and his Mormon followers were planning to emigrate either to Hudson's Bay or to Russian-America. If the rumor was true, noted Stoeckl, it "would place before us the alternative of providing armed resistance or of giving up part of our territory." When the czar read this dispatch, he penned on the margin: "This supports the idea of settling henceforth the question of our American possessions."[11]

By the end of 1859, Senator Gwin once more suggested to Stoeckl that Russia sell its American territory, mentioning that $5 million would be a fair price. Stoeckl transmitted Gwin's offer to Foreign Minister Gorchakov, adding that American Assistant Secretary of State John Appleton (who was on intimate terms with Buchanan and actually ran the Department of State) had supported his bid. The Russian minister thought his government should accept the offer. "The conquest of California dealt a fatal blow to the predominance of the English in the Pacific, and at the present time," Stoeckl believed, "the United States exercises there a control almost without limit." If it were not for the colony's small value, he argued, "they would not be safe from American filibusterers."[12] Stoeckl missed the point. For many United States citizens, Russian-America was quite valuable. Before serious negotiations could begin, however, American domestic events intervened.

Even after the Russians realized that the impending American civil strife had won a reprieve for Russian-America, influential Russian policy makers were planning for the day when the area would become a territory of the United States. Admiral Ivan Popov, who commanded the Russian fleet in the Pacific and enjoyed the confidence of Grand Duke Constantine, saw the question not in terms of whether Russian-America should be ceded to the United States, but rather, how much would have to be ceded to sate the American appetite. In a long memorandum to the Ministry of Foreign Affairs in February 1860, Popov noted: "Whatever they may say in Europe about . . . the 'Monroe Doctrine,' or the doctrine of 'manifest destiny,' anyone who has lived in the North American life cannot fail to understand instinctively that this principle is entering more and more into the blood of the people, and that new generations are sucking it in with their mother's milk." Popov pointed out that the Yankees "try to maintain . . . advantage by all the means at their disposal and the question of the destruction of the influence of neighbors leads in practice to the principle of not having any." Sale of Russian-America, urged the Admiral, was a suitable alternative to its seizure by the Americans. Popov, like Constantine and Muraviev, urged the czar to concentrate his nation's energies in Asia where Russia's manifest destiny was to be found. He suggested that Russia should cede the mainland, the Aleutians, and the islands of the Bering Sea, "because . . . geographically all these are American—but let us retain the Commander Islands so as not to have the Yankees too near us."[13]

In 1863, the czar convened an extraordinary commission headed by Minister of Interior and Trade Butovsky to make recommendations about the future of the American colony. The commission concluded that "all the financial resources of the country [Russian-America] could hardly be sufficient to repay the expenses of its defense or even simple administration." Nevertheless, the report argued, "in spite of the small value to us of the American possessions as far as industries and trade are concerned, there are political reasons which make their preservation by us an absolute necessity." The commission alleged: "Only by strengthening our foothold in North America can we call ourselves masters of the Northern precincts of the Pacific Ocean which . . . is a very desirable object for a powerful Empire." The report saw the retention of Russian-America as necessary for "a more intimate intercourse with Japan and altogether would serve as a support to our power in the Far East." Moreover, continued possession of the American colonies could "be turned to a certain advantage for the revival and reinforcement of our navy.'' (This argument seems to have been aimed at Grand Duke Constantine, chief admiral and minister of the navy, who favored the cession of Russian-America.) The commission concluded that the North American possessions should no longer be administered by the Russian-American Company. It suggested instead the formation of a civil government and the removal of "the Company's grasping and all-powerful monopoly.''[14]

The report of the commission urging reorganization and retention of Russian-America was a rebuttal to Constantine's and Popov's urgings to cede the colonies to the United States. Both sides in the controversy, however, cited Russian interest in the Far East as intimately related to the future of the Russian holding. The commission concluded that only by continued Russian sovereignty in North America could the Asian Pacific be secured, while Constantine and his allies argued that only by divestment of Russian-America and consolidation along the Amur could Russia's Asian future be assured.

Events in Russian-America added weight to Constantine's arguments. When rumors spread in 1863 that gold had been discovered along the Russian part of the Stikine River, the Russian-American Company, fearing a stampede of American miners, appealed to the St. Petersburg government for a man-of-war. In 1865, Stoeckl wrote to Gorchakov reporting a conversation with a Professor Whitney, a geologist from California, who assured the Russian minister that due to the geological coastal formations of the territory, it was almost certain that gold could be found in Russian-America.[15] Stoeckl later admitted that one of the prime motives for the sale was the fear of a mass of American prospectors invading the Russian possession as they had California. Stoeckl pointed to an incident that had occurred in 1858 in British Columbia, when some veins of gold were discovered along the Fraser River. A colony of some thousands of Americans was established quickly. They wanted to form a government, Stoeckl related, and the British sent in troops and frigates to drive them out. Nevertheless, it was not the British troops, but the insufficient amounts of gold that caused the colony to disperse. If it had not been for that lack of gold, Stoeckl conjectured, the area

would surely be American today.[16] In 1866, a man digging a telegraph post hole for the Collins Overland Line Company in Sitka
accidently struck gold.[17] This discovery, no doubt, added a sense
of urgency to the Russians' willingness to cede their North
American possession.

The accelerated American interest in Russian-America made it
painfully obvious to the Russian government that earlier urgings
and decisions to sell had indeed been correct. On December 12,
1866, Foreign Minister Gorchakov submitted to Czar Alexander
the opinions of three prominent Russian policy makers—Grand
Duke Constantine, Minister of Finance Michael de Reutern, and
Baron de Osten-Saken of the Asian department of the foreign
office—dealing with the future of the Russian possessions in
North America. Constantine, consistent with the view he had
advocated since 1857, urged his brother to cede the possessions
to the United States before the Yankees took them. He urged that
Russia concentrate its efforts on the Amur region. De Reutern,
the minister of finance, argued that not only were the colonies in
North America a financial failure, but they could not be defended
against any action taken by the United States. Only Osten-Saken
did not fear the United States would take the territory.[18]

Osten-Saken expanded his views in a longer memorandum
dated December 16, 1866. He warned that if Russia sold its possessions to the United States, "America will jump over the bar-
rier with one step. Are we in a position," he asked, "to oppose
them with any counter-action in the Eastern Siberian territories?"
Osten-Saken argued that the United States would use its possession of Russian-America, along with the Collins telegraph line, as
a stepping-stone to Japan and China. Once Americans had their
telegraph line, along with Russia's North American territory,
they would, he predicted, have a "sufficiently strong motive for
gaining access to Japan and China along the chain of volcanic
islands connecting America with Kamchatka, Kamchatka with
Sakalin, etc."[19]

Gorchakov and Alexander decided to accept the arguments of
Constantine and de Reutern. Ten more years of conflict with the
Americans over the Russian possessions had swayed the aging

foreign minister. Writing to the czar at the end of December 1866, Gorchakov agreed that the Russian-American territory was a financial failure. More important, he observed, "in the political aspect the position of our colonies is scarcely more advantageous. The means of defense are insufficient to protect them against American filibusterers who swarm the Pacific and whom the recall of our squadron renders still more bold in committing depredations on our coasts." Gorchakov believed that a proper reading of American history would point the correct course for the Russian government to follow. He recalled that "the Americans bought Louisiana and Florida from France and from Spain and quite recently Texas from Mexico, and they have previously proposed to us some years ago to do the same for our colonies."[20] Gorchakov must have realized that the United States purchased Louisiana, Florida, Texas, and California by a combination of cash and force. Now the story seemed to be repeating itself in Alaska, with, no doubt for the Russians, frightening consistency.

II

The czar accepted Gorchakov's analysis, and Stoeckl returned to the United States to conclude the sale. When he arrived in the United States in February 1867, he did not go immediately to Washington, but remained in New York City to allow a broken leg to heal. As he wrote to Gorchakov, Congress had just adjourned, and he wanted to wait for commencement of the next session. Stoeckl, fearing the growing impotency of the Johnson administration, decided that working through influential Senators was the best way to get a treaty accepted.[21] He did not waste time in New York, for upon his arrival he contacted Secretary of State William H. Seward "by the intermediary of one of his political friends who exercises great political influence over him."[22] This presumably was Thurlow Weed, who was in New York City at the time negotiating for the purchase of the *Commercial Advertiser.*[23]

Well before the discussions between Seward and Stoeckl began, the issue had been decided. All that remained was to set the price. Even an American Civil War had not deterred Yankee enterprise in Russian-America. The bipartisan nature of the interest in the purchase of the Russian colony, which had developed in the 1850s, assured the success of the Alaska negotiations.

10

The Resolution of a Rivalry

When Seward and Stoeckl met on March 11, 1867, in Washington, D.C., the Secretary of State was, by Stoeckl's own admission, already aware of the nature of the Russian minister's visit. Stoeckl told Seward "of the difficulties that the incursion of Americans [in Russian-America] could create between the two Governments." For this reason, the imperial government had decided "that the time has arrived" to enter into negotiations with the United States government leading to the cession of Russia's North American possessions. The Secretary of State, contrary to popular reports and later historians, did not fall into a swoon when he heard the offer;[1] rather, he explained to the Russian minister that President Johnson would have to be consulted prior to any decision.[2] Three days later, Seward informed Stoeckl that the President agreed to allow Seward to negotiate for the purchase of Russian-America. Stoeckl suggested to the Secretary of State that the best means of concluding this affair was by consulting influential members of the two houses of Congress, and if it were possible, engaging the Congress to take the initiative. The Secretary of State would have none of this. In effect, he told the Russian minister to keep his hands off American politics for, "it was up to the Administration, i.e. to him [Seward] to run this affair." Stoeckl reluctantly agreed to Seward's plea for secrecy.[3]

I

Seward was wise to demand that Stoeckl agree to allow the negotiations to be "conducted in the greatest secrecy."[4] Stoeckl soon realized any open discussion would destroy all chances for the treaty's confirmation by the Senate. Soon after the treaty was made public, but before Seward had convinced Senator Charles Sumner to guide it swiftly through the Senate, Stoeckl observed great opposition to the treaty. "This opposition," he noted, "is not aimed at the 'transaction' itself as from the passionate animosity which reigns in the Congress against the President and even more against the Secretary of State."[5] Stoeckl feared the Senate would not consent to the treaty. After Seward had succeeded in obtaining Senate approval of the treaty, Stoeckl had to admit, although grudgingly, that Seward "hastened the negotiations . . . thanks to the promptness that he took to conclude the treaty."[6]

Once Seward was confident of secrecy, he worked quickly and quietly to gain influential support for the cession. The Johnson cabinet approved the treaty on March 15.[7] On March 18, the Secretary of State wrote a note to Julius Hilgard of the Coast Survey, requesting him to report to the Department of State the following day and to bring with him the map of the Russian possessions on the Northwest Coast of America.[8] Seward also wrote to Benjamin Pierce, superintendent of the Coast Survey, on the same day for "a copy of any map of the Russian possessions in the Northwest Coast of America."[9] On the following day, Seward talked to both men about the impending purchase.

The treaty, signed on the night of March 29, was ready the next day for submission to the Senate. With the treaty signed, Seward began an all-out publicity campaign. The *New York Commercial Advertiser*'s ownership and editorship had recently been assumed by Seward's closest friend and political ally, Thurlow Weed.[10] If any newspaper could be considered a spokesman for Seward in March and April 1867, it was the *Advertiser*. The day the treaty was made public, March 31, Weed's paper ran the first story on the agreement, describing the acquisition in detailed terms. Weed praised the purchase, proclaiming: "It is a valuable fur country . . . the possession of which will influence in our favor the vast trade of the Pacific."[11] Henry Raymond's *New York Times,* a strongly pro-Seward sheet, followed Weed's lead and ran a long editorial on April 1 lauding the purchase: "While narrow-minded political bigots have been exhausting all their resources in branding him [Seward] as a traitor to his party, he has been quietly pursuing great objects of permanent and paramount importance for his Country." Raymond believed "the main importance of this acquisition grows out of its bearing upon our future trade with Japan, China, and the other countries of Eastern Asia."[12] The following day Raymond wrote to Lorenzo L. Crounse, the *Times* Washington correspondent, ordering him to "see Mr. Seward about the Russian Treaty," because Raymond wanted to "get his (S's) views of its advantages."[13] Meanwhile, the *Times* continued to plug the treaty. The April 2 editorial called the purchase "a natural though perhaps unexpected consummation of negotiations dating back to the time of Monroe."[14]

The traditional tale of the newspaper opposition to Seward's purchase had been distorted over the years. Many newspapers, like Bennett's *New York Herald,* while referring to the purchase as "Walrussia," urged Senate approval in their editorial columns. For instance, the *Herald* was "satisfied that the proposed purchase will be at once approved by the public sentiment and will . . . be considered a bargin at seven million."[15] The *New York Post,* which in its early edition on April 1 called the territory a "frozen sterile desert," in its second edition that day supported the treaty by noting that the Russian territory had valuable fishing along its shores and "will develop its value with the advance of our population."[16]

Strong opposition to the treaty was limited to a few, but influential, newspapers. Horace Greeley's *New York Tribune* launched the loudest and bitterest attack on the purchase, claiming that the administration was attempting to divert public attention from its domestic disasters. "Russian-America is a good way off," commented the *Tribune* on April 1, "and so a good place on which to fix the public eye." The *Tribune* could find "no advantages" in the cession.[17] While there was newspaper opposition to the treaty in all sections of the nation, save the Far West, the opposition was clearly in the minority.[18]

The advocates of the purchase employed three main arguments to urge the Senate to ratify. The first was the value of the fishing and whaling trade. New England newspapers were especially adamant on this point. The *Boston Advertiser* pointed to "the great whale fishing of the Northern Pacific and of Behring Straits, in which Massachusetts is deeply interested."[19] The *Boston Herald* found the Russian-American "rivers and bays on its coast swarm with fine fish"; it believed the purchase price a steal: "it is dog cheap."[20] The *National Intelligencer* also noted that the Russian-American "seas are alive with all the fish that enter into the commerce and consumption of the world."[21] The *Commercial Advertiser* agreed with the *New York Herald* that the purchase price was a bargain "simply as a speculation in fish oil and the fur business."[22] Even strong opponents of the treaty, such as the *New Orleans Daily Picayune,* admitted that "this acquisition . . . includes valuable fisheries."[23]

Second, many newspapers supported the cession because, like the *New York World,* they agreed "we must regard the purchase of the Russian possession as wise [for] . . . it is an advancing step in that manifest destiny which is yet to give us British North America." The *World* predicted, "The purchase of the Russian territory renders it morally certain" that the United States would acquire British Columbia, because that strip between American possessions "will always be an eyesore to the nation, whose sense of symmetry will be offended by the ragged look of the map."[24] The *New York Post* agreed: "The purchase of the Russian Territory is a step toward the retrieval of this blunder [the Oregon Compromise] not only by giving us the undisputed prominence on the American Coast of the Pacific, but by pushing it out of the power of England."[25] Bennett's *Herald* could not help noting that Britain would now find its possessions "in the uncomfortable position of a hostile cockney with a watchful Yankee on either side of him."[26] If Americans were surprised by the purchase, noted the *Connecticut Courant,* "England will have a shock of another sort. It lies between the British possessions and Asia," the *Courant* continued, "and cuts off communication with Asia across the Behring Straits."[27] The *San Francisco Chronicle,* representative of West Coast opinion, believed "our English friends won't like the move to be sure. . . . It will also place British Columbia in a rather awkward position—sandwiched right between our Washington Territory and our new acquisition."[28]

The third argument offered in favor of the cession was that it provided a natural bridge to the commerce of the Pacific and Asia. The *Commercial Advertiser*'s and the *New York Times*' advocacy of this view has already been noted. This view also found wide support across the nation. The *San Francisco Chronicle* wrote editorially that by the acquisition of "this valuable territory," the United States was "thus extending the area of freedom to the point where 'young America brisk and spry, shakes hands with old Asia withered and dry.' "[29] The Connecticut *Courant* saw the territory as "likely to become important if we have telegraphic communication with Asia by that route."[30]

The main thrust of the opposition to the purchase did not derive solely from the belief that Alaska would be worthless to the United States but centered on the type of foreign policy the United States would pursue as a result of the Alaska purchase. The *Tribune*'s main policy disagreement over the Russian treaty was with "the manifest destiny mob who believe we ought to annex British America at a week's notice." Greeley disagreed with the "suggestion, which is put forward at least semi-officially, that the occupation of Russian-America will be a sort of menace to Great Britain by interposing between her American possession and the Pacific."[31] The *New Orleans Daily Picayune* was more precise. It understood the implications of Seward's larger policy and attacked them head on: "The principle the purchase will establish is that it is a part of the duty and a good policy for the Government to hold distant colonies for the improvement of commerce." The *Picayune* noted this was "the same ground on which Great Britain established that wide colonial empire of which her most intelligent statesmen of the day are desirous to get rid."[32] The analysis of the *Picayune* was not typical, however. Most of the journals that opposed the treaty of cession agreed with *Harper's Weekly* that the purchase "would necessarily expose the friendly relations of this country and England to disturbance." The editor added: "Undoubtedly . . . it is our 'manifest destiny' ultimately to rule the continent; but that is no reason why we should immediately annex Mexico, or make war upon Canada, or buy Russian-America."[33]

Seward knew his real battle was not with the press but with the Senate Committee on Foreign Relations and Charles Sumner, its chairman. Seward prepared the treaty so the Senate could act on it on Saturday, March 30. The regular session of Congress ended on that day at noon. The President and his cabinet went to Capitol Hill at ten in the morning. Conversations with several Senators, including Senator Cole of California, convinced Seward that the Senate would not pass his treaty on that day. Seward and Johnson therefore quickly presented to the Senate a proclamation calling on it to convene on Monday, April 1, due to an "extraordinary occasion." The Senate then went into executive session, Sumner sending the treaty to the Committee on Foreign Relations, while the rest of the Senate adjourned.[34]

Seward did not neglect the other Senators or the public. While the treaty was being considered, the Department of State issued a five-page publication, "The Purchase of the Russian Possessions in North America: Papers Relating to the Value and Resources of the Country." The pamphlet contained seven pieces, including letters from Professor Spencer Baird of the Smithsonian Institution, Perry M. Collins, Civil War heroes General Henry W. Halleck and Commodore John Rogers, as well as Quartermaster General Montgomery C. Meigs.[35] Former Assistant Navy Secretary Gustavus V. Fox, one of the key Seward publicists, reported to Assistant Secretary of State Frederick Seward on April 8, referring to the "splendid project of acquiring Russian-America," that "I have got my leading men to telegraph in its favor to New England Senators and have even gone into newspaper writing myself to advocate it."[36] John Pruyn, another Seward confidant, reported in on the same day that he had "written several Senators urging the confirmation of the Russian-American Treaty."[37] The day before the confirmation of the treaty, the *Tribune* lamented: "It cannot be denied that the chances of ratification of the Esquimaux Acquisition Treaty, which were utterly desperate when it was presented to the Senate, improve daily." Greeley angrily pointed to the cause: "Mr. Seward is engineering with all of his personal influence . . . to win the vote of the Senate and to create a public opinion that shall justify and sustain that vote."[38]

Seward concentrated his efforts on Charles Sumner. When Sumner first learned of the treaty, he was convinced it could never be ratified and went to see Stoeckl requesting that it be withdrawn. The Russian minister refused.[39] At this point, chances for Senate approval looked hopeless. Stoeckl wrote that the "personal animosity of the Senators to the Secretary of State" made his (Stoeckl's) own task more difficult.[40] The Secretary of State, aware of "strong opposition in the Senate," launched his campaign to convert Charles Sumner to his side. Seward believed that with Sumner as his ally, the nation and the Senate would follow.[41]

Beginning on April 2, Sumner was bombarded with letters, telegrams, and appeals from persons working with Seward to gain confirmation of the treaty. On April 2, Sumner received three telegrams from key Seward supporters urging ratification: Former Assistant Secretary of the Navy G. V. Fox; Quartermaster General Meigs; and Julius Hilgard of the Coastal Survey.[42] In the next few days, Sumner's mail continued to support the cession heavily. Professor Spencer Baird of the Smithsonian Institution, Commander John Rogers, Congressman Thaddeus Stevens, and Perry Collins, all addressed themselves to persuading Sumner. Aside from adding their powerful voices, many of the writers included convincing testimony about the future of Alaska, which tended to sway Sumner.[43] Baird of the Smithsonian was particularly persuasive in pointing out to Sumner that "the shores of the North Pacific are swarming with animals of economic import," while the islands abounded in coal. Baird forwarded information obtained by Collins' Russian-American telegraph line explorations, adding, "The [Smithsonian] Institution had for several years been diligently engaged in gathering . . . and collecting information to illustrate the character of the northwest portion of the American Continent."[44] On April 9, armed with new facts, Charles Sumner offered a three-hour oration in support of the purchase of Russian-America by the United States.

As late as April 4, the *Albany Argus,* a strongly pro-Seward paper, attacked Sumner's apparent opposition to the treaty. The *Argus* said such opposition harkened back to "the traditional policy of Federalism," which had "opposed the acquisition of Louisiana and Florida. It organized against the annexation of Texas. It regarded the purchase of California as a calamity." As for the chairman of the Senate Committee on Foreign Relations, "Sumner is a mere echo of the sentiments of a small class of English politicians. . . . It is a pity that the foreign policy of a great country should be in the hands of such a flunky."[45]

The Massachusetts Senator was no intellectual lightweight, nor, in this instance, could one dismiss him as a Seward lackey. By 1867, he was entering the last phase of an active political and scholarly life. Like Seward, Sumner had been greatly influenced by John Quincy Adams.[46] Like Seward, Sumner had pursued an ambiguous attitude toward the Russian monarchy, criticizing its suppressions against Hungary in 1848 and joining with Seward in the senatorial welcome for Kossuth in 1851.[47] The Senator was suspicious of the Russian fleet visit of 1863, noting the fleet had come not out of any friendly attitude toward the United States, but rather out of fear that a European war over the Polish revolt could lead to the Russian fleet's being "sealed up at Cronstadt."[48] Nevertheless, in 1867, Sumner described the earlier fleet visit as "intended by the Emperor and accepted by the United States as a friendly demonstration."[49]

In supporting the Alaska purchase, Sumner argued that he opposed "indiscriminate and costly annexation." Nevertheless, he believed that the continent was destined to be under the rule of the United States. Of course, Sumner added, "There is no territorial aggrandizement which is worth the price of blood."[50] Sumner, however, ended where the manifest destinarians had begun, by rejecting overt force for "democratic pressure" in order to acquire territory. He was willing to be persuaded by Seward that Alaska fit into his definition of acquisition "by attraction of republican institutions" as well as by being a place worthy of attraction. Once he was convinced, he employed all his powers of persuasion to present a strong brief in favor of the cession.

Sumner opened his famous speech in defense of the cession with a quotation from John Adams, who had proclaimed in 1787 that the new nation was "destined to spread over the northern part of that whole quarter of the globe." The Senator then declared that one could not help noting that the mainland of Russian-America was "flanked by that narrow Aleutian range which, starting from Alaska, stretches far away to Japan, as if America were extending a friendly hand to Asia." At this point, Sumner presented, in surprising detail, the history of the discovery of Russian-America and Russia's title to it, as well as French and Spanish claims. He reviewed the various American attempts to purchase the territory, which, he said, began in the Polk administration. He told of Gwin's attempt, the memorial of the Washington Territory, and Cole's exertions on behalf of the Goldstone group. Sumner could not avoid mentioning the bipartisan aspect of the attempts to acquire Russian-America, noting "the exertions at different times of two Senators from California who, differing in political sentiments, and in party relations, took the initial steps which ended in this treaty."[51]

The advantages of the treaty were many, the Senator continued: "Since 1854 the people of California have received their ice from the Fresh water lakes in the islands of Kodiak." The fishing and whaling trade of Russian-America he believed to be incomparable. Most important, Sumner proclaimed, "all are looking to the Orient, as in the time of Columbus, although like him they sail to the west. To them, China, and Japan, those ancient realms of fabulous wealth, are the Indies." Sumner had to admit that this was no new idea. He emphasized that, for the Russian-American Company, "China was the best customer." As Sumner concluded this part of his brief:

The advantages to the Pacific Coast have two aspects, one domestic and the other foreign. Not only does the treaty extend the coasting trade of California, Oregon, and Washington Territory northward, but it also extends the base of commerce with China and Japan.[52]

In expounding another advantage of the cession, Sumner revealed his ambiguous attitude toward American friendship with Russia. In the speech, the Senator had urged the purchase so as not to weaken the amity between Russia and the United States, but he could not avoid noting that a friendly despot is best kept at a distance. He, therefore, listed among the advantages of the treaty that "we dismiss one more monarch from this continent." With this treaty, America could also thwart the schemes of Great Britain. Sumner, like most of the press that supported the treaty, saw the purchase of Russian-America as the best way to check the growth of British power on the Pacific Coast of North America.[53]

The day after Sumner's speech, the Senate approved Seward's treaty by a vote of 37 to 2. The cession still had to go to the House of Representatives in order that the $7.2 million purchase price be appropriated. The bill did not receive House approval until July 1868, and its passage was due once more, in no small part, to an immense propaganda effort by the Secretary of State. The *New York Herald* noted: "The illustrious Premier is working the telegraph and the Associated Press in the manufacture of public opinion night and day."[54]

The forces of opposition again quickly appeared. The *New York Tribune*, which had urged Senate rejection, began a campaign on April 10 urging the House to nullify the Senate action. Seward immediately had Sumner's speech printed with funds from the Department of State, making sure that it was widely distributed to both members of the House and their constituents.[55] One of Seward's aids, Simon Stevens, reported to his chief that he even tried to "get an article on *our* side of the question in the *Tribune*."[56] The Secretary of State sent out a team of scientists from the Smithsonian Institution to Alaska to make a survey of the new territory. Seward instructed the team's director, Professor Joseph Henry, to make the survey with all possible speed so that a report could be presented to the Congress at the opening of the next session.[57] When the survey was ready, Seward forwarded it to Congress along with Sumner's speech and reams of other propurchase propaganda. Seward's report, delivered on February 17, 1868, in its two sections covered 380 pages of material.[58] The appropriation for the purchase finally passed the House in July 1868 by a vote of 113 to 43.

II

Some Americans did not wait until the House of Representatives made up its mind. Stoeckl reported on May 27, 1868, that Senators Cole and Conness of California had assured him that "Americans will be in a hurry in opening commercial relations" with the newly acquired territory. "This is in effect what has happened," the Russian minister noted. "Hardly was the treaty made known to San Francisco than the exploration of the ceded territory caught the attention of American speculators."[59] Seward wrote to Stoeckl on May 20, 1867, asking if an American steamer sent to Sitka by a Mr. Holiday, "one of the richest businessmen of California, could sell merchandise there before the formal occupation of the territory."[60] Stoeckl acquiesced. He explained to Gorchakov that Russian-America would soon be filled with Americans "who will go in the course of this year . . . in order to exploit it."[61]

The purchase of Russian-America was only one part of Seward's vision of a commercial empire, which, as he noted in 1852, required "adequate expansion." Once the Russian territory became American property, Seward believed that British Columbia, sandwiched between United States territory, would fall into American hands. While Stoeckl assured the British minister to the United States, Frederick Bruce, that this would not be the result of the sale, the Russian minister wrote to Gorchakov, "there is no doubt" that the British possessions along the Pacific Coast would soon fall to the United States; "The English government cannot prevent this." Stoeckl noted that Seward was not adverse to starting rumors that the cession was aimed at England in order to thwart the Canadian federation then in the process of formation.[62]

Bruce wrote Lord Stanley, the British foreign minister, that the

Russian-American treaty was an attempt to cooperate to drive Britain out of North America. The United States, Bruce relayed, was "land-hungry" and would use its acquisition of Russian-America as a wedge against England. He was positive the United States would ask for British Columbia.[63] He was correct. The United States consul at Halifax, Nova Scotia, Mortimer Mellville Jackson, wrote a "private and official" letter to Seward enclosing the prospectus of the Hudson's Bay Company. Jackson believed "it was of the highest importance to American interests that the vast territory owned by this Company should be occupied by American citizens and under the control and jurisdiction of the Government of the U.S."[64] Seward agreed, and he sounded out Bruce about setting off America's *Alabama* claims in return for the cession of British Columbia. Bruce failed to see any connection. Lord Bruce wrote to his government that Seward had gone so far as urging an important American businessman to form a company in order to buy up the rights of the Hudson's Bay Company.[65] Seward obviously hoped to move into the British Pacific Coast possessions in the same manner that his predecessors and fellow countrymen undercut Russian rule in North America.

The second stage of Seward's larger plan assumed that with the Russian and British Pacific possessions assured, the United States, under the Secretary of State's direction, would purchase the Danish West Indies[66] and abrogate the Clayton-Bulwer Treaty with England in order to obtain an American canal to the Pacific.[67] With the Pacific Coast controlled by the United States and opened by rail and canal to the eastern industrial states, the way would be clear for the commercial, nonterritorial aspect of Seward's new empire. This integrated empire could then, Seward believed, capture and retain the legendary markets of Asia.[68] If the vision was not larger than the man, at least it was greater than the times. Seward could not, try as he would, escape the domestic troubles of the administration or the mood of the nation toward expansion. Once before, in 1861, Seward had suggested external solutions to internal tribulations. Then he proposed an attack on a European nation and a war in Latin America in order to avoid American civil war. Lincoln rejected the idea. In 1867, Seward had to lay his plans not before a sympathetic, yet unwilling, Lincoln, but before a hostile Congress and a divided, albeit victorious, section.

Seward succeeded in Russian-America while meeting failure in the other aspects of his drive for an integrated empire. The purchase of Russian-America resulted from events that occurred between the 1780s and 1867. The contemporary who most clearly wrote the story was the Russian minister to the United States, Edward de Stoeckl, in a long memorandum to Prince Gorchakov in July 1867. Stoeckl noted that Russian-America might not have been worth keeping, but "aside from these difficulties, we would have encountered serious obstacles from our American neighbors." Stoeckl traced the history of United States–Russian relations in Russian-America. Beginning with the Treaty of 1824, the Russian minister noted how, time and again, the United States government pushed to keep Russian-America open to Yankee commerce. "But another problem," Stoeckl proclaimed, "menaced our possessions. I am speaking of American filibusterers who swarm in the Pacific. To their eyes this continent is their patrimony." Stoeckl explained that "it was hoped that the little resources of our colonies would shelter them from the rapacity of the filibusters, but it has been otherwise." While American citizens had many rich areas of their own to exploit, "the fish, the forests, and several other products [of Alaska] . . . have not escaped the lust of the Americans." The government of the United States, declared Stoeckl, was as culpable as its zealous citizens. Whenever the Russian government complained about encroachments by Americans, the United States government would reply, "If they [American citizens] commit disorders on your territory, it is up to you to defend it," knowing full well that that was impossible.

Stoeckl concluded that Russia had been forced out of its American possessions: "Menaced by American neighbors our possessions would entangle us in serious disputes with the Federal Government and finish by becoming American property." When Gorchakov read this dispatch he wrote "*trés remarquable*" on top and sent it on to Alexander. The Czar added a notation below Gorchakov's: "Yes, and we must make an extract and publish it."[69]

11

Conclusion

Commercial activity by United States citizens in Russian-America began in the 1790s as an adjunct to the China trade. For the next eighty years, Americans penetrated the Russian colony in search of trade, sea otter furs, whales, ice, fish, and coal, as well as commercial and communications routes to link North America to Asia. Some United States citizens like William McKendree Gwin, William H. Seward, and Perry M. Collins saw Russian-America as part of the larger "battle for Asia." Others, like the whalers and traders of the antebellum period, viewed Alaska in a narrower sense as a place to make profits.

From the very beginnings, private American enterprise in Russian-America caused friction to develop between the governments of Russia and the United States. With the possible exception of the Polk administration in 1845, federal officials gave unflagging support to the protection of American commercial rights against repeated Russian governmental demands that United States citizens cease their commercial operations in Russian-America. This was not pro forma support either. In 1822–1823, Secretary of State John Quincy Adams informed the Russians that closing Russian North America to United States traders and whalers could lead to war. In 1838, when the Russian government again attempted to close its possession to American citizens, Secretary of State John Forsyth repeated

Adams's earlier warning. No less vigorous was federal support for particular commercial enterprises ranging from the sea otter trade in the early 1800s to the ice trade and Collins's project of the 1850s.

Russian government officials were as consistent in their predictions of a United States takeover of Russian-America as American policy was in bringing about that result. In 1805, Grand Chamberlain Nikolai Rezanov, then touring the colony, urged the czar to rid Russian-America of the Yankees before they seized the colony. Rezanov's warning was repeated time and again in the next sixty years by Russian-American Company officials as well as by important Russian government leaders. In the 1850s, such influential figures as Nikolai Muraviev, conqueror of the Amur region, Ivan Popov, commander of the Russian Pacific fleet, and Grand Duke Constantine Nikolaevich, the czar's brother, urged Alexander II to cede Russian-America to the United States because Rezanov's earlier fears seemed confirmed. Ultimately, the Russian government concluded that retention of Russian-America was an overextension of the Russian empire and that the colony's value was not sufficient when measured against the cost of defending it against continued American encroachments. Nevertheless, when Russia sold Alaska to the United States in 1867, it did so reluctantly. As Russian Minister Stoeckl pointed out to Russian critics of the sale, his government was forced to sell: "It was a question of our selling them or our seeing them [the United States] seize it." Russian-America was ceded to the United States because of its value. If, by 1867, the colony had proved a millstone around the Russian neck, that was due to a combination of American enterprise and federal support for that enterprise.

Surely the traditional story that the United States bought Alaska because the czar was able to capitalize on America's friendship in order to "unload this bothersome liability on the Americans for a substantial sum"[1] needs serious revision. The history of the United States–Russian rivalry in the Pacific Northwest from 1790 to 1867 must call into question as well the view that the early nineteenth century was a period of "a realistic romance" during which "the relations between the United States and Russia were in large measure cordial."[2] Those historians who have claimed that Russian-America was purchased as a stepping-stone to Asia must also revise their story to include the fact that Alaska was sought for its own value as well. The Alaska purchase, long relegated as a curiosity in American history, must be placed in proper perspective as a transitional phase of American expansion. If the Alaska purchase was the culmination of continental expansion, it was also the affirmation of Gwin's and Seward's view that continentalism did not stop at the water's edge.

Notes

CHAPTER 1

1. See, for instance, Frank A. Golder, "The Purchase of Alaska," *American Historical Review* 25 (1920): 411-425; Thomas A. Bailey, "Why the United States Purchased Alaska," *Pacific Historical Review* 3 (March 1934); Victor J. Farrar, *Purchase of Alaska* (Washington, 1935), p. 19; A. G. Mazour, "The Prelude to Russia's Departure from America," *Pacific Historical Review* 10 (September 1941): 316; Peter M. Buzanski, "Alaska and Nineteenth Century Diplomacy," *Journal of the West* 6 (1967): 452. Buzanski, unlike the others, does find that some Americans desired the acquisition of Russian-America before 1867. A Soviet historian, Mikhail Belov, published a brief essay in *Soviet Woman* (1967), in which he blames the sale of Alaska on a combination of czarist degeneracy and American imperialism. Belov, however, offers no evidence beyond Leninist faith to substantiate his thesis. An American professor, Henry R. Huttenbach, has written a reply to Belov (*Alaska Review* [Spring-Summer 1970]: 33-45) which repeats the Golder-Bailey thesis. Huttenbach concludes that "the Russian government, freely, without pressure from the United States, disengaged itself from Alaska." The debate over the purchase of Alaska has thus reached the point where a Soviet historian has argued that the United States acquired Russian-America because it was shrewd, while an American historian has attributed it to his nation's mindlessness.

2. Stoeckl to de Westman, July 1867, "Papers Relating to the Cession of Alaska," Record Group 59, Annex 42, National Archives. (These manuscripts were obtained from the Soviet government in 1936 in typed copy.)

160   Conflict on the Northwest Coast

3. Kenneth S. Latourette, "The History of Early Relations Between the United States and China, 1784-1844," *Transactions of the Connecticut Academy of Arts and Sciences* 22 (New Haven, 1917), pp. 27-28; Samuel Eliot Morison, *The Maritime History of Massachusetts* (Boston, 1921), pp. 43-46.

4. The stockholders for the first voyage of the *Columbia* were Joseph Barell, Samuel Brown, Fulfinch, John Derby, Crowel Hatch, and John M. Pintard; Hubert H. Bancroft, *History of the Northwest Coast* (San Francisco, 1884), 1: 185-192; Latourette, "Early Relations with China," pp. 31-33; Morison, *Maritime History of Massachusetts*, pp. 46-47.

5. Morison, *Maritime History of Massachusetts*, pp. 49-50.

6. Timothy Pitkin, *A Statistical View of the Commerce of the United States* (New Haven, 1835), pp. 245-249, 303; Latourette, "Early Relations with China," pp. 33-35; Morison, *Maritime History of Massachusetts*, chapter 6, esp. pp. 49-50, 53-54, 56-57, 69-70; Bancroft, *Northwest Coast*, 1: 359.

7. Robert Greenhow, *The History of Oregon and California* (Boston, 1845), pp. 266-267; J. C. Hildt, *Early Diplomatic Negotiations of the United States with Russia*, Johns Hopkins University Studies, vol. 24 (1906), pp. 157-158; Richard Van Alstyne, "International Rivalries in the Pacific Northwest," *Oregon Historical Quarterly* 46 (September 1945), 193-194. From 1790 until 1818, 108 American vessels were engaged in trading along the Northwest Coast and only twenty-two English vessels were so engaged (most of them before 1800). The French had three vessels there and the Portuguese, two. Bancroft, *Northwest Coast*, 1: 359.

8. Bancroft, *Northwest Coast*, 1: 318-319.

9. Adele Ogden, *The California Sea Otter Trade* (Berkeley, 1941), pp. 32-35, 41-42.

10. Ibid., pp. 45-47; Hector Chevigny, *Russian America* (New York, 1965), pp. 101-102; Morison, *Maritime History of Massachusetts*, pp. 60-61; Adele Ogden, "Russian Sea-Otter and Seal Hunting on the California Coast," *California Historical Quarterly* 12 (September 1933): 217-220.

11. Bancroft, *Northwest Coast*, 1: 324-325.

12. Nikolai Petrovich Rezanov, *The Rezanov Voyage to Neuva California in 1806* (San Francisco, 1926), pp. 69-72, 81-86; Bancroft, *Northwest Coast*, 1: 324-325; Bancroft, *History of Alaska* (reprint ed.: New York, 1959), pp. 480, 446. Chevigny in both his recent monograph—*Russian America* (New York, 1965)—and in his earlier work,

Lost Empire: Life of Nikolai Rezanov (Portland, Oregon, 1938), discussed the Rezanov mission. In neither work does he offer any documentation, and, in *Lost Empire*, he edited the letters of Rezanov in such a manner as to destroy the substance of the messages to the czar. Neither his work on Rezanov nor the one on Baranov (*Lord of Alaska* [New York, 1942]) can be considered more than popular history. Indeed, the author makes no other claims. Chevigny's more recent work on Russian-America, though more scholarly in approach than his earlier works, in no way measures up to Bancroft's much earlier efforts, which still remain the most authoritative in the English language on the subject of Russian America.

13. Rezanov, *Voyage*, pp. 56-58, 72-73; Bancroft, *Alaska*, p. 451; Ogden, *California Sea Otter Trade*, p. 47; Ogden, "Russian Sea-Otter Hunting," pp. 226-227.

14. Rezanov, *Voyage*, pp. 71-73. Rezanov's mention of sixty Americans was an apparent reference to the Lewis and Clark expedition, which was crossing the continent at that time. Bancroft, *Northwest Coast*, 1: 321-322.

15. Rezanov, *Voyage*, pp. 5-7; John Stanton, "The Foundations of Russian Foreign Policy in the Far East, 1847-1875" (Ph.D. diss., University of California, Berkeley, 1932), p. 485; Bancroft, *Alaska*, p. 481; Chevigny, *Russian-America*, pp. 115-117.

16. Ogden, "Russian Sea-Otter Hunting," pp. 226-227.

17. Ibid., pp. 228, 233.

18. S. B. Okun, *The Russian-American Company*, trans. Carl Ginsburg (Cambridge, Massachusetts, 1951) pp. 153-154. Chevigny, *Russian-America*, pp. 133-134.

19. Rumiantsev to Harris, May 17, 1808, American State Papers, *Foreign Relations* (Washington, D.C., 1833-1859), 5: 439 (hereafter cited as ASP, FR).

20. Ibid., pp. 455-456; Rumiantsev to Harris, June 13, 1808, ASP, FR, 3: 298; Harris to Madison, July 7/19, 1808, ASP, FR, 3: 298. Hildt, "Early Relations," p. 38, asserts the czar established diplomatic relations at this particular time to aid Russia in persuading the United States to carry its trade after Tilsit. American carriers (who were not government agents in any sense) had been carrying Russian goods since the beginning of the Napoleonic wars, and American captains did not need official diplomatic representatives in Washington to convince them that they could make a profit carrying Russian goods. On the other hand, the Russians did need to have stronger diplomatic ties to the United States if

they desired to halt American penetration of the Pacific Northwest territory.

21. Hildt, "Early Relations," pp. 42-43; Dashkov to Smith, January 4, 1810, ASP, FR, 5: 438-439.

22. Robert Smith had served the previous eight years as Jefferson's Secretary of the Navy. He was the brother of the prominent Baltimore merchant and Republican party leader, Samuel Smith. Smith, however, was not James Madison's personal choice for Secretary of State. The President-elect desired that Albert Gallatin take that post, but a faction of Madison's party headed by Samuel Smith and another financial contributor to the Republican cause strongly opposed Gallatin's appointment. Reluctantly, Madison tendered the Department of State to Robert Smith. In March 1811, at Gallatin's insistence, Smith was removed as Secretary of State. The decision to retire Robert Smith was due to political differences, not diplomatic policy. Gallatin, an enemy of the Smith brothers, made it clear to Madison that either Smith must resign or he (Secretary of Treasury Gallatin) would. Madison chose Gallatin. The President, however, did offer Smith the mission to Russia, which the Secretary of State declined. There is no biography of Robert Smith except for Charles C. Tansill's section on Smith in S. F. Bemis, ed., *American Secretaries of State and Their Diplomacies* (New York, 1928), 3: 151-197.

23. Dashkov to Smith, April 24, 1810, ASP, FR, 5: 441.

24. Smith to Dashkov, May 5, 1810, ASP, FR, 5: 441-442.

25. Ibid.

26. President James Madison offered the Russian mission to Adams in March 1809. Adams arrived in St. Petersburg in October. Earlier, Madison's predecessor, Thomas Jefferson, had attempted to send William Short to Russia as minister. The Senate, however, rejected Short's nomination in February 1809. The decision to appoint Short was made before news of Dashkov's appointment became known in Washington. Jefferson decided to send Short to Russia in the hope that an American mission might serve to gain Russian support for American neutral rights against Britain and France. Short was instructed that the "primary object" of his mission was to secure Russia's backing in maintaining the just rights of neutrals. President Jefferson hoped to maintain open trade with Russia despite French and British policies. John Quincy Adams's instructions were the same as those given to Short. See John Quincy Adams, *Memoirs,* ed. Charles Francis Adams (Philadelphia, 1874-1877), 1: 544-545; Hildt, "Early Relations," 38-45; Madison to Short, Sep-

tember 8, 1808, "Instructions, Russia," Record Group 59; National Archives; Jefferson to Madison, July 29, 1808, *The Writings of Thomas Jefferson,* ed. A. A. Lipscomb (Washington, 1903), 12: 111-112; Madison to Jefferson, July 4, 1809, *Writings of James Madison* (Philadelphia, 1867), 2: 445-446.

27. Smith to Adams, May 5, 1810, *Writings of Madison,* 2: 440; also, Smith to Adams, May 5, 1810, "Diplomatic Instructions," National Archives, Record Group 59.

28. John Quincy Adams came from Boston, the home of Sturgis, Perkins, O'Cain, Winship, and other Northwest Coast traders. Adams was a close personal friend of Perkins, with whom he had organized an intellectual society called the Crackbrain Club in the late 1790s. As minister to Russia, Adams maintained a close and amiable relationship with Czar Alexander. See Samuel F. Bemis. *John Quincy Adams and the Foundations of American Foreign Policy* (New York, 1949), pp. 26, 156-179.

29. Adams to Smith, October 5, 1810, ASP, FR, 5: 442.

30. Ibid., October 30, 1810, ASP, FR, 5: 442.

31. Ibid., October 12, 1810, ASP, FR, 5: 443.

32. Bancroft, *Alaska,* p. 480; Chevigny, *Russian-America,* pp. 127-130, and *Lord of Alaska,* pp. 227-232.

33. Okun, *Russian-American Company,* pp. 69-71. Kramer served on the board of directors of the Russian-American Company for twenty years (1805-1825).

34. Chevigny, *Russian-America,* p. 132.

35. Bancroft, *Alaska,* pp. 470-471; Kenneth W. Porter, *John Jacob Astor, Businessman* (Cambridge, Massachusetts, 1931), pp. 176-177. Porter argues that Baranov read Golovnin's report and, thinking it ludicrous, never sent it on. But Okun, *Russian-American Company,* p. 25, shows that Golovnin's, as well as similar reports, did reach the board of directors. Chevigny, *Russian-America,* p. 181, argues that Golovnin's motives for warning of the imminent American takeover rested upon his desire to persuade the government to send patrolling warships to the Pacific and frequent around-the-world voyages. All this would prevent the peacetime deterioration of the navy. While Chevigny may be correct, such a motive on Golovnin's part does not exclude the fear of the Russian captain of an American seizure.

36. "Memorandum of the Governing Board to the Tsar," December 18, 1811, in Okun, *Russian-American Company,* p. 75; *Guide to Materials for American History in Russian Archives,* ed. F. A. Golder (Washington, 1917), p. 139 (see 1811, #47). Another reason that board

members opposed the American trade with the company in North America had to do with the huge profits to be made in outfitting ships from Russia for around-the-world expeditions to the colonies. Whenever such an expedition was set up, the contract for it would invariably be given to a company board member, who made a large return on his investment. These voyages, of course, were more costly than were the supplies brought from America, and, more often than not, these voyages resulted in losses to the company's stockholders. See Okun, *Russian-American Company,* p. 71.

37. Okun, *Russian-American Company,* pp. 76-77.

38. Ibid., pp. 77-78.

39. Porter, *Astor,* 1: 164-166.

40. Astor to De Witt Clinton, January 25, 1808, in Porter, *Astor,* 1: 166.

41. Henry Dearborn to Jefferson, April 8, 1808, Thomas Jefferson Papers, Manuscript Division, Library of Congress.

42. Astor to Jefferson, February 27, 1808, Jefferson Papers.

43. Jefferson to Astor, April 13, 1808, *Writings of Thomas Jefferson,* Andrew A. Lipscomb (Washington, 1903), 12: 28.

44. Porter, *Astor,* 1: 167.

45. Jefferson to Meriwether Lewis, July 17, 1808, *Writings,* 12: 97-100.

46. Astor to Jefferson, March 11, 1812, Jefferson Papers.

47. Ibid. (Many letters and documents relating to this section are reproduced in full in the appendix and documents section of Porter, *Astor;* hereafter, such documents will be cited as Porter, *Doc.*) In a letter to Thomas Jefferson on March 14, 1812, Astor gave the history of his early dealings with Dashkov. Ibid., pp. 508-510.

48. Bancroft, *Alaska,* pp. 468-469.

49. Dashkov to Astor, November 7, 1809, Porter, *Doc.,* 1: 428-429. Most of the letters concerning Astor's dealings with the Russian-American Company are at the Baker Library of the Harvard Business School.

50. Porter, *Astor,* 1: 173-176.

51. Ibid.; Bancroft, *Alaska,* pp. 470-471.

52. Baranov to Astor, July 27, 1810, Porter, *Doc.,* 1: 442-445.

53. Porter, *Astor,* 1: 192.

54. Bentzon to Astor, July 9, 1810, Porter, *Doc.,* 1: 439-442.

55. Ibid.

56. Gallatin to Madison, January 5, 1811, Madison Papers, Manuscript Division, Library of Congress.

57. Gallatin to Madison, September 5, 1810, *Writings of Albert Gallatin,* ed. Henry Adams (Washington, 1879), 1: 486; Madison to Gallatin, September 12, 1810, *Writings of Gallatin,* pp. 489-490.

58. Porter, *Astor,* 1: 196.

59. Astor to Bentzon, January 11, 1811, Porter, *Doc.,* 1: 454-459.

60. Astor to Jefferson, March 14, 1812, Jefferson Papers; also reproduced in Porter, *Doc.,* 1: 508-513. For the terms of the contract between the American Fur Company and the Russian-American Company, see footnote 38.

61. Bancroft, *Northwest Coast,* 1: 329; Porter, *Astor,* 1: chapter 8, esp. pp. 228-229, 267-268.

62. Chevigny, *Russian-America,* pp. 151-152.

CHAPTER 2

1. Kenneth W. Porter, *John Jacob Astor* (Cambridge, Mass., 1931), 1: 241-242; S. B. Okun, *The Russian-American Company,* trans. Carl Ginsburg (Cambridge, 1951), p. 78.

2. The number of American trading vessels in the Northwest Coast by year: 1815, 10; 1816, 10; 1817, 18; 1818, 12; 1819, 10; 1820, 14; 1821, 13; 1822, 18 (F. W. Howay, "A List of Trading Vessels in the Maritime Fur Trade, 1815-1825," *Proceedings and Transactions of the Royal Society of Canada,* sec. 2, 3d series, 27 (1933), 119-147, sec. 2, 3d series, 28 (1934), 11-49).

3. Ibid.

4. *Annals of Congress,* 17 Cong., 2 sess., p. 403. January 18, 1822.

5. Ibid.

6. Ibid. Value of American nonspecie items traded at Canton: 1816 1817, $1,064,600; 1817-1818, $2,675,828; 1818-1819, $2,803,151; 1819-1820, $2,317,795.

7. *Historical Statistics of the United States* (Washington, 1949), p. 243.

8. See n. 2.

9. Charles M. Wiltse, *John C. Calhoun, Nationalist* (New York, 1944), pp. 221-222.

10. William Nesbet Chambers, *Old Bullion Benton: Senator from the West Coast* (Boston, 1956), pp. 883-884.

11. Wiltse, Calhoun, *Nationalist,* p. 221.

12. Astor and his cohorts also feared too much governmental supervision. They had become alarmed by Secretary of War Calhoun's proposal to establish a federal agency to supervise and license all fur traders dealing with the Indians. Calhoun suggested placing all American fur companies under governmental regulation. Such a system, Astor feared, would severely hamper his peltry business. Astor, Crooks, and Farnham, as well as Benton, desired their government's protection against the British and the Russians, not regulation of their business transactions. Calhoun had submitted a report in December 1818 requesting Congress to create an agency to supervise all fur traders. The Secretary of War believed this to be necessary in order to avoid recurring conflicts with the Indian tribes, which resulted from the often dishonest practices of fur traders. Furthermore, Calhoun predicted that national direction "would, in a few years push our trade [fur] to the Pacific Ocean." In the 1820s, Astor and the other fur traders did not receive federal protection in the Pacific Northwest, nor were governmental regulations, like those suggested by Calhoun, imposed. See Wiltse, *Calhoun, Nationalist,* pp. 221-222; John C. Calhoun, *The Papers of John C. Calhoun,* ed. W. E. Hemphill (Columbia, S.C., 1967), 3: 341-355; *Annals of Congress,* 15 Cong., 2 sess., pp. 2464-2466.

13. Edward C. Bourne, "Aspects of Oregon History Before 1840," *Oregon Historical Review* 6 (September 1905): 261-263. Surprisingly little else is known about the impetus of Floyd's outspoken support for American expansion to Oregon. Lester Burell Shippee, who did extensive research on Floyd's congressional career, concluded that "in the case of Dr. Floyd there seems to be left no direct personal evidence" for his motives in supporting the acquisition of Oregon for so many years with such consistency ("Federal Relations of Oregon," *Oregon Historical Society Quarterly* 19 [June 1918]: 112). This writer suspects that there are other reasons for Floyd's unaltering stance on the Northwest Coast issue than those presented here, but, so far, attempts to uncover them have proved fruitless. When Jackson passed him up for a cabinet position in 1829, Floyd returned to his home state to run for governor. After 1830, Floyd's ideas took a different turn. As governor of Virginia at the time of Nat Turner's revolt, Floyd seems to have turned more and more toward a state's rights position at the end of his years. By 1832, he had repudiated the Jackson administration and supported Calhoun's nullification. In that year, the state of South Carolina cast its votes for Floyd for the presidency in the electoral college. A recent article by John H. Schroeder, "Rep. John Floyd, 1817-1829: Harbinger of Oregon

Territory," *Oregon Historical Quarterly* 70 (December 1969): 333-346, sheds no new light upon Floyd's motives for such vehemence on the Oregon question.

14. Thomas H. Benton, *Thirty Years' View* (New York, 1854), 1: 13.

15. Ibid.; *Annals of Congress,* 16 Cong., 2 sess., January 1821, pp. 946-959 (see esp. 955-956 for fear of Russia). The Russian-American Company established the Ross colony ninety-four miles north of San Francisco in 1812. For a discussion of the Russian attempt to gain a sphere of influence in the Sandwich Islands during this period see Okun, *Russian-American Company,* pp. 156-165.

16. Benton, *Thirty Years,* p. 13.

17. Shippee, "Federal Relations of Oregon," 116-117; Samuel Flagg Bemis, *John Quincy Adams and the Foundations of American Foreign Policy* (New York, 1949), pp. 488-489.

18. Porter to Madison, October 31, 1815, Madison Papers, Manuscript Division, Library of Congress.

19. Bemis, *Adams and Foreign Policy,* pp. 488-489.

20. Poletica to Nesselrode, January 21/February 2, 1821, Okun, *Russian-American Company,* pp. 79-80; *Guide to Materials for American History in Russian Archives,* ed. F. A. Golder (Washington, 1937), p. 37.

21. Archives of the Chancery of the Minister of Foreign Affairs, 1817, in Okun, *Russian-American Company,* pp. 75, 78.

22. Vasilli Golovnin, "Letters of Captain Golovnin on the Condition of Russian-America in the Year 1818," Mss., Bancroft Library, University of California. Golovnin also blamed the Russian-American Company's management for much of the trouble with the Yankees. The captain alleged that the company had "powers of a certain extent . . . unheard of in Russia." He accused the company's administration of being pompous. Golovnin's letter displayed the clear antagonism of a career officer toward businessmen and merchants; see also Golovnin to the Directors of the Russian-American Company, September 10, 1819, in Okun, *Russian-American Company,* pp. 78-79; Hector Chevigny, *Russian America* (New York, 1965), pp. 160, 180. In a recent article, Mary E. Wheeler suggests that internal conflicts between the leaders of the Russian-American Company in St. Petersburg and its managers in the colony allowed Boston traders to succeed in becoming the chief suppliers of the Russian colony. Golovnin's letters, though not cited by Professor Wheeler, seem to give some credence to her argument. See

Wheeler, "Empires in Conflict and Cooperation: The 'Bostonians' and the Russian-American Company," *Pacific Historical Review* 40 (November 1971): 419-441.

23. Wheeler, "Empires in Conflict," 181-183.

24. "Ukase of September 4/16, 1821," American State Papers, *Foreign Relations* 4: 857-867 (hereafter cited as ASP, FR); *Proceedings of the Alaska Boundary Tribunal* (Washington, 1904) 2: appendix, pp. 26-28 (hereafter cited as *Alaska Trib.*).

25. "Ukase of September 16," ASP, FR, 4: 857-861.

26. Nesselrode to Poletica, October 7, 1821, "Correspondence of the Russian Ministers in Washington, 1818-1825," *American Historical Review* 18 (January 1913): 329-331 (my translation); Nesselrode to Lieven (Russian Minister to England), October 7, 1821, *Alaska Trib.*, 2: appendix, 99-100.

27. Nesselrode to Poletica, October 7, 1821, "Correspondence of the Russian Ministers," 331-333 (my translation).

28. Bagot to Marquis of Londonderry, November 17, 1821, *Alaska Trib.*, 2: 100-101.

29. *Niles Weekly Register,* December 29, 1821, pp. 278-279.

30. *Annals of Congress,* 17 Cong., 1 sess., December 10, 1821, 1: 529.

31. Ibid., December 17, 1821, 553.

32. For Floyd's January 1821 report see footnote 15; *Annals of Congress,* 17 Cong., 1 sess., January 18, 1822, 1: 744; "Floyd Committee Report on Pacific Northwest," *House Report* #18, 17 Cong., 1 sess., January 18, 1822.

33. *Annals of Congress,* 17 Cong., 1 sess., February 16, 1822, 1: 1073.

34. For Monroe's correspondence dealing with the Pacific Northwest, see ibid., 17 Cong., 1 sess., April 17, 1822, appendix, pp. 2129-2160.

35. Ibid., December 17, 1822, pp. 396-409.

36. Ibid.

37. Ibid., pp. 411-413.

38. Ibid., pp. 413-422.

39. Ibid.

40. Ibid., pp. 422-424.

41. See Bemis, *Adams and Foreign Policy,* pp. 487, 495-496, 514, for a discussion of the political implications of Floyd's bill.

42. Ibid., pp. 423.

43. *Boston Daily Advertiser,* January 28, 31, February 6, 20, 1822.

44. Bemis, *Adams and Foreign Policy,* pp. 510-511.

45. William Sturgis (unsigned), "Examination of the Russian Claims

to the Northwest Coast of America," *North American Review* 15 (October 1822), pp. 370-401.

46. Adams to Middleton, July 22, 1823, American State Papers, 5: 436-437.

47. Ivanov to Nesselrode, November 1822, January 1823, *Guide to Russian Archives*, 1: 77.

48. *Niles Weekly Register*, December 29, 1821, pp. 278-279, July 27, 1822, p. 349, November 9, 1822, p. 157.

49. *National Intelligencer*, December 22, 1821, February 12, 13, 1822.

50. *Newburyport Herald*, quoted in *Niles Weekly Register*, June 8, 1822, pp. 226-227.

51. *Baltimore Chronicle*, quoted in *Niles Weekly Register*, May 10, 1823, p. 146.

CHAPTER 3

1. John Quincy Adams, *Memoirs*, ed. Charles Francis Adams (Philadelphia, 1874-1877), 4: 130-131, 5: 53.

2. Glyndon Van Deusen, *The Life of Henry Clay* (Boston, 1937), pp. 116-130.

3. Clay to John J. Crittenden, December 14, 1819, *The Papers of Henry Clay*, ed. John F. Hopkins (Lexington, 1961), 2: 732-733; Clay to Amos Kendall, January 8, 1820, April 16, 1820, *Papers of Henry Clay*, 2: 752-753, 822-824; Jonathan Russell to Clay, December 17, 1820, *Papers of Henry Clay*, 2: 782-784; *Annals of Congress*, 16 Cong., 1 sess., March 28, 1820, 1691; ibid., April 31, 1820, 1730-1731.

4. For a presentation of Adams' continentalist views in document form, see Walter F. LaFeber, ed., *John Quincy Adams and American Continental Empire* (Chicago, 1965).

5. Adams to Abigail Adams, *The Writings of John Quincy Adams*, ed. Worthington C. Ford (New York, 1913-1917), 4: 129.

6. For Adams' tenure at St. Petersburg, see Samuel F. Bemis, *John Quincy Adams and the Foundations of American Foreign Policy* (New York, 1949), pp. 156-179.

7. Adams to Robt. Smith, September 5, 1810, *Writings*, 3: 486-487; Adams to Monroe, September 30, 1812, *Writings*, 4: 389-391; Monroe to Adams, April 26, 1813, *Writings*, 4: 476-478.

8. Adams to Abigail Adams, May 12, 1814, *Writings*, 5: 43.

170   Conflict on the Northwest Coast

9. Adams to Louisa C. Adams, July 2, 1814, *Writings,* 5: 55.
10. Adams to Campbell, June 28, 1818, *Writings,* 6: 366-377. Monroe, on the other hand, was less hopeful. In 1816, he noted that the "only circumstances in which a difference of interest is anticipated between the United States and Russia related to their respective claims on the Pacific Ocean" (Monroe to William Pinkney, May 10, 1816, *The Writings of James Monroe,* ed. S. M. Hamilton [New York, 1903], 5: 383).
11. John Quincy Adams, *Memoirs,* ed. Charles F. Adams (Philadelphia, 1874-1877), 4: 437-439.
12. For a discussion of specie outflow as a major cause of the 1819 depression, see Walter B. Smith, *The Second Bank of the United States* (Cambridge, Massachusetts, 1953), pp. 102-105. U.S. specie outflow in Canton trade from 1816-1821 was:

Year	Total Value	Specie	Other
1816-1817	5,609,600	4,545,000	1,064,600
1817-1818	7,076,228	5,601,000	2,675,828
1818-1819	10,217,151	7,414,000	2,803,151
1820-1821	5,392,795	2,995,000	2,317,795

"Other" refers mainly to Northwest furs and sandalwood (*Annals of Congress,* 17 Cong., 2 sess., December 17, 1822, p. 403). The total export of specie in 1821 amounted to $10.5 million, while the total specie import was $8.1 million. The balance of specie outflow was $2.4 million. The amount of specie traded at the Canton in 1821 was $2,995,000, which put it higher than the total outflow of specie. The specie traded at Canton was, therefore, a significant factor in the economy's health. See *Historical Statistics of the United States* (Washington, 1949), p. 245.
13. Adams, *Memoirs,* 5: 237-238.
14. Ibid., pp. 250-253.
15. Poletica to Adams, January 30 (February 11), 1822, *American State Papers, Foreign Relations* 4: (Washington, 1833-1859), 856-857.
16. Adams to Poletica, February 25, 1822, ASP, FR, 4: 861.
17. Poletica to Adams, February 28, 1822, ASP, FR, 4: 861-863.
18. Adams to Poletica, March 30, 1822, ASP, FR, 4: 863.
19. LaFeber, ed., *Adams and Empire,* pp. 48-50.
20. Poletica to Adams, April 2, 1822, ASP, FR, 4: 863-865.
21. Ibid., April 16, 1822, "Notes from Foreign Legations, Russia," National Archives, Record Group 59. Some European newspapers reported that Poletica had left the United States because relations between

the United States and Russia were strained to the brink of war over the issue of the emperor's ukase. See Nesselrode to D. Anstett (Frankfort), July 13, 1822, *Guide to Materials for American History in Russian Archives,* ed. F. A. Golder (Washington, 1917), p. 109.

22. Adams to Poletica, April 24, 1822, "Notes to Foreign Ministers, 1793-1834," National Archives, Record Group 59.

23. Adams to Middleton, May 13, 1822, *Proceedings of the Alaska Boundary Tribunal* (Washington, 1904), 2: appendix, pp. 39-40 (hereafter cited as *Alaska Trib.*).

24. Middleton to Adams, August 8/21, 1822, ibid., pp. 42-45 (includes enclosure #1: Middleton to Nesselrode, July 24 [August 5], 1822, "note verbale" [prepared but not delivered], pp. 44-45).

25. Ibid.

26. Middleton to Adams, August 8/21, 1822, ibid., 2: 42-45.

27. Guriev (Minister of Finance) to Chief Manager of Russian-American Co., memorandum, July 18/30, 1822, "Secret," ibid., pp. 40-41.

28. Board of Administration of Russian-American Co. to Chief Manager of Colonies, July 31 (August 12), 1822, ibid.

29. Ibid.; see especially enclosure #481, Great Britain's attitude toward the ukase played a very small role, if any, in the Russian decision to back down from enforcing it.

30. See Guriev to Russian-American Co., July 18/30, 1822, ibid., pp. 40-41.

31. The British government did not even formally protest against the decree until November 1822; see Wellington to G. Canning, November 28, 1822, ibid., pp. 113-117.

32. Tuyll to Adams, April 18, 1823, "Notes from Foreign Legations," ASP, FR, 5: 435.

33. S. Canning to G. Canning, May 3, 1823, *Alaska Trib.*, 2: appendix, pp. 120-121.

34. Adams to Tuyll, May 7, 1823, ASP, FR, 5: 435-436.

35. Stratford Canning to G. Canning, May 3, 1823, *Alaska Trib.*, 2: appendix, pp. 120-121.

36. Bagot to G. Canning, October 17/29, 1823, ibid., pp. 129-131.

37. Adams, *Memoirs,* 6: 157-158; see also Adams to Middleton, July 22, 1823, ASP, FR, 5: 436-437. Adams told Middleton to read Sturgis's October 1822 article in the *North American Review.* The Secretary said "the article written by a person fully master of the subject" should prove useful in arguing the case of the United States. In a special enclo-

sure Secretary of State Adams presented his own views to Middleton on the matter: "There can, perhaps, be no better time for saying frankly and explicitly, to the Russian Government, that the future peace of the world, the interests of Russia herself, cannot be promoted by Russian settlements upon any part of the American Continent." See enclosure 3-K, ibid.

Sturgis's article was also read by the Russian minister of foreign affairs. The Russian consul in Philadelphia, Ivanov, sent the foreign minister two copies of the article. See Ivanov to Nesselrode, November 1822 and January 1823, 16189, 17036, *Guide to Russian Archives,* 1: 77.

38. Adams to James Lloyd, January 15, 1823, in Bemis, *Adams and Foreign Policy,* p. 515. Lloyd served in the Senate from 1808 to 1813 and again from 1822 to 1826.

39. Ibid., p. 515.

40. Lloyd to Adams, July 28, 1823, ibid., pp. 515-516.

41. Adams, *Memoirs,* 6: 163.

42. Ibid., p. 186; Worthington C. Ford, "John Quincy Adams and the Monroe Doctrine," *American Historical Review* 8 (October 1902): 28-29.

43. Tuyll to Adams, November 15, 1823, "Notes from Russian Legation," National Archives, Record Group 59.

44. Nesselrode to Tuyll, August 30, 1823, in Ford, "Adams and the Monroe Doctrine," pp. 29-32.

45. Adams, *Memoirs,* 6: 194.

46. Adams to Tuyll, November 27, 1823, "Notes to Russian Legation." While parts of Adams' original draft were not sent to Tuyll, I have quoted only from the final draft. What was left out was even more direct and, possibly, personally insulting to the czar. Adams had intended to instruct the czar in "Republican Principles," but agreed to leave that section out at Wirt's insistence. For a copy of the complete rough draft see Ford, "Adams and the Monroe Doctrine," pp. 41-44.

47. Adams, *Memoirs,* 6: 200-203, 208.

48. Ibid., p. 208.

49. Ibid., pp. 206-207. In August 1823, the British foreign minister, George Canning, proposed that the United States and Great Britain issue a joint declaration of policy with regard to Latin America. Canning suggested that both nations should declare: (1) the recovery of the colonies by Spain was hopeless; (2) the problem of recognizing the former colonies as independent states was one of "time and circumstances"; (3) they would not oppose amicable negotiations between Spain and her

former colonies; (4) they did not desire the possession of any of Spain's former colonies; (5) they would oppose the transfer of any of Spain's former colonies to any other power. Adams had not formally answered Canning's proposal before December of 1823. See Dexter Perkins, *The Monroe Doctrine, 1823-1826* (Cambridge, Mass., 1927), pp. 62-64.

50. William Appleman Williams, *The Contours of American History* (Chicago, 1961), p. 216. A Soviet historian, Nikolai N. Bolkhovitinov, has reaffirmed William's arguments. Bolkhovitinov asserts that the "Monroe Doctrine was directed to Great Britain." See N. N. Bolkhovitinov, "Russia and the Declaration of the Non-Colonization Principles: New Archival Evidence," *Oregon Historical Review* 72 (June 1971): 125-126.

51. G. Canning to Bagot, January 15, 1824, *Alaska Trib.*, 2: 144-149. A recent essay by Irby C. Nichols and Richard A. Ward, "Anglo-American Relations and the Russian Ukase: A Reassessment," *Pacific Historical Review* 41 (November 1972): 444-459, affirms the view that the Monroe Doctrine served as the impetus for the end of joint Anglo-American negotiations with Russia over the czar's ukase.

52. Middleton to Adams, November 1/13, 1/23, ASP, FR, 4: 449.

53. S. B. Okun, *The Russian-American Company*, trans. Carl Ginsburg (Cambridge, 1951), pp. 67-68, 186.

54. P. A. Tikhmenev, *The Historical Review of the Russian-American Company* (St. Petersburg, 1861-1863), 1: 397-399; Hubert H. Bancroft, *History of Alaska* (San Francisco, 1886), p. 541; Hector Chevigny, *Russian-America: The Great Alaskan Venture, 1741-1867* (New York, 1965), p. 186. There is a strange sidelight to all this since one of the directors, Benedict Kramer, was an American, the representative in Russia of the New York banking firm of Kramer and Smith. Kramer had been a strong advocate of excluding foreign shipping from the Russian colonies. As soon as the ukase was issued in 1821, Kramer outfitted an around-the-world expedition to supply the colony. He procured the vessel *Yelena* for the company in the United States for a commission amounting to 6 percent of the cost of the vessel. Kramer also purchased another ship, the *Yelizavila*, which was known to be completely unseaworthy. That vessel had belonged to an insolvent debtor of Kramer. He purchased that ship (actually from himself) at a cost of 30,000 rubles. The *Yelizavila* cost the company an additional 70,000 rubles in repairs. In 1825, at a stockholder's meeting, Kramer was appropriately made the scapegoat for much of the company's financial plight since 1821. He resigned. It must have seemed to the stockholders

of the Russian-American Company that no matter what actions they took, they could not avoid the Americans eager to take part of the profits. For more on Kramer, see Okun, *Russian-American Company,* pp. 69-71; Chevigny, *Russian-American,* p. 186.

55. Middleton to Adams, February 5, 1824, ASP, FR, 5: 457; December 1/13, 1823, contains "Confidential Memorial," enclosure 8 (a), pp. 449-452; February 25 (March 8), 1824, "Private," *Alaska Trib.*, 2: appendix, pp. 68-69.

56. Ibid., pp. 10-12.

57. Middleton to Adams, April 7/19, 1824, ASP, FR, 5: 457-462. The convention was ratified by the Senate on January 7, 1825, by a vote of 41 to 1. The only dissenter was James De Wolf of Rhode Island, who did not explain his reason for voting no. James Lloyd of Massachusetts privately objected to the treaty in a letter to Adams on December 25, 1824. Lloyd opposed the ban on liquor trade because it deprived Yankee captains of their "most alluring traffic." He suggested that United States ratification be contingent upon Britain's acceptance of the same restrictions. The Massachusetts Senator also believed the ten-year clause might later prove to be a limitation on American trade. Nevertheless, Lloyd voted for ratification. See Bemis, *Adams and Foreign Policy,* p. 525.

58. Adams to Rush, July 22, 1823, in Bemis, *Adams and Foreign Policy,* pp. 446-448.

59. Nesselrode to Mordinov (large and prominent stockholder in the Company), 1824, Okun, *Russian-American Company,* p. 89.

CHAPTER 4

1. P. A. Tikhmenev, *The Historical Review of the Russian-American Company* (St. Petersburg, 1861-1863), 1, pp. 434-435.

2. Mordvinov to Nesselrode, February 1824, S. B. Okun, *Russian-American Company,* ed. Carl Ginsburg (Cambridge, 1951), pp. 88-89. For more on Mordvinov, see Basil Dmytryshyn, "Admiral Nikolai S. Mordvinov: Russia's Forgotten Liberal," *Russian Review* 30 (January 1971): 54-63.

3. Ryleyev to Kankrin, March 1824, Okun, *Russian-American Company,* pp. 90-91.

4. Kankrin to Nesselrode, May 16, June 14, August 15, 1824, in *Guide to Materials in American History in Russian Archives,* 2 vols. (Washington, 1917 and 1937), 2, p. 17.

5. Nesselrode to Kankrin, August, 18, 1824, ibid.

6. Okun, *Russian-American Company,* pp. 91-92.

7. Ibid., p. 88.

8. For a detailed discussion of the background, founding, and growth of Fort Ross, see ibid., chap. 6, pp. 119-133; also John Clarence Du Four, "The Russian Withdrawal from California," *California Historical Society Quarterly* 12 (September 1933): 240-276.

9. Adele Ogden, *California Sea Otter Trade* (Berkeley, 1941), p. 86; Ogden, "Russian Sea-Otter and Seal Hunting," p. 233; Frederick Howay, ed., "William Sturgis: The Northwest Fur Trade," *British Columbia Historical Society Quarterly* 8 (January 1944), p. 15; Samuel Eliot Morison, *The Maritime History of Massachusetts* (Boston, 1921), pp. 260-261. For the statistics of the general decline of the American fur trade at Canton from 1821 to 1840, see *Congressional Globe,* 28 Cong., 1 sess., February 27, 1844, Appendix, p. 226.

10. Tikhmenev, *Russian-American Company,* 1: 398.

11. Ibid., pp. 398-399; Kenneth S. Latourette, "The History of the Early Relations Between the United States and China," *Transactions of the Connecticut Academy of Arts and Sciences* 22 (1917): 55.

12. Hector Chevigny, *Russian-America* (New York, 1965), p. 189.

13. Morison, *Maritime History of Massachusetts,* p. 261.

14. Krudener to Minister of Foreign Affairs, July 1835, nos. 16283, 16354, *Guide to Russian Archives,* p. 61.

15. Tikhmenev, *Russian-American Company,* 1: 408.

16. Chevigny, *Russian-America,* p. 189. The 1825 Anglo-Russian treaty was essentially the same as the 1824 Russian-American convention with one exception: the Anglo-Russian treaty specifically recognized the 54° 40' line as the southern boundary of the Russian possession, while the Treaty of 1824 provided only that the United States agree to establish no settlements north of 54° 40'. For the Anglo-Russian Treaty, see *Proceedings of the Alaska Boundary Tribunal* (Washington, 1905), 2: appendix, pp. 12-16 (hereafter cited as *Alaska Trib.*).

17. Adams, "First Annual Message," December 6, 1825, in *A Compilation of the Messages and Papers of the Presidents,* ed. James D. Richardson (New York, 1897), 2: 875-879.

18. Jackson, "First Annual Message," December 8, 1829, ibid., 3: 1008.

19. See "Report of Baylies' Committee," *Debates of Congress,* 18 Cong., 2 sess., December 16, 1825, p. 813; Francis Baylies, House Report #213, 19 Cong., 1 sess., May 15, 1825, p. 22.

20. *Debates of Congress,* 18 Cong., 1 sess., December 20, 21, 1824, pp. 13, 39.

21. The vote in the House was 111 yeas and 58 nays. See *House Journal,* 18 Cong., 2 sess., December 23, 1824, p. 78. The bill had majority support from every section. For the purposes of tabulating this vote, I have arbitrarily broken down the nation into the following sections: West, in which I have placed Kentucky, Tennessee, Ohio, Indiana, Illinois, and Missouri; Northeast: Maine, New Hampshire, Massachusetts, Connecticut, Rhode Island, Vermont, New York, New Jersey, and Pennsylvania; South: Delaware, Maryland, Virginia, North Carolina, South Carolina, Georgia, Louisiana, Mississippi, and Alabama. The vote in favor of the bill would therefore show:

	Yeas	Nays
West	28	9
Northeast	54	33
South	29	16
	111	58

22. *Debates in Congress,* 18 Cong., 2 sess., March 1, 1825, p. 713. The vote in the Senate to table was 25 yeas and 14 nays; the vote to table the bill, as I have set it up sectionally in n. 21, would therefore show:

	Yeas		Nays
West	2	(Brown of Ohio & Barton of	7
Northeast	13	Mo.)	2
South	10		5
	25		14

23. For Trimble's view, see ibid., December 21, 1824, pp. 39-42.

24. See *Debates of Congress,* 20 Cong., 2 sess., January 9, 1829, pp. 168-175, 187-192. The final vote on January 9, 1829, was 80 in favor and 99 opposed. The vote could not be considered sectional and was not divided along party lines. Analysis of the vote by section would show competitive voting on this bill in all sections. In n. 21, I placed New England together with the other northeastern states. In the following sectional breakdown I have separated New York, Pennsylvania, New Jersey, and Delaware and labeled them North.

	Yeas	Nays
New England	15	19
North	20	33
South	26	30
West	19	17

25. For a discussion of the Commercial Treaty of 1832, see Benjamin P. Thomas, *Russian-American Relations, 1815-1867,* Johns Hopkins University Studies 48 (1930), pp. 68-91; "Commissions to Private Armed Vessels," *House Exec. Doc.* #111, 33 Cong., 1 sess.; *Washington Globe,* October 1, 1832.

26. Osten-Sacken to Secretary of State Livingston, October 14, 1832, "Notes from Russian Legation," National Archives, Record Group 59.

27. Livingston to Osten-Sacken, December 4, 1832, "Notes to Foreign Ministers," National Archives, Record Group 59.

28. Krudener to Acting Secretary of State A. Dickens, May 19/31, 1835, "Correspondence with Russia, 1835-1838," *House Executive Document* 2, 25 Cong., 3 sess., p. 47; *Alaska Trib.,* 2: appendix, pp. 236-237.

29. Forsyth to Wilkins, July 30, 1835, House Document 2; see also Dickens to Krudener, June 3, 1835, in ibid., and Krudener to Forsyth, June 29, 1835, ibid., p. 48.

30. Okun, *Russian-American Company,* p. 140; DuFour, "Russian Withdrawal from California," pp. 243-244.

31. Wrangell to the Governing Board, report, April 1834, Okun, *Russian-American Company,* pp. 140-144.

32. Wrangell to Governing Board, April 1834, House Document 2, pp. 142-145.

33. Ibid., pp. 146-147; DuFour, "Russian Withdrawal from California," p. 244.

34. Dimitry Zavalishnin, "The Affairs of the Ross Colony," 1866 report, Bancroft Library, University of California, Berkeley.

35. For a discussion of the political implications of Forsyth's support of the "Force Bill," see Alvin LaRoy Duckett, *John Forsyth, Political Tactician* (Athens, Ga., 1962), pp. 161-163.

36. There is no good biography of John Forsyth. Eugene I. McCormac's essay in Samuel Flagg Bemis, ed., *The American Secretaries of State and Their Diplomacies,* 10 vols. (New York, 1928), IV, pp. 201-

243, is an adequate sketch, but no more. Alvin LaRoy Duckett's more recent biography, while more complete than McCormac's on Forsyth's earlier life, adds little if anything in discussion of Forsyth as Secretary of State. Duckett does not even mention Forsyth's concern or actions about the attempt by Russians to exclude United States citizens from Russian-America from 1834 to 1838.

37. William Wilkins was a United States Senator from Pennsylvania at the time of his appointment to the Russian post. Wilkins was from Pittsburgh and served as the western leader of the Dallas (Senator George M. Dallas of Philadelphia) faction of the Pennsylvania Democratic party. The Dallas faction's opposition in the Democratic party was led by former Minister to Russia James Buchanan. By 1833, the Pennsylvania Democratic party seemed hopelessly split. The Jackson administration decided to send Wilkins to Russia in order to open a Senate seat for the Buchanan faction in hopes that, by so doing, the Pennsylvania Democrats would end their feuds. See Philip S. Klein, *President James Buchanan* (University Park, Pa., 1962), pp. 73, 96-99.

38. See House Document 2, p. 53 (emphasis added).

39. Wilkins to Forsyth, November 23, 1835, ibid., p. 61.

40. Ibid.

41. Wilkins to Nesselrode, November 1/13, 1835, ibid., pp. 63-64. Wilkins dismissed Nesselrode's claim that Americans had been selling spirituous liquors, firearms, and gunpowder to the natives by pointing out that such sales were prohibited by the 1824 treaty and that "there have been no infractions . . . complained of in representations of the [Russian] Government at Washington." Wilkins saw the real opposition to American commerce in this area as coming from the Russian-American Fur Company, which feared American competition.

42. Report of the Board of Directors of the Russian-American Company to the Department of Trade and Manufacturers, November 26, 1835 (no. 1298), *Alaska Trib.*, 2: appendix, pp. 234-236. The report also urged denial of these rights to British subjects as well for many of the same reasons, yet the board was less harsh in its discussion of the British actions in Russian-America. The report did urge, however, allowing foreigners to continue to come to Novo-Archangelesk to trade solely at the offices of the Russian Company.

43. Wilkins to Forsyth, December 11, 1835, House Document 2, pp. 66-70.

44. George M. Dallas, *Diary* (Philadelphia, 1892), p. 209.

45. Wilkins to Forsyth, December 11, 1835, enclosure of Nesselrode to Wilkins, November 28, 1835, House Document 2, p. 71.

46. George M. Dallas of Philadelphia was then serving in the United States Senate. He was the leading member of the "family," or Dallas faction, of the Pennsylvania Democrats. By 1837, however, the Buchanan forces seemed triumphant over those of Dallas. No doubt Dallas, like Wilkins before him, was sent to Russia by the Democratic administration more with an eye toward Pennsylvania politics than for any reasons relevant to American-Russian relations. See Klein, *Buchanan*, pp. 112-113.

47. Forsyth to Dallas, April 19, 1837, House Document 2, p. 54.

48. Forsyth to Dallas, May 4, 1837, ibid., p. 55.

49. Dallas to Forsyth, August 16, 1837, ibid., pp. 73-74.

50. Forsyth to Dallas, November 3, 1837, ibid., pp. 58-59.

51. Dallas to Forsyth, September 8, 1837, ibid., p. 74.

52. Nesselrode to Dallas, February 23, 1838 (O.S.) House Document 2, pp. 80-81.

53. Dallas to Forsyth, January 22, 1838, "Despatches Russia," National Archives, Record Group 59.

54. Dallas to Nesselrode, March 5/17, 1838, House Document 2, pp. 82-83.

55. Nesselrode to Dallas, March 9, 1838, ibid., pp. 91-92.

56. Dallas to Forsyth, April 16, 1838, ibid., pp. 87-89

57. There is some evidence that in November 1838 the Russian government was attempting to persuade the United States to join with it in open support of the Canadian Revolt. See Van Buren Papers, November 12, 1838, Library of Congress, Manuscript Division. Van Buren saved an editorial from the *New York Morning Herald* of November 12, 1838, which described the Russian attempts to get American support in aiding the Canadian rebels. The editorial also warned Americans that "Russia is now reaching across the Atlantic, and is actually encouraging the elements of discord on the New York frontier."

58. Van Buren, "Annual Message," December 3, 1838, *Messages of the Presidents*, 4: 1702. See also Bancroft, *Alaska*, pp. 556-557; Chevigny, *Russian-America*, pp. 190-191.

59. Nesselrode to Kankrin, January 4, 1839, *Alaska Trib.*, 2: p. 312.

60. Bodisco to Foreign Affairs, August 10/22, 1839, May 1840, *Guide to Russian Archives*, 1: 65-66.

61. The 1839 agreement between the Hudson's Bay Company and the Russian-American Company provided that a lisiere from Cape Spencer south to 54° 40' was to be leased to the British company for a period of ten years. In return, the Hudson's Bay Company promised to deliver to the Russian company a rental payment of 2,000 landed otter skins annu-

ally and also to provide an additional 2,000 skins at 23 shillings each. The lessee was also required to provide the Russian-American Company with food and supplies. While the British company was able to fulfill the first part of the agreement, it proved unable to supply the Russian colony with needed foodstuffs and supplies. As a result, the Russian settlement remained dependent upon Yankee traders for necessities. See Tikhmenev, *Russian-American Company,* 1: 411-412; Tikhmenev reproduces the contract with the Hudson's Bay Company in 1: appendix, pp. 323-325.

CHAPTER 5

1. Herman Melville, *Mardi* (1849; reprint ed., New York, 1964), p. 18.

2. Alexander Starbuck, *History of American Whale Fishery* (1878; reprint ed., New York, 1961), 1: 98; Walter S. Tower, *A History of American Whale Fishery* (Philadelphia, 1907), p. 59; Clarence L. Andrews, "Alaska Whaling," *Washington Historical Quarterly* 9 (January 1918): 4-5.

3. Starbuck, *Whale Fishery,* 1: 98-100; Andrews, "Alaska Whaling," 4-5; Tower, *American Whale Fishery,* p. 59.

4. Starbuck, *Whale Fishery,* 1: 364-407, 2: 408-435; Tower, *American Whale Fishery,* pp. 121, 129. Since Northwest Coast whaling voyages lasted two to three years, the number of ships sent out was less than the total number of the fleet.

5. Tower, *American Whale Fishery,* p. 51.

6. Starbuck, *Whale Fishery,* 2: 660.

7. Samuel Eliot Morison, *The Maritime History of Massachusetts* (Boston, 1921), p. 319.

8. For instance, see Douglass C. North, *Economic Growth of the United States, 1790-1860* (New York, 1961), p. 200, or the newer interpretation offered by Peter Temin, *The Jacksonian Economy* (New York, 1969), pp. 136-147.

9. For a discussion of the business aspect of whaling, see chapters 11 and 12 of Elmo Paul Hohman, *The American Whaleman* (New York, 1928).

10. Temin, *Jacksonian Economy,* pp. 160-161.

11. For a discussion of the leaders of the Massachusetts cotton-textile industry in the late 1830s and early 1840s, see Thomas H. O'Connor,

Lords of the Loom: The Cotton Whigs and the Coming of the Civil War
(New York, 1968), chap. 2, pp. 29-35.

12. Peter Temin argues in *Jacksonian Economy*, pp. 156-157, that the period 1838 to 1843 was deflationary but not depressionary: "Gross investment . . . declined by less than one quarter from 1839 to 1843. Consumption . . . actually rose in the early 1840's." The gross national product also rose. Temin sees a decline in production in some industries such as cotton-textiles, but his data allow for the existence of sufficient funds for investment in other nonindustrial sectors of the economy (with the exception of cotton). The significant increase in investment and profit in whaling suggests that New England investors turned away from cotton-textiles and shipping, putting their money into other enterprises such as whaling.

13. Tower, *American Whale Fishery*, pp. 121, 143.

14. Temin, *Jacksonian Economy*, p. 161.

15. Morison, *Maritime History of Massachusetts*, pp. 316-318; Tower, *American Whale Fishery*, p. 54; Starbuck, *Whale Fishery*, 1: 372-476, 2: 675-684.

16. Starbuck, *Whale Fishery*, 1: 372-476; Tower, *American Whale Fishery*, p. 123.

17. Joseph Grinnell, "Speech on the Tariff, with Statistical Tables of the Whale Fishery," Washington, 1844; Hohman, *American Whaleman*, appendix, pp. 323-325. Figures calculated using 1844 as a base year.

18. Timothy Pitkin, *Statistical View of the Commerce of the United States of America* (New Haven, 1835), p. 45.

19. Starbuck, *Whale Fishery*, 2: 700-701; *Historical Statistics of the United States* (Washington, 1949), p. 245.

20. Hohman, *American Whaleman*, pp. 278-279, 286-287.

21. For a list of owners and investors, see Starbuck, *Whale Fishery*, 1: 372-407, 2: 408-476. Some large investors had acquired their money in textiles.

22. See *Dictionary of American Biography* (New York, 1928), 21 vols., 8: 3-4.

23. Ibid., 9: 312-313.

24. Morison, *Maritime History of Massachusetts*, p. 318; *Dictionary of American Biography*, 13: 164-165.

25. Hohman, *American Whaleman*, p. 279.

26. The congressional voting records of Barker Burnell (Whig from the Tenth Congressional District of Massachusetts representing New Bedford and Nantucket) and Thomas W. Williams (Whig and whaling

magnate representing the Third Congressional District of Connecticut, which included New London) bear this out. Both men strongly supported high tariffs and federal government aid for internal improvements. Both also voted for the reestablishment of the Bank of the United States. See Joel Silbey, *The Shrine of Party, Congressional Voting Behavior, 1841-1852* (Pittsburgh, 1967), appendix, pp. 155, 158. Since these votes coincided with Whig party voting, no special conclusions about whaling districts can be drawn except that they elected men who supported national Whig policies to the Twenty-seventh Congress. Furthermore, these policies had the backing of investors in whaling such as Howland and Morgan. See n. 23 and 24 above.

27. Richard N. Current, *Daniel Webster and the Rise of National Conservatism* (Boston, 1955), pp. 119-126; Claude M. Fuess, *Daniel Webster* (Boston, 1930), 2: 105-116.

28. See *Whig Almanac* (New York, 1843), pp. 51-64; (1845), pp. 53-54.

29. In 1842, Connecticut turned all its Whig Congressmen out of office. This statewide trend followed the national trend of reacting unfavorably to the first year of the Tyler administration. However, George H. Catlin, who was elected from the Third Congressional District (New London) voted against expansion and supported internal improvements. Catlin's case will be discussed later in this section.

30. *Biographical Directory of the American Congress, 1774-1971* (Washington, D.C., 1971), p. 1932.

31. *Whig Almanac* (1843), p. 51; (1845), p. 53.

32. See Silbey, *Shrine of Party,* pp. 155-171.

33. Ibid., p. 166.

34. *Congressional Globe,* 28 Cong., 2 sess., December 17, 1844, p. 39.

35. See *Dictionary of American Biography,* 8: 3-4. In 1846 Grinnell obtained a charter for a cotton factory in New Bedford and became the first president of that enterprise.

36. Joseph Grinnell, "Speech on the Tariff," *Hunt's Merchant's Magazine* 12 (January 1845): 96-97; *Congressional Globe,* 28 Cong., 1 sess., May 1, 1844, p. 570.

37. P. A. Tikhmenev, *The Historical Review of the Russian-American Company* (St. Petersburg, 1861-1863), 2: 149-150; H. H. Bancroft, *History of Alaska* (San Francisco, 1886), pp. 583-584.

38. Ministry of Finance to Ministry of Foreign Affairs, November 30, 1842, *Guide to Materials for American History in Russian Archives,* ed. F. A. Golder (Washington, 1917), 1: 19.

39. Ministry of Foreign Affairs to Ministry of Finance, December 9, 1842, *Guide to Russian Archives,* 1: 19; Bancroft, *Alaska,* pp. 583-584. Less obtrusive, but no less persistent than the whalers, were such Boston traders as William H. Boardman. Boardman, having found it profitable to supply the Russians in North America, extended his trading interests in 1835 to Kamchatka along the Asian coast. Kamchatka, like the other Asian coastal possessions of the czar, fell under the jurisdiction of the Russian-American Company. Boardman's successes quickly impelled other Yankee traders to follow him into Russian Asia. By 1843, American traders dominated the trade of Kamchatka and threatened to destroy the internal commerce of the area. In 1842, the Russian government informed United States Minister Charles S. Todd that Kamchatka would be closed to Yankee traders beginning in spring 1843. Minister Todd, at Webster's instruction, protested the Russian action. Receiving no satisfactory answer, Todd again wrote to Russian Foreign Minister Nesselrode in April 1843, requesting a speedy reply since "the season for American trade on that coast is rapidly approaching." Nesselrode soon realized what Todd and Webster knew all along: the Russian decree would not halt the determined Yankee traders and would create diplomatic enmity where none need exist. During the 1843 season, the American traders were as abundant as ever in Kamchatka. In September 1843, the czar's government agreed to defer any decision about foreign traders in Kamchatka for two more years. That decision, in effect, left Kamchatka open indefinitely to Yankee traders. Krudener to Nesselrode, July 1835, *Guide to Russian Archives,* 1: 61; Papers to Department of Internal Relations of Ministry of Foreign Affairs, 1835, II-3, 7, *Guide to Russian Archives,* p. 112; Tikhmenev, *Russian-American Company,* 1: 408; Todd to Webster, December 15/17, 1842, "Despatches, Russia," National Archives, Record Group 59; Todd to Webster, March 23/April 4, 1843; Todd to Nesselrode, March 20/April 1, 1843; Todd to Webster, September 7/19, 1843; Todd to Calhoun, October 22/November 3, 1844, "Despatches, Russia."

40. Tikhmenev, *Russian-American Company,* 2: 152.

41. Ibid., pp. 152-153.

42. Enclosure of St. Petersburg *Journal* (my translation) in Todd to Webster, February 22, 1843, "Despatches, Russia."

43. Enclosure in Todd to Calhoun, May 5/17, 1844, "Despatches, Russia" (my translation).

44. Tikhmenev, *Russian-American Company,* 2: 153-157.

184   Conflict on the Northwest Coast

45. Ibid.
46. Starbuck, *Whale Fishery,* 2: 364-407, 2: 408-435; Tower, *American Whale Fishery,* pp. 121, 129.
47. Tikhmenev, *Russian-American Company,* 2: 153.
48. For a discussion of the importance of the Okhotsk and Kamchatka grounds, see Tower, *American Whale Fishery,* p. 52, and Tikhmenev, *Russian-American Company,* 2: 156-157.
49. Starbuck, *Whale Fishery,* 2: 660.
50. Ibid., pp. 420-491.
51. Ibid., p. 660.
52. Muraviev to Chief of Staff of Navy, September 26, 1848, in Tikhmenev, *Russian-American Company,* 2: 164.
53. Ibid., p. 157.
54. Muraviev to Minister of Finances, March 7, 1846, ibid., p. 162; Finance to Foreign Affairs, March 11, 1846, *Guide to Russian Archives,* 1: 19; Tikhmenev, *Russian-American Company,* 2: 163-164.
55. Papers of the Ministry of Finance, 1847, #12/24, *Guide to Russian Archives,* 1: 137; Tikhmenev, *Russian-American Company,* 2: 164-165; Bancroft, *Alaska,* p. 585.
56. Hallie M. McPherson, "The Interest of William McKendree Gwin in the Purchase of Alaska," *Pacific Historical Review* 3 (March 1934), pp. 20-30.

CHAPTER 6

1. See Ray Allen Billington, *The Far Western Frontier* (New York, 1956), p. 156; Frederick Merk, *The Oregon Question* (Cambridge, Mass., 1967), p. 236.
2. Merk, *Oregon Question,* p. 247; H. H. Bancroft, *Oregon* (San Francisco, 1886), 1: 393, 454-456.
3. Merk, *Oregon Question,* p. 248; Bancroft, *Oregon,* 1: 446-449.
4. Merk, *Oregon Question,* p. 247.
5. Charles M. Wiltse, *John C. Calhoun, Sectionalist, 1840-1850* (New York, 1951), pp. 204-206.
6. Merk, *Oregon Question,* p. 339.
7. Charles Sellers, *James K. Polk, Continentalist, 1843-1846* (Princeton, 1966), p. 99.
8. James D. Richardson, ed., *A Compilation of the Messages and Papers of the President* (New York, 1900), 4: 381.

9. Merk has suggested that Polk differed from his predecessors not in goals, but in the manner of reaching them. See Merk, *Oregon Question,* pp. 337-363, 410-411.

10. James Buchanan, *The Works of James Buchanan,* ed. John Bassett Moore (Philadelphia, 1909), 5: 452-480. On other matters, such as the tariff, Buchanan's views were not as antagonistic to northeastern Whigs. The Pennsylvania Senator supported high tariff rates for both iron and coal, which his home state produced in sufficient quantities. Only after strong-armed persuasion by President Polk did Buchanan agree to support the lower rates of the 1846 Walker tariff. See Philip S. Klein, *President James Buchanan* (University Park, Pa., 1962), pp. 144-145, 172-174.

11. Samuel Flagg Bemis, *John Quincy Adams and the Foundations of American Foreign Policy* (New York, 1949), pp. 510-511.

12. William Sturgis, *The Oregon Question: Substance of a Lecture Given Before the Mercantile Library Association* (Boston, 1845).

13. Richard N. Current, *Daniel Webster and the Rise of National Conservatism* (Boston, 1955), pp. 136-137. Those most concerned with whaling generally viewed Webster as the national political leader who came closest to supporting the general views held by whaling investors and Congressmen from whaling districts. Webster was also seen by many who had trading interests on the Northwest Coast as their particular political leader. Daniel Webster received the Federalist nomination for Congress in 1822 as the hand-picked candidate of a Boston committee of five. Thomas Handsayd Perkins, who owed his wealth to the Northwest Coast fur trade, served as chairman, while William Sturgis was another member of the committee. As Secretary of State in 1841, Webster refused to support a Russian request that he use his powers as Secretary of State to keep Yankee traders and whalers from landing along the coasts of Russian-America. In 1843 he successfully beat off an attempt by the Russian government to exclude Unites States traders from Kamchatka, a Russian-Asian coastal possession which fell under the jurisdiction of the Russian-American Company. See Claude M. Fuess, *Daniel Webster* (Boston, 1930), 1: 309; Nesselrode to Bodisco, March 18/30, 1841, "Notes from the Russian Legation," Record Group 59, National Archives; Todd (U.S. Minister to Russia) to Webster, December 15/17, 1842; Todd to Webster, March 23/April 4, 1843; Todd to Nesselrode, March 20/April 1, 1843; Todd to Webster, September 7/19, 1843, "Despatches, Russia," Record Group 59, National Archives.

14. Daniel Webster, *Writings and Speeches of Daniel Webster* (New York and Boston, 1903), 13: 312-318.

15. Ibid., 9: 60-62, 63-69, 70-77.

16. Winthrop, who represented the Boston district in Congress, retained a strong interest in both whaling and Northwest Coast trading. The old Northwest Coast fur trade had originated from Boston, and Winthrop remained a close political ally of both Sturgis and Perkins. Moreover, many of whalings' most important investors resided in Boston and took a strong interest in maintaining peace in the Pacific Northwest.

17. Robert C. Winthrop, *Addresses and Speeches* (Boston, 1852-1886), 1: 416-417.

18. For Rockwell's views on whaling, see his speech of January 16, 1846, in *Congressional Globe,* 29 Cong., 1 sess., 213-214.

19. Ibid., April 25, 1846, 726-727. On April 18, 1846, Grinnell voted against the bill "to protect the rights of American settlers in the territory of Oregon" (ibid., 690). On April 24, along with the other whaling Whigs, he supported a joint resolution instructing Polk to end the joint occupation and to seek a compromise settlement with Great Britain (ibid., 720-721).

20. Hunt, from upstate New York, of course was not a whaling-district congressman. Nevertheless, he expressed sentiments with which those from whaling districts readily agreed.

21. Congressional Globe, 29 Congr., 1 sess., February 6, 1846, pp. 330-331. All sides in the Oregon debate agreed on one point: Oregon's possession would be a boost to the China trade. The whaling forces argued that a settlement at 49° would give the United States all it needed in Oregon for China commerce, that is, a good port on the Pacific. Those calling for the whole of Oregon pointed to the potential of the China market as a reason to demand the territory up to 54° 40'. They refused to accept the whaling interests' argument that there was no harbor north of 49° or south of 54° 40' that could be useful for any commerce. Congressman Samuel Gordon, Democrat from New York, arguing for all of Oregon, called that territory the "key to the Pacific. It will command the trade of the Isles of the Pacific, of the East and of China" (ibid., January 6, 1846, appendix, pp. 115-117). Robert Winthrop, on the other hand, argued that "we need ports on the Pacific. . . . As to land, we have millions of acres of better land still unoccupied on this side of the Mountains" (ibid., January 3, 1846, pp. 99-100). Washington Hunt agreed. He observed that all the United States needed in Oregon were the ports south of 49°. Such "possession will ultimately secure us an ascendancy in the trade of the Pacific thereby making 'the upper most part of the earth' tributary to our enterprise, and pour into our lap, 'the

wealth of Ormus and of India'" (ibid., February 6, 1846, pp. 238-241). There were, of course, many sides to the Oregon debate. Some southerners followed the lead of John C. Calhoun, who opposed the whole of Oregon sentiment because it could lead to war with Britain, the South's biggest customer for cotton. See Norman Graebner, "Political Factors in the Oregon Compromise," *Pacific Northwest Quarterly* 52 (1961): 7-14.

22. For more on Buchanan, see Klein, *Buchanan;* for Buchanan's tenure as minister to Russia, see pp. 78-96. Buchanan was instrumental in negotiating the first treaty of commerce between the two nations in 1832.

23. For the provisions of the United States treaty with Russia of April 17, 1824, see *Proceedings of the Alaska Boundary Tribunal* (Washington, 1904), 2: appendix, pp. 10-12 (hereafter cited as *Alaska Trib.*).

24. Bodisco to Buchanan, July ?, 1845, "Notes from the Russian Legation."

25. *Washington Daily Union,* September 26, 1845 (italics added); *Alaska Trib.*, 2: appendix, p. 250; Bodisco to Buchanan, September 26, 1845, "Notes from the Russian Legation."

26. Buchanan to Bodisco, September 25(?), 1845, "Notes from the Russian Legation."

27. Relations with Mexico had steadily deteriorated since February 1845 when Congress passed a joint resolution annexing Texas. In October 1845, Polk sent John Slidell to Mexico to settle outstanding differences. The mission was doomed from the start. By January 1846, war with Mexico seemed unavoidable. While Grinnell and others concerned with whaling were not pleased at the prospect of war, they found the pill less bitter because the war might effect the annexation of the harbor of San Francisco. Polk had privately committed himself to the acquisition of California from the first days of his administration. With the addition of San Francisco, the President hoped to remove northeastern opposition to his continentalist ambitions. He believed the northeastern Whigs could oppose no expansionist designs which included the ports of the California coast. Webster, after all, had attempted to acquire San Francisco in 1842. When word leaked out that Slidell's mission to Mexico might result in the forcible seizure of California, the Whig *American Review* lamely protested that if California were acquired, they would "prefer to see it accomplished, at once more direct and less questionable in the point of national morality." Nevertheless, the editor made it abundantly clear that California's harbors should be possessed by the United States. The passing of California to any other nation, exclaimed the writer, "would be inconsistent with the interests and safety of the United

States . . . it is an event which they 'CANNOT PERMIT IN ANY CONTINGENCY WHATEVER.' '' For Polk's views, see Sellers, *Polk,* pp. 213, 231-232; see also *American Review* 3 (January 1846): 82-99, esp. pp. 82, 98-99.

28. On April 24, the Congress adopted by overwhelming majorities a Senate-sponsored measure giving the British notice of the American intention to terminate the joint occupation of Oregon territory. This resolution urged the President to seek a peaceful compromise with Great Britain. Polk decided to send this notice to London, although he could have withheld it. The British government was able to use this conciliatory resolution as a basis for a proposal to partition Oregon at 49°. Polk submitted this new offer to the Senate in June saying that if the Senate decided to accept it, he would sign such a treaty. Polk was able to keep his announced pledge not to compromise, claiming the Senate had decided the issue. The Senate, on the other hand, could believe that its notice of termination of joint occupancy had won the day. See Merk, *Oregon Question,* pp. 346-347.

29. Norman Graebner, *Empire on the Pacific* (New York, 1955), p. 105.

30. Sellers, *Polk,* p. 232.

31. See Webster to Fletcher Webster, June 10, 16, 19, 1846 (and two of June 1846, undated), *Writings of Daniel Webster,* 16: 495-497. Webster told his son (ibid., p. 497) that he had talked with Grinnel who "says, the Whigs, generally, and a good many Democrats of *property,* will vote for Gen. T. to keep out Gen. C. thro [*sic*] fear that the latter will bring *war,* with some nation or another." Three days later Webster told Fletcher he would reluctantly support Taylor: "I see no way but to *fall in,* and acquiesce."

32. Opposition to Polk's policies in Mexico played an important part in the Whig presidential victory. In the congressional elections of 1846, the Whigs gained control of the Congress due, in part, to voters' hostile reaction to the war with Mexico. While most Whigs opposed the war, they felt obliged to vote for the declaration of war lest they be described as traitors. The lesson of the Federalists' opposition to the War of 1812 still lingered in Whig political memories. Fourteen Whigs in the House, however, refused to vote in favor of the declaration of war, one being Joseph Grinnell (*Congressional Globe,* 29 Cong., 1 sess., May 11, 1846, 794-795). All nay votes came from the North; Massachusetts, 5; Ohio, 5; New York, Pennsylvania, and Rhode Island, each 1. The vast majority of Whigs, including Grinnell, voted to extend support for the troops during

the war. The fact that the two most prominent generals, Zachary Taylor and Winfield Scott, were Whigs made this task easier. While the Whig party opposed Polk's desire to annex all of Mexico, they eagerly supported the addition of California to the union. See Frederick Merk, *Manifest Destiny and Mission in American History* (New York, 1963), esp. pp. 90-91, 153.

33. Mary W. Williams, "John Middleton Clayton," in Samuel F. Bemis, *Secretaries of State and Their Diplomacies* (New York, 1928), 7: esp. pp. 3-18; Joseph P. Comegys, *Memoir of John Clayton* (Wilmington, Del., 1882).

34. Folsom to Clayton, October 29, 1849, "Miscellaneous Letters of the State Department," Record Group 59, National Archives.

35. *Annals of San Francisco* (San Francisco, 1854), pp. 754-757; bond of John L. Folsom to M. Hall McAllister, December 31, 1854, John L. Folsom Papers, California Historical Society, San Francisco.

36. Folsom was referring to the ten-year agreement between the Hudson's Bay Company and the Russian-American Company. This agreement gave to Hudson's Bay Company a lease to a coastal strip on the mainland and the right of exclusive sale of land otters to the Russian company. In return, the British company promised to become the exclusive supplier of food and other supplies for the Russian colony. See P. A. Tikhmenev, *Historical Review of the Russian-American Company* (St. Petersburg, 1863), 1: appendix, pp. 323-325. Contrary to Folsom's allegation, the British company did not retain the exclusive right for all carrying trade between Russian-America and the United States. Moreover, the Hudson's Bay Company proved unable to supply the Russian colony's needs, and American traders continued to be the chief suppliers of necessities for Russian-America. See ibid., 1: 411-412. Folsom may not have been aware of the intricacies of the Hudson's Bay Company lease, but he certainly must have known, as he indicated when he alluded to the large trade between San Francisco and Sitka, that the British were not successfully closing Russian-America off to United States traders. When the agreement between the Hudson's Bay Company and the Russian company expired in 1849, the two companies concluded a revised pact, which deleted the provision that the English company supply foodstuffs and supplies, as well as the promise to sell the increasingly scarce land otters to the Russians. Essentially the new agreement was only an extension of the previous lease of land. See ibid., 2: 174-178; see also John S. Galbraith, *The Hudson's Bay Company* (Berkeley, 1957), esp. pp. 161-162.

37. Folsom to Clayton, October 29, 1849, "Miscellaneous Letters of State Department," Record Group 59, National Archives.

38. Ibid., Thurston to Clayton, January 26, 1850. Thurston, like Folsom, must have been aware that United States citizens, and not the Hudson's Bay Company, were the chief suppliers of Russian-America. He seems to have chosen, nevertheless, to use the existence of the Hudson's Bay Company's lease to make his case seem both stronger and more urgent.

39. Clayton to Stoeckl, March 20, 1850, "Notes to the Russian Legation," Record Group 59, National Archives; Stoeckl to Nesselrode, March 19/31, 1850, *Guide to Russian Archives,* 1: p. 72.

40. Stoeckl to Clayton, March 21, 1850, "Notes from the Russian Legation."

41. Nesselrode to W. Bodisco, May 15/27, 1851, *Guide to Materials for American History in Russian Archives,* ed. F. A. Golder (Washington, 1917), 1: 73.

42. Webster, *Writings,* 4: 212-213.

43. Webster to Bodisco, January 25, 1851, "Notes to the Russian Legation"; Bodisco informed Nesselrode of Webster's assistance. On March 9, Bodisco told his foreign minister that, thanks to Webster, the Russian-American Company had been "put in touch with one of the best American commercial houses in China." The company ships, added Bodisco, might count on the support of the American consul there (*Guide to Russian Archives,* 1: p. 73). On June 10, 22, 1851, the Russian minister informed Nesselrode of Webster's offer of services of United States diplomatic and consular agents in China and the Sandwich Islands to Russian subjects (ibid., p. 74); see also Bodisco to Webster, June 17, 1851, "Notes from the Russian Legation."

44. Tikhmenev, *Russian-American Company,* 2: 194. In his many real-estate ventures, John Folsom, who had written the 1849 report for Clayton, "American Interests on the Pacific Coasts," established a close working relationship with Charles J. Brenham and Archibald C. Peachy. The latter two, in 1851, were among the founders of the American-Russian Commercial Company of San Francisco, which in February 1852 obtained a contract to import coal and ice from the Russian colony. See Charles Wilkins to A. C. Peachy, March 5, 1851, Folsom Papers, California Historical Society, San Francisco.

45. Everett to Bodisco, December 14, 1852, "Notes to the Russian Legation."

46. *Newark Sentinel,* reprinted in *Niles National Register,* February 21, 1849.

CHAPTER 7

1. Joel H. Silbey, "The Civil War Synthesis in American Political History," *Civil War History* 10 (June 1964): 130-140.

2. Frederick Merk, *Manifest Destiny and Mission in American History* (New York, 1963), p. 227.

3. Samuel Flagg Bemis has argued that "the crowding vehemence of sectional politics in the United States broke down the expansionist program of the Democratic Party" in the 1850s (*American Foreign Policy and Diplomacy* [New York, 1959], p. 200). Thomas A. Bailey believes that "if the slavery issue had not appeared as an apple of discord," Cuba, Mexico, and much of Latin America would have been annexed (*A Diplomatic History of the American People* [New York, 1969], p. 267), Arthur Ekirch concludes that "prospects for territorial growth" were dim by the mid-1850's because antislavery opinion in the North refused to support any further expansion to new territories which might be open for the extension of slavery (*Ideas, Ideals, and American Diplomacy* [New York, 1966], p. 57).

4. Charles Vevier has pointed out that American continentalism in the 1850s acquired a two-part meaning. First, it signified a "nation-continent created through the interaction of foreign policy and territorial acquisition of contiguous territory in North America." Second, and, in turn, "it projected the concept of the second American world, the continental domain that was fated to extend its influence over the entire world through the expansion of commerce and the control of international communications." Both parts, argued Vevier, were reciprocal. This, as we shall see, is a good working definition of both Gwin's and Seward's view of expansion in the Pacific Northwest ("American Continentalism, An Idea of Expansion, 1845-1919," *American Historical Review* 65 [January 1960]; 329-330).

5. Even after moving to California, Gwin retained his plantation in Mississippi. When the war broke out, his son Willie enlisted in the Confederate army. After Gwin was released from federal custody in 1861, he returned to his Mississippi home. See Lately Thomas, *Between Two Empires* (Boston, 1969), pp. 257-276.

6. Hallie M. McPherson, "The Interest of William McKendree Gwin in the Purchase of Alaska, 1854-1861," *Pacific Historical Review* 3 (March 1934): 31; *Congressional Globe*, 33 Cong., 1 sess., April 10, 1854, pp. 881-882.

7. Gwin dictated his memoirs in 1878 and presented them to the Bancroft Library, *Memoirs of William McKendree Gwin*, MSS Collec-

tion, Bancroft, University of California, Berkeley. These memoirs were completely republished in 1940 in the *California Historical Society Quarterly* in four parts. In a recent biography of Gwin, *Between Two Empires,* Lately Thomas seems to have relied rather strongly on Gwin's memoirs, which are, of course, an apologia. In all fairness to Thomas, he makes no pretension that his offering is a scholarly work. To serious students of Gwin's exploits, Thomas's effort is of rather limited value. Much more valuable is Hallie M. McPherson's Ph.D. dissertation (University of California, Berkeley, 1931), "William McKendree Gwin, Expansionist."

8. William H. Seward, *Works,* ed. G. E. Baker (Boston, 1884-1885), 3: 281.

9. For background on Seward, see Glyndon Van Deusen, *William Henry Seward* (New York, 1967). Van Deusen largely neglects Seward's relationship with Gwin as does Walter G. Sharrow in his otherwise interesting article, "William Henry Seward and the Basis for American Empire, 1850-1860," *Pacific Historical Review* 36 (1967): 325-342. Walter LaFeber presents Seward's views on the need for an integrated American empire in *The New Empire* (Ithaca, 1963), pp. 24-32.

10. Gwin, *Memoirs,* p. 3.

11. Ibid., pp. 15-16.

12. In 1881, Gwin wrote a long letter to Evan J. Coleman, his son-in-law, in which Gwin noted that "very intimate personal relations had existed between Mr. Seward and myself for many years prior to those unhappy days [outbreak of Civil War]." See Evan J. Coleman, "Gwin & Seward—A Secret Chapter in Ante-Bellum History," *Overland Monthly* (November 1891): 465-471.

13. Seward to Weed, December 20, 1845, Thurlow Weed Papers, Rush Rhees Library, University of Rochester.

14. *Congressional Globe,* 32 Cong., 1 sess., August 30, 1852, p. 2452. While the survey was sent, no armaments accompanied it.

15. Van Deusen, *Seward,* p. 140.

16. Seward, *Works,* 4: 442.

17. See Seward's speech before the Phi Beta Kappa Society of Yale College, July 16, 1854, for his views on American expansion, in Seward, *Works*, pp. 160-178; see also Van Deusen, *Seward,* p. 147.

18. *Congressional Globe,* 32 Cong., 1 sess., July 29, 1852, pp. 1873-1876, reprinted as *The Whale Fishery & American Commerce in the Pacific Ocean* (Washington, 1852); see also Seward, *Works,* 1: 236-253.

19. Van Deusen, *Seward,* p. 532.

20. Gwin to Marcy, April 20, 1855, in Ivor D. Spencer, *The Victor and the Spoils: A Life of W. L. Marcy* (Providence, R.I., 1959), pp. 387-397.

21. Van Deusen, *Seward,* p. 533.

22. *House Executive Document* 177, "Russian-America," 40 Cong., 2 sess., February 17, 1868, p. 46. For more on Gwin's 1854 offer, see chap. 9.

23. Charles Vevier has written an interesting and informative article about Collins's designs on the Amur and its relation to American expansionism. See "The Collins Overland Line and American Continentalism," *Pacific Historical Review* 28 (August 1959): 237-253.

24. Gwin and Scott to Cass, June 4, 1858, "Consular Despatches, Amoor River," Record Group 59, National Archives.

25. Vevier, "Collins Line," 247; Van Deusen, *Seward,* pp. 326, 513-514; Seward to Chandler, May 14, 1864, Seward Papers, Rush Rhees Library, University of Rochester.

26. Stoeckl to Gorchakov, January 4, 1860, "Cession of Alaska," Annex 6, National Archives Record Group 59 (my translation). Gwin worked with Beverley C. Sanders, head of the American-Russian Commercial Company, during the Crimean War to get Sanders's company the trading rights to supply the Russian company, and, in the process, a more favorable contract from the Russians. See B. P. Thomas, *Russian-American Relations, 1815-1867,* Johns Hopkins University Studies 48 (Baltimore, 1930), p. 115. Captain N. Golovnin, who was sent to Russian-America by Czar Alexander in 1860, complained about Gwin's enthusiasm for the Russian colony: Senator Gwin and others had advanced the argument that "the Americans would have a perfect right to close their ports to Russian ships as long as our ports in Russian-America will not admit American vessels." Golovnin pointed out that "Senator Gwin was canvassing for a four-year term and therefore raised several questions to show their electors to what degree he was occupied with his country's welfare. With this object he advanced also the alleged desires of California businessmen to obtain free access to the Russian colony." As far as Golovnin was concerned, Gwin was just another of those American politicians "whose whole working and striving is bent to the means of obtaining . . . the largest number of voters and by their help to be elected Representatives to Congress, I.E., to get a profitable position with all facilities for filling their pocket" (N. Golovnin, "Review of the Russian Colonies in North America," Office of the Marine Ministerium, St. Petersburg, 1861, MSS translated by Ivan Petrov, Bancroft Library, University of California, Berkeley, pp. 202-203).

27. Buchanan, Second Annual Message, December 6, 1858, in James D. Richardson, *A Compilation of the Messages and Papers of the Presidents* (New York, 1897), 5: 479-529.

28. Philip S. Klein, *President James Buchanan* (University Park, Pa., 1962), pp. 313-327. Klein points out that, from the very beginning of his administration, Buchanan opted for a policy of status quo at home and active diplomacy abroad in order to divert public attention from sectional interest to foreign adventure. To that end, Buchanan decided that he would personally direct the Department of State and appointed Secretary of State Cass with the explicit understanding that the President and John Appleton (Assistant Secretary of State) would make all policy decisions. See also Frank B. Woodford, *Lewis Cass* (New Brunswick, 1950), pp. 315-316. For Gwin's close ties with the Buchanan administration, see Klein, *Buchanan,* pp. 326, 333-334.

29. Stoeckl to Gorchakov, January 4, 1860, "Cession of Alaska," Record Group 59, Annex 8, National Archives (my translation). Stoeckl wrote two letters to Gorchakov dated January 4, 1860—the earlier one (Annex 6) favorable to the sale, the latter (Annex 8) citing American domestic problems as excluding the sale for the present; see also Stoeckl to Gorchakov, July 4/16, 1860, in ibid., Annex 10, in which Stoeckl noted that proposed sale of Russian-America should be put off until a more opportune time.

30. Gwin to Seward, February 20, 1856, January 8, 1858, Seward Papers.

31. Seward, *Works,* 4: 442.

32. Ibid., 1: 58, 60.

33. Ibid., pp. 248-250 (emphasis added).

34. Ibid., 4: 333.

CHAPTER 8

1. Joel H. Silbey, ed., *The Transformation of American Politics, 1840-1860* (Englewood Cliffs, N.J., 1967), pp. 22-33.

2. For a view of the economic development of the United States during this period, see Douglas North, *The Economic Growth of the United States, 1790-1860* (New York, 1961), pp. 204-210; see also George R. Taylor, *The Transportation Revolution, 1815-1860* (New York, 1951), esp. chaps. 7, 8, 9, 15.

3. See North, *Economic Growth of the United States,* pp. 210-213.

4. Walter Tower, *A History of American Whale Fishery* (Philadelphia, 1907), p. 66; P. A. Tikhmenev, *Historical Review of the Russian-American Company* (St. Petersburg, 1863), 2: 159-161.

5. Tower, *American Whale Fishery,* pp. 66, 121, 129; Hubert Bancroft, *History of the Northwest Coast* (San Francisco, 1884), p. 668; Tikhmenev, *Russian-American Company,* 2: 159-161. According to the Department of Foreign Commerce's *Report of the Commission on the Organization of the Russian-American Colonies* (St. Petersburg, 1863), pt. 1, p. 162, from 1850 to 1860 there was an average of 600 United States vessels annually in Russian colonial waters. In 1854, the report claims that 525 Yankee vessels were counted, while 468 appeared in 1855. These figures seem a little inflated, but they are an indication, nevertheless, of the magnitude of the Yankee whaling effort in Russian-America as viewed by the Russian company.

6. Alexander Starbuck, *History of American Whale Fishery* (1878; reprint ed., New York, 1961), 2: 660.

7. Tikhmenev, *Russian-American Company,* 2: 174-178.

8. *Annals of San Francisco,* pp. 735-739. Also see Norman E. Saul, "Beverley C. Sanders and the Expansion of American Trade with Russia, 1853-1855," *Maryland Historical Magazine* 67 (Summer 1972): 156-170. Professor Saul kindly supplied me with a complete list of the stockholders, which he obtained from the Sanders Papers.

9. *Annals of San Francisco* (San Francisco, 1855), pp. 735-739.

10. For Burling and Hill, see: William Burling Papers, California Historical Society, San Francisco; *Sketches of Leading and Representative Men of San Francisco,* ed. "Eminent Editors" (1875), p. 806; *Early Days in California,* ed. G. W. Sullivan (San Francisco, 1888), 1: 218.

11. For Samuel Hensley, see obituary of S. J. Hensley, January 4, 1866, California Historical Society.

12. For Abel Guy, see Abel Guy Papers, California Historical Society.

13. For Folsom's report on Russian-America and his relationship with Brenham and Peachy, see chap. 6. Among the other San Franciscans who owned a large number of shares in the company were: John Caperton, notary public for the County of San Francisco (see John Caperton Papers, California Historical Society); James C. Ward and Robt. Wells, partners in a rather successful real estate speculation business (see James C. Ward Papers, California Historical Society); J. Mora Moss, who succeeded Sanders as president of the company was involved in numerous enterprises in the 1850s, including the New Almaden-Quicksilver Mining Company (of which he was president) and the Sacramento Valley Railroad (see J. Mora Moss Papers, New Almaden Mining Co. Papers, 1854-1864, and Sacramento Valley Railroad Papers, California Historical Society). In November 1852, Moss joined with

Sanders to found the San Francisco Gas and Coal Company, incorporated with a capital stock of $450,000. See *Annals of San Francisco*, p. 518.

14. N. Golovnin, "Review of the Russian Colonies in North America," *Material for the History of Russian Settlements on the Shores of the Eastern Ocean* (St. Petersburg, 1863), pp. 182-184, trans. Ivan Petrov, Bancroft Library, University of California; Department of Foreign Commerce, "Report of the Commission on the Organization of the Russian-American Colonies" (St. Petersburg, 1863), 2 pts., trans. by Petrov, Bancroft Library, 1: 126-129; Tikhmenev, *Russian-American Company,* 2: 194; Hubert H. Bancroft, *History of Alaska, 1730-1885* (San Francisco, 1886), p. 587; Andrews, "Alaska Under the Russians," *Washington Historical Quarterly* 8 (October 1916): 289; E. L. Keithahn, "Alaska Ice, Inc.," *Pacific Northwest Quarterly* (April 1945): 121; Saul, "Beverley C. Sanders," pp. 157-158. Tikhmenev (*Russian-American Company,* 2: 194) says that in the first contract the American company agreed to take 1200 tons of ice per year at $20.25 per ton.

15. Golovnin, "Review of the Russian Colonies," p. 183; Stoeckl to Gorchakov, March 10/22, 1854, *Guide to Materials for American History in Russian Archives,* ed. F. A. Golder (Washington, 1937), 2: 2; Saul, "Beverley C. Sanders," p. 159.

16. Tikhmenev, *Russian-American Company,* 2: 195; Golovnin, "Review of the Russian Colonies," pp. 183-184; Saul, "Beverley C. Sanders," pp. 159-164.

17. Saul, in "Beverley C. Sanders," pp. 162-164, argues that the Russian government was pleased to sign the agreement with the American-Russian Ice Company. Saul's evidence, however, rests upon Sanders's diary. On the other hand, both Tikhmenev, *Russian-American Company,* 2: 195, and Russian sources show that the Russians reluctantly agreed to the contract because of the circumstances of the Crimean War. See memorandum of Baron F. Wrangell to czar, April 9, 1857, "Cession of Alaska," Annex 2, Record Group 59, National Archives. The czar, in a memorandum of April 29, 1857, noted that the contract with the American-Russian Ice Company had "exceedingly reduce[d] the value of our possession in North America" ("Cession of Alaska," Annex 3).

18. Tikhmenev, *Russian-American Company,* 2: 178, 197-198; Andrews, "Alaska Under the Russians," p. 289; Bancroft, *Alaska,* p. 287; Keithahn, "Alaska Ice, Inc.," pp. 123, 128; *Alaska Herald* (September

15, 1868). Golovnin's report, pp. 184-185, claimed that the 1860 contract was made because Sanders's company had defaulted on the 1854 agreement. Evidence for such a view is sketchy. Since the 1860 contract provided for the American company to purchase more ice at a cheaper price per ton, one suspects that Golovnin's analysis is incorrect. Nevertheless, the 1860 agreement does not deal with the sale of timber, coal, and fish. It may well be that the American company and the Russian company found that aspect of the previous agreement unworkable, especially after the Russian-American coal mining operation at Kenai Bay was destroyed by fire in early 1860. See F. A. Golder, "Mining in Alaska before 1867," *Washington Historical Quarterly* 7 (July 1916): 236.

19. Keithahn, "Alaska Ice, Inc.," p. 126. Apparently no bargain was reached with the Hong Kong merchants.

20. Collins to Pierce, February 29, 1856, "Amoor River," National Archives, Record Group 59. Charles Vevier has written a most interesting and informative article about Collins's designs on the Amur and its relation to American expansion ("The Collins Overland Line and American Continentalism," *Pacific Historical Review* 28 [August 1959]: 237-253). While I have borrowed heavily from Vevier's work, I have rechecked the sources in order to understand the particular relationship of the Collins scheme to United States interest in Russian-America.

21. By the end of 1843, the Russian-American Company had given up its earlier attempts to exclude Yankee traders in Russian Asia. See Todd to Webster, April 20/May 2, 1843; Todd to Upshur, August 7/19, 1843, "Despatches, Russia," National Archives, Record Group 59. Yet as late as 1860 the Russian company was lodging complaints against the behavior of Yankees in Russian Asia. See Cass to Stoeckl, December 8, 1860, "Notes to Russian Legation," National Archives, Record Group 59.

22. Collins to Pierce, February 29, 1856, "Amoor River."

23. Cass to James R. Clay, July 15, 1859, "P. McD. Collins," 35 Cong., 2 sess., *House Executive Document* 53, pp. 1-4.

24. Seymour to Marcy, November 1/13, 1856, "Despatches, Russia."

25. Collins to Marcy, July 24, September 10, November 18/30, 1856, extract from Collins' notes, February 28, 1857, enclosed in Collins to Cass, March 6, 1858, "Amoor River."

26. Collins to Marcy, December 17, 1857, Collins to Cass, February 12, 1858, "Amoor River."

27. Vevier, "Collins Line," p. 243; *New York Herald*, April 8, 1858;

198 Conflict on the Northwest Coast

Gwin and Chas. L. Scott to Cass, June 4, 1858, "Amoor River"; *Congressional Globe*, 35 Cong., 2 sess., January 19, 1859, pt. I, p. 471.

28. Collins to Cass, September 20, 1859, "Amoor River"; "Collins Amoor River Report," 37 Cong., 2 sess., H. Doc. 45, p. 215.

29. Collins to Cass, October 8, 1859, May 1, 1860; Collins to F. W. Seward, September 18, 1861, "Amoor River."

30. Victor J. Farrar, "Joseph Lane McDonald and the Purchase of Alaska," *Washington Historical Quarterly* 12 (April 1921): 83-84; McDonald to Seward, July 15, 1867, "Russian-America," 40 Cong., 2 sess., *House Executive Document* 177, p. 58.

31. Tower, *American Whale Fishery*, pp. 52, 70-72.

32. Ibid., p. 67.

33. *Dictionary of American Biography*, 21 vols. (New York, 1928), 8: 4.

34. Tower, *American Whale Fishery*, pp. 76-77.

35. Andrews, "Alaska Whaling," p. 6.

36. Tower, *American Whale Fishery*, p. 129.

37. Tikhmenev, *Russian-American Company*, 2: 197-198.

38. Frederick Whymper, *Travel and Adventure in the Territory of Alaska* (New York, 1871), pp. 104-105.

39. "U.S. Coast Survey, 1867," 40 Cong., 2 sess., H. Doc. 275, Appendix 18, pp. 210-211.

40. *Alta California*, November 21, 1867; see also Keithahn, "Alaska Ice, Inc.," pp. 125-128.

41. Collins to Cass, October 8, 1859, May 1, 1860, "Amoor River."

42. Collins to F. W. Seward, September 18, 1861 (and memorandum to Cameron), June 9, 1862, "Amoor River."

43. Vevier, "Collins Line," p. 244.

44. Seward to Cameron, June 9, 1862, "Instructions, Russia"; Cameron to Seward, July 23, 1862, "Despatches, Russia," National Archives, Record Group 59.

45. Clay to Seward, May 19, June 17, 1863, "Despatches, Russia."

46. Vevier, "Collins Line," 245-246.

47. Ibid., p. 247. Since the telegraphic cable would have to pass through British Columbia also, the approval of the British government was necessary. Seward instructed Charles F. Adams, United States Minister to Great Britain, to aid Collins in obtaining such rights. Adams was successful. See Seward to Adams, July 13, 1863, "Instructions, G. B.," National Archives, Record Group 59; Collins to F. W. Seward, August 18, December 31, 1863, February 8, 1864, "Amoor River." The

Russian minister to the United States, Edward de Stoeckl, was awarded 300 shares in the Collins Line for "his distinguished aid and good offices . . . which greatly contributed to the advancement of the enterprise." Another 1000 shares were sent to Minister Cassius Clay for distribution to influential Russians.

48. Vevier, "Collins Line," pp. 248-250.

49. Ibid., p. 252.

50. Clay to Seward, November 14, 1864, "Despatches, Russia."

51. Seward to Clay, December 26, 1864, "Instructions, Russia."

52. H. Doc. 177, 40 Cong., 2 sess., p. 5.

53. In the winter of 1867, Western Union cancelled the building of the Collins overland line. The combination of Cyrus Field's successful laying of an Atlantic cable and the continued unwillingness of the Russian government to agree to a rebate rate of less than 40 percent doomed the line's chances for success. See Vevier, "Collins Line," pp. 250-251.

54. Farrar, "McDonald and Alaska," pp. 85-86.

55. Ibid., pp. 86-87.

56. "Memorial of the Legislature of Washington Territory to the President," received February, 1866, H. Doc. 177, pp. 4-5. While the memorial was still before the Washington legislature, McDonald forwarded a printed copy to Secretary of State Seward with a long letter urging Seward to acquire such fishing privileges in Russian-America for United States citizens as were enjoyed by them along the coasts of British America (McDonald to Seward, July 15, 1867, p. 58). In this letter McDonald refers to the earlier letter discussed, but I have found no copy of it.

57. Farrar, "McDonald and Alaska," p. 89.

58. H. Doc. 177, p. 4.

59. Lewis Goldstone, "Memorial of Louis Goldstone," MSS, Cornelius Cole Papers, Powell Library, Department of Special Collections, UCLA; Goldstone, "Testimony before the House Ways and Means Committee," H. Rept. #623, "Hearings on the Alaska Commercial Company," 44 Cong., 1 sess., May 1, 1876, pp. 120-121; Cornelius Cole to Victor J. Farrar, September 10, 1923, in Farrar, "Senator Cole and the Purchase of Alaska," *Washington Historical Quarterly* 14 (October 1923): 243-244. Cole was 101 years old when this letter was written. Farrar claims that Cole was still very lucid. See also Cornelius Cole, *Memoirs* (New York, 1908), pp. 281-282. Samuel Brannan was a very active partner in the Goldstone group. Brannan had come to San Francisco in 1846, and in 1847 he founded the *California Star,* the

parent newspaper of the *Alta California*. His numerous real estate ventures made him, according to the 1855 edition of the *Annals of San Francisco*, p. 752, "the wealthiest man . . . in all California." In the late 1850s and early 1860s Brannan invested his wealth establishing banking, railway, telegraph, and express companies. See *Dictionary of American Biography*, 2: 601-602. See also Cole to Burke, October 22, 1867, Cornelius Cole Papers, Powell Library, UCLA. For more on the company's founding, see Rudolf Glanz, *The Jews in American Alaska, 1867-1880* (New York, 1953), p. 7.

60. Goldstone, "Memorial."

61. Goldstone or Sullivan to Cole, April 10, 1866, H. Doc. 177, p. 133. Cole was born in Lodi in upstate New York in 1822. He read law in the Auburn office of William H. Seward (Seward, Morgan, and Blatchford) in 1847-1848. For the rest of his life, Cole regarded Seward as his mentor. He left for California in 1849 to seek his fortune in gold. For the next twelve years, he maintained a constant correspondence with Seward on the conditions—political and economic—of California and the Pacific Northwest. In the early 1850s Cole urged Senator Seward to push for a Pacific Coast survey, which Seward did in his 1852 report on whaling discussed in the previous chapter. The Seward Papers, at the University of Rochester, contain over fifty letters between the two men beginning in 1849 and continuing until Seward's tenure as Secretary of State ended. See esp. Cole to Seward, December 14, 1849, June 17, 1850, November 15, 1850, June 19, 1856, June 3, 1860; Seward to Cole, December 25, 1867. Also see Cole, *Memoirs*, pp. 3, 97-98.

62. Cole to Burke, December 4, 1866, Cole Papers.

63. H. Doc. 177, p. 133.

64. Cole to Burke, January 24, 1867, H. Doc. 177.

65. Clay to Cole, February 1, 1867, H. Doc. 177, p. 133.

66. Cole to Burke, February 23, 1867, Cole Papers.

67. Cole, *Memoirs*, pp. 282-283.

68. Cole to Burke, April 1, 1867, Cole Papers.

69. Ibid., April 10, 1867.

70. Gorchakov to Alexander, December 1866, "Cession of Alaska," Annex 13.

CHAPTER 9

1. Hallie M. McPherson, "The Interest of William McKendree Gwin in the Purchase of Alaska, 1854-1861," *Pacific Historical Review* 3

(March 1934): 29-30; Stuart R. Tompkins, *Alaska, Promyshlennik & Sourdough* (Norman, Okla., 1945), pp. 174-175.

2. *New York Herald,* July 20, 25, 1854; *London Times,* August 8, 1854; H. Doc. 177, 40 Cong., 2 sess., February 17, 1868, p. 46; F. A. Golder, "The Purchase of Alaska," *American Historical Review* 25 (April 1920): 412.

3. "Russian-America," 40 Cong., 2 sess., H. Doc. 177, p. 46; Stoeckl quoted in Golder, "The Purchase of Alaska," p. 412 (my translation from the French).

4. Stoeckl to Nesselrode, January 1856, in "The Purchase of Alaska," p. 413 (my translation).

5. For a discussion of some particular aspects of Constantine Nikolaevich's plans for redirection of Russian policy, see W. E. Mosse, "Russia and the Levant, 1856-1862; Grand Duke Constantine Nicholaevich and the Russian Steam Navigation Company," *Journal of Modern History* 26 (March 1954): 39-48.

6. Constantine to Gorchakov, December 7, 1857 (o.s.), Manuscript Division, Library of Congress.

7. Gorchakov to Constantine [December 1857], "Cession of Alaska," Annex 1, National Archives, Record Group 59. The National Archives lists this undated letter as December 1856, but since it is a response to Constantine's letter of December 7, 1857, dealing with the cession of Russian-America, this letter must have been written in December 1857 and not in 1856.

8. Baron Ferdinand von Wrangell, "Concerning the Cession of the American Colonies to the Government of the United States," April 9, 1857, "Cession of Alaska," Annex 2.

9. "Memorandum Concerning the Cession to the United States of Our Possessions in North America," April 1857 (czar's notation date, April 29, 1857), "Cession of Alaska," Annex 3. The czar was particularly annoyed that the American-Russian Commercial Company had been able to use the Crimean War as a lever to obtain a more favorable treaty in 1855 from the Russian company.

10. Stoeckl to Gorchakov, November 13, 1857, "Cession of Alaska," Annex 5.

11. Ibid., December 2, 1857, "Cession of Alaska," Annex 4.

12. Ibid., January 4, 1860, "Cession of Alaska," Annex 6 (my translation).

13. Popov, memorandum, February 7, 1860, "Cession of Alaska," Annex 9. In 1860, the czar sent a commission headed by State Counselor

Sergie Kostlivtsev and Captain N. Golovnin to Russian-America to make a thorough investigation of the situation and condition of the colony. In 1863 Golovnin submitted his report to the czar, which urged retention of the colony. Golovnin suggested the opening of the ports of New Archangel and St. Paul to Yankee traders. Any other United States vessel "hunting and fishing in our waters should be considered as a smuggler, arrested and subjected either to a fine in money or confiscation." Russian-America could be protected from Yankee penetration, he added, by "the stationing of some of our men of war at Honolulu and San Francisco, where whalers and smugglers are generally fitted out."

14. *Report of Commission on Organization of Russian-America* (St. Petersburg, 1863), 1: 233-237.

15. P. A. Golder, "Mining in Alaska Before 1867," *Washington Historical Quarterly* 7 (July 1916): 238.

16. Stoeckl to Gorchakov, April 19, 1867, "Cession of Alaska," Annex 29.

17. The accidental discovery of gold in 1866 by the Collins people received coverage in the Russian press. Also, coal mining was initiated by the Russians in 1857, but the coal could not compete with English or Hong Kong–Japanese coal. A mining fire in 1860 wiped out this Russian-American industry, but by this time the coal potential of the Russian possessions had attracted considerable interest on the part of some Americans. See Golder, "Mining in Alaska," pp. 236-238.

18. Gorchakov to Alexander, December 12, 1866 (o.s.), "Cession of Alaska," Annex 12.

19. Osten-Saken to Gorchakov, December 16, 1867 (o.s.), "Cession of Alaska," Annex 18.

20. Gorchakov to Alexander, December 1866, "Cession of Alaska," Annex 13; see also "cession of Alaska," item 5.

21. Stoeckl to Gorchakov, February 26, 1867, "Cession of Alaska," Annex 19.

22. Stoeckl to Gorchakov, April 19, 1867, "Cession of Alaska," Annex 30 (my translation).

23. Hansen Risley to Weed, March 27, 1867; Frederick Seward to Weed, March 31, 1867, Weed Papers, Rush Rhees Library, University of Rochester, Rochester, New York.

CHAPTER 10

1. See, for example, Thomas A. Bailey, *A Diplomatic History of the American People* (New York, 1964), p. 366.

2. Stoeckl to Gorchakov, March 6/16, 1867, "Cession of Alaska," Annex 21, Record Group 59, National Archives (my translation).

3. Ibid., April 19, 1867, "Cession of Alaska," Annex 30 (my translation).

4. Ibid., March 6/16, 1867, "Cession of Alaska," Annex 21 (my translation).

5. Ibid., March 22/April 3, 1867, "Cession of Alaska," Annex 26 (my translation).

6. Ibid., April 19, 1867, "Cession of Alaska," Annex 30 (my translation).

7. Gideon Welles, *Diary of Gideon Welles*, ed. Howard K. Beale (New York, 1968), 3: 66, 68; "Notes of W. G. Moore" (Secretary to President Johnson), *American Historical Review* 19 (October 1913): 106.

8. Seward to Julius E. Hilgard, March 18, 1867, "Domestic Letters of the State Department," Record Group 59, National Archives.

9. Seward to Benjamin Pierce, March 18, 1867, "Domestic Letters."

10. James Kelly to Seward, March 22, 1867, Papers of Andrew Johnson, Manuscript Division, Library of Congress. Kelly informed Seward that Weed had successfully obtained the *Commercial Advertiser* and that Seward could count on this paper's being a "friend" of the administration.

11. *Commercial Advertiser*, March 31, 1867.

12. *New York Times*, April 1, 1867.

13. Henry J. Raymond to Crounse, April 2, 1867, William Seward Papers, Rush Rhees Library, University of Rochester, Rochester, New York.

14. *New York Times*, April 2, 1867.

15. *New York Herald*, April 1, 1867.

16. *New York Post*, April 1, 1867.

17. *New York Tribune*, April 1, 1867.

18. Also opposed, but not as strongly as the *Tribune*, were the *Boston Daily Evening Transcript*, April 3, 1867; *New Orleans Daily Picayune; Cincinnati Daily Gazette*. Many newspapers took no stand at all: see *Philadelphia Public Ledger*, April 1, 11, 1867; *Connecticut Courant*, April 11, 1867. R. E. Welch, Jr. ("American Public Opinion and the Purchase of Russian America," *American Slavic and East European Review* 17 [December 1958]: 481-494), examines forty-eight newspapers from all sections and concludes that most supported the treaty, which is true. But in his enthusiasm to build his case, Welch has often overstated the early support given the treaty—many newspapers simply remained neutral—and often misquotes or fails to read through the

editorials he cites. Also, he neglects to distinguish between early editorial support and that support which grew as a result of Seward's propaganda campaign. He does this by telling us that for his purposes Seward's influence is "irrelevant." Welch claims that editors and citizens knew about Alaska from means other than Seward's propaganda. While that is certainly correct, Welch makes the error of citing as evidence for that view the publicity about the Collins Line and the Smithsonian survey of 1867, projects which Seward vigorously sponsored.

19. *Boston Advertiser,* April 6, 1867.

20. *Boston Herald,* April 11, 1867.

21. *National Intelligencer,* April 5, 1867.

22. *Commercial Advertiser,* March 31, 1867; *New York Herald,* April 1, 1867.

23. *New Orleans Daily Picayune,* March 31, 1867.

24. *New York World,* April 1, 1867.

25. *New York Post,* April 1, 1867.

26. *New York Herald,* April 1, 1867.

27. *Connecticut Courant,* April 6, 1867.

28. *San Francisco Chronicle,* April 11, 1867. See also *Boston Daily Telegraph,* April 11, 1867.

29. *San Francisco Chronicle,* April 11, 1867.

30. *Connecticut Courant,* April 6, 1867.

31. *New York Tribune,* April 1, 1867. Greeley's opposition to the purchase of Russian-America was, of course, tempered by his longstanding feud with Seward. See Glyndon Van Deusen, *William Henry Seward* (New York, 1967), pp. 229-230, 423-424.

32. *New Orleans Daily Picayune,* April 2, 1867.

33. *Harper's Weekly,* April 13, 1867, p. 266.

34. See Van Deusen, *Seward,* pp. 541-542; *National Intelligencer,* April 1, 1867.

35. David Hunter Miller, "The Alaska Treaty," Department of State, National Archives, p. 305; H. Doc. 177, 40 Cong., 2 sess., February 17, 1868, pp. 25-33.

36. Fox to F. W. Seward, April 8, 1867, Seward Papers.

37. John Pruyn to Seward, April 8, 1867, Seward Papers.

38. *New York Tribune,* April 8, 1867.

39. Sumner to Bright, April 16, 1867, *Memoir and Letters of Charles Sumner,* ed. E. L. Pierce (Boston, 1877-1893), 4: 318-319; Stoeckl to Gorchakov, April 19, 1867, "Cession of Alaska," Annex 30, Record Group 59, National Archives.

40. Stoeckl, of course, was exaggerating his own mission to the Senate for the benefit of his superiors in St. Petersburg. Stoeckl to Gorchakov, April 19, 1867 (two letters of that date), "Cession of Alaska," Annexes 28, 30 (my translation).

41. *New York Tribune*, April 8, 1867; John B. Weller to Seward, April 3, 1867, Seward Papers.

42. Fox to Sumner, April 2, 1867, Sumner Papers, Houghton Library, Harvard University, vol. 81, #51-60, cited in Hunter-Miller, "Alaska Treaty," p. 321. After the treaty was signed, Assistant Secretary of State Frederick Seward wrote to Fox declaring: "The Secretary desires me to thank you heartily . . . for the public services rendered. The treaty seems to grow in popular favor and I think we have just reason to exchange congratulations" (F. W. Seward to Fox, April 12, 1867, Seward Papers). Meigs to Sumner, April 2, 1867, Sumner Papers, vol. 81, #61, cited in Hunter-Miller, "Alaska Treaty," p. 321; Julius Hilgard to Sumner, Sumner Papers, vol. 81, #68. Hilgard, it will be remembered, was called in by Seward on March 18 to plan strategy and compile data for the passage of the treaty (Seward to Hilgard, March 18, 1867, "Domestic Correspondence of State Department," National Archives).

43. Sumner, *Memoir and Letters*, 4: 326, lists most of the letters written to Sumner from March 31 to April 8 urging passage of the treaty.

44. Baird to Sumner, March 31, 1867, Sumner Papers, vol. 81, #55, Hunter-Miller, "Alaska Treaty," p. 316. In an otherwise excellent book, David Donald, *Charles Sumner and the Rights of Man* (New York, 1970), pp. 304-310, neglects Seward's role in Sumner's final decision to support the purchase treaty. Donald argues that the letters Sumner received "from the representatives of New England commercial and mercantile interests" and from "scientists connected with the Smithsonian Institution" softened Sumner's "aversion to the treaty." Seward's orchestration of the letter writing campaign directed at Sumner is overlooked by Donald.

45. *Albany Argus*, April 4, 1867. John Pruyn sent a copy of the editorial to Seward noting that he had "written several Senators urging the confirmation of the Russian-American Treaty." Pruyn to Seward, April 4, 1867, Seward Papers. The editorial went on to note: "The fur trade and the fisheries constitute the principle value of this territory. But the day is coming when the commerce of the Pacific will rival that of the Atlantic and will be almost entirely under our control. When that day comes the ports of the northwest coast will be indispensible to us."

46. David Donald, *Charles Sumner and the Coming of the Civil War* (New York, 1960), pp. 153-154, 211.

47. Sumner, *Works,* 3: 3-9.

48. Sumner to Bright, October 6, 1867, *Memoir and Letters,* 4: 146. For more on the fleet visit, see Howard I. Kushner, "The Russian Fleet and the American Civil War: Another View," *Historian* 34 (August 1972): 633-649.

49. Sumner, *Works,* 11: 228-230.

50. Ibid., pp. 232-233.

51. Ibid., pp. 181-349.

52. Ibid.

53. Ibid. Sumner also mentioned the value of timber and minerals of Russian-America, especially coal and copper and possibly gold, iron, silver, and lead, as other inducements for the purchase.

54. *New York Herald,* April 9, 1867.

55. Sumner, *Memoir and Letters,* 4: 327.

56. Simon Stevens to Seward, April 27, 1867, Seward Papers.

57. Seward to Joseph Henry, April 10, 1867, Seward Papers.

58. H. Doc. 177.

59. Stoeckl to Gorchakov, May 15/27, 1867, "Cession of Alaska," Annex 37 (my translation).

60. Seward to Stoeckl, May 20, 1867, "Notes to Russian Legation," Record Group 59, National Archives.

61. Stoeckl to Seward, May 22, 1867, "Notes from Russian Legation," Record Group 59, National Archives.

62. Stoeckl to Gorchakov, April 19, 1867, "Cession of Alaska," Annex 29 (Stoeckl wrote four despatches on April 19).

63. Bruce to Lord Stanley, "Confidential," April 2, 1867, Library of Congress, Proceedings Foreign Office, 115; 465 (filed with Foreign Office, 5: 1106, Box 2, #102; Hunter-Miller, "The Alaska Treaty," p. 266).

64. Mortimer Melville Jackson to Seward, March 25, 1867, Seward Papers.

65. Van Deusen, *Seward,* pp. 548-549. Van Deusen notes that in January 1867, two months before the cession of Alaska, Seward sent to the Senate a report of E. H. Derby, special agent of the United States in Canada. Derby urged the cession of British Columbia and Vancouver Island to the United States in payment for the claims against England. In Jackson's letter to Seward, cited above, Jackson relates that he discussed the cession of the British province with Derby.

66. Seward attempted to purchase the Danish West Indies as early as July 12, 1866, when he made such an offer to General Raasloff, the

minister to the United States from Denmark. Raasloff and his government were vague in their reply, and the offer remained open when Seward negotiated the treaty of cession for Alaska in March 1867. On the same day (March 14) that Seward and Stoeckl agreed to the Alaska sale, Seward requested Stoeckl to see "if the Imperial Government could use its influence with the Court of Copenhagen in order to urge it to cede . . . the Danish possessions in the Antilles." When Stoeckl tried to beg off, the Secretary of State replied that he would write out a personal note to Gorchakov for Stoeckl to forward to St. Petersburg. Gorchakov, noting that he "did not want to burden himself making suggestions to the Danish," instructed Stoeckl to avoid the issue or to "decline politely using the argument that at the moment we do not have a Minister at Copenhagen and Denmark does not have a ministry here." See Van Deusen, *Seward*, p. 527; Seward to George H. Yeaman, "Confidential," March 28, 1867, Seward Papers; Stoeckl to Gorchakov, March 6/18, 1867, "Cession of Alaska," Annex 22 (my translation); Gorchakov to Stoeckl, March 26/April 8, 1867, "Cession of Alaska," Annex 27 (my translation).

67. G. V. Fox to F. W. Seward, April 8, 1867, Seward Papers.

68. Seward hoped that the new American Pacific Coast, running from California to Alaska, would be opened by rail and canal to the eastern industrial United States. This empire could then, he believed, capture and retain the markets of Asia. Seward moved swiftly, often in concert with other powers, to maintain stability in eastern Asia. Van Deusen, *Seward*, pp. 519-522.

69. Stoeckl to Gorchakov, July 12/24, 1867, "Cession of Alaska," Annex 43 (my translation).

CHAPTER 11

1. Thomas A. Bailey, *A Diplomatic History of the American People* (New York, 1969), p. 365.

2. William A. Williams, *American-Russian Relations, 1781-1947* (New York, 1952), p. 4.

Selected Bibliography

MANUSCRIPT SOURCES

Burling, William. California Historical Society. San Francisco.

Caperton, John. California Historical Society. San Francisco.

Cole, Cornelius. Department of Special Collections, Powell Library, University of California. Los Angeles.

Guy, Abel. California Historical Society. San Francisco.

Gwin, William McKendree. Bancroft Library, University of California. Berkeley.

_____. California Historical Society. San Francisco.

Folsom, John L. California Historical Society. San Francisco.

Jefferson, Thomas. Library of Congress. Washington, D.C.

Johnson, Andrew. Library of Congress. Washington, D.C.

Lincoln, Abraham. Library of Congress. Washington, D.C.

Madison, James. Library of Congress. Washington, D.C.

Moss, J. Mora. California Historical Society, San Francisco.

Pierce, Franklin. Library of Congress. Washington, D.C.

Polk, James K. Library of Congress. Washington, D.C.

Seward, William H. Rush Rhees Library, University of Rochester. Rochester, N.Y.

Stoeckl, Edward. Correspondence to Prince Alexandre Gorchakov. Archives of Russian Ministry of Foreign Affairs, Leningrad. Microprint in Rush Rhees Library, University of Rochester, Rochester, N.Y.

Sullivan, Eugene. California Historical Society. San Francisco.

Taylor, Zachary. Library of Congress. Washington, D.C.

Van Buren, Martin. Library of Congress. Washington, D.C.

Ward, James C. California Historical Society, San Francisco.
Weed, Thurlow. Rush Rhees Library, University of Rochester. Rochester, N.Y.

ARCHIVAL MATERIALS

Alaska Collection. Bancroft Library, University of California. Berkeley.
New Almaden Quicksilver Mining Company. California Historical Society. San Francisco.
Record Group 59. General Records of the Department of State. National Archives. Washington, D.C.
Record Group 261. Records of the Russian-American Company, 1802-1867. National Archives. Washington, D.C.
Sacramento Valley Railroad. California Historical Society. San Francisco.

PUBLISHED ARCHIVAL AND OTHER
GOVERNMENTAL RECORDS

United States

American State Papers. Foreign Relations. Washington, D.C., 1833-1859. 6 vols.
Annals of Congress. Washington, D.C., 1879-1824.
Biographical Directory of the American Congress, 1774-1961. Washington, D.C., 1961.
A Compilation of the Messages and Papers of the Presidents. Edited by James D. Richardson. Washington, D.C., 1900. 10 vols.
Congressional Globe. Washington, D.C., 1833-1873.
Debates of Congress. Washington, D.C., 1824-1833.
Proceedings of the Alaska Boundary Tribunal. Washington, D.C., 1904. 7 vols.
Records of the Russian-American Company, 1802, 1817-1867. Edited by Raymond H. Fisher. Washington, 1971.
Report of the United States Commissioner of Fish and Fisheries. Edited by Alexander Starbuck. Washington, D.C., 1878. 2 vols.
U.S. Congress. House. *Commissions to Private Armed Vessels.* 33 Cong., 1 sess., June 12, 1854. H. Doc. 111.

————. *Correspondence with Russia, 1835-1838.* 25 Cong., 3 sess., December 3, 1838. H. Doc. 2.

————. *Explorations of the Amoor River.* 35 Cong., 1 sess., April 7, 1858. H. Doc. 98.

————. *Floyd Committee Report on Pacific Northwest.* 17 Cong., 1 sess., January 18, 1822. H. Rept. 18.

————. *Hearings on Alaska Commercial Company.* 44 Cong., 1 sess., June 3, 1876. H. Rept. 623.

————. *P. McD. Collins.* 35 Cong., 2 sess., January 18, 1859. H. Doc. 53.

————. *Report of the Superintendent of the U.S. Coast Survey—1867.* 40 Cong., 2 sess., December 28, 1867. H. Doc. 275.

————. *Report on the Islands Discovered by Whalers in the Pacific.* 23 Cong., 2 sess., January 24, 1835. H. Doc. 105.

————. *Report on the Survey and Reconaissances of Behring's Straits by John Rogers.* 34 Cong., 1 sess., December 3, 1855. H. Doc. 1.

————. *Russian-America.* 40 Cong., 2 sess., February 16, 1868. H. Doc. 177.

————. *The Treaty with Russia.* 40 Cong., 2 sess., May 18, 1868. H. Rept. 37.

U.S. Congress. Senate. *Memoir, Geographical, Political, and Commercial . . . on Siberia, Manchuria, and the Asiatic Islands of the Northern Pacific Ocean; and on the Importance of Opening Commercial Intercourse with those Countries.* 30 Cong., 1 sess., March 8, 1848. S. Doc. 80.

U.S. Department of State. *Foreign Relations.* Washington, D.C., 1861-1870.

Russia

Golovnin, N. *Review of the Russian Colonies in North America.* Office of the Marine Ministerium, St. Petersburg, 1861. Translated by Ivan Petrov, Bancroft Library, University of California. Berkeley.

Golovnin, Vasilli. *Condition of Russian-America in the Year 1818.* Bancroft Library, University of California. Berkeley.

Report of the Committee on the Organization of the Russian-American Colonies. St. Petersburg, 1863. Bancroft Library, University of California. Berkeley.

Rossiiko-Amerikanskaia Kompaniia. *Instructions to Baranov, Aug. 20, 1802.* Bancroft Library, University of California. Berkeley.

————. *Inventory of Documents and Communications Received, Per-*

*taining to the Affairs of the Russian-American Company, August 17,
1781-August 27, 1824.* Bancroft Library, University of California.
Berkeley.

Zavalishin, Dimitry. *The Affairs of Ross Colony.* Moscow, 1866. Translated by Martin Klinkofstrom. Bancroft Library, University of California. Berkeley.

PUBLISHED PRIVATE PAPERS AND LETTERS

Adams, John Quincy. *Memoirs.* Edited by Charles Francis Adams. Philadelphia, 1874-1877. 12 vols.

_____. *The Writings of John Quincy Adams.* Edited by Worthington C. Ford. New York, 1913-1917. 7 vols.

Benton, Thomas Hart. *Thirty Years' View.* New York, 1854.

Buchanan, James. *The Works of James Buchanan.* Edited by John Bassett Moore. Philadelphia, 1909. 12 vols.

Clay, Henry. *The Papers of Henry Clay.* Edited by John F. Hopkins. Lexington, Kentucky, 1961. 2 vols.

Correspondence of the Russian Ministers in Washington, 1819-1825. "Documents." *American Historical Review* 18: 309-345.

Dallas, George M. *Diary.* Edited by Susan Dallas. Philadelphia, 1892.

Gallatin, Albert. *The Writings of Albert Gallatin.* Edited by Henry Adams. Washington, 1879. 3 vols.

Gwin, William M. "Memoirs of the Honorable William M. Gwin." Edited by William H. Ellison. *California Historical Society Quarterly* 19 (March-December 1940).

Jefferson, Thomas. *Writings of Thomas Jefferson.* Edited by A. A. Lipscomb, Washington, 1903. 20 vols.

Madison, James. *Writings of James Madison.* Philadelphia, 1867. 4 vols.

Miller, David Hunter, ed. "Russian Opinion on the Cession of Alaska." *American Historical Review* 48 (April 1943): 521-531.

Monroe, James. *Writings of James Monroe.* Edited by S. M. Hamilton. New York, 1903. 7 vols.

Moore, William G. "Notes of Colonel William G. Moore, Private Secretary to President Johnson." *American Historical Review* 19 (October 1913): 98-132.

"The Projected Purchase of Alaska, 1859-1860." *Pacific Historical Review* 3 (March 1934): 80-87.

Rezanov, Nikolai Petrovich. *The Rezanov Voyage to Neuva California in 1806.* San Francisco, 1926.

Seward, William H. *Works.* Edited by George E. Baker. Boston, 1884-1885. 5 vols.

Sumner, Charles. *Memoir and Letters of Charles Sumner.* Edited by E. L. Pierce. Boston, 1877-1893. 4 vols.

_____. *Complete Works.* Boston, 1900. 20 vols.

Webster, Daniel. *Writings and Speeches of Daniel Webster.* Edited by C. H. Van Tyne. New York and Boston, 1903. 18 vols.

Winthrop, Robert C. *Addresses and Speeches.* Boston, 1852-1886. 4 vols.

BOOKS

Annals of San Francisco, 1855. San Francisco, 1855.

Babey, Anna M. *Americans in Russia, 1776-1917.* New York, 1938.

Bailey, Thomas A. *America Faces Russia.* Ithaca, New York, 1950.

Bancroft, Hubert H. *History of Alaska, 1730-1885.* San Francisco, 1886.

_____. *History of the Northwest Coast.* San Francisco, 1884. 2 vols.

_____. *History of Oregon, 1834-1848.* San Francisco, 1886.

Bemis, Samuel F. *John Quincy Adams and the Foundations of American Foreign Policy.* New York, 1949.

_____. *John Quincy Adams and the Union.* New York, 1856.

Billington, Ray A. *The Far Western Frontier, 1830-1860.* New York, 1956.

Bolkhovitinov, Nikolai N. *Stanovlenie russko-amerikanskikh otnoshenii, 1775-1815.* Moscow, 1966.

Brauer, Kinley J. *Cotton Versus Conscience: Massachusetts Whig Politics and Southwestern Expansion, 1843-1848.* Lexington, Kentucky, 1967.

Callahan, J. M. *The Alaska Purchase and American-Canadian Relations.* Morgantown, West Virginia, 1908.

Chambers, William Nisbet. *Old Bullion Benton, Senator from the New West.* Boston, 1956.

Chevigny, Hector. *Lord of Alaska: Baranov.* New York, 1942.

_____. *Lost Empire: Life of Nikolai Rezanov.* Portland, Oregon, 1938.

_____. *Russian-America, The Great Alaskan Venture, 1741-1867.* New York, 1965.

Comegys, Joseph P. *Memoir of John M. Clayton*. Wilmington, Delaware, 1882.

Current, Richard N. *Daniel Webster and the Rise of National Conservatism*, Boston, 1955.

Dangerfield, George. *The Awakening of American Nationalism*. New York, 1965.

Donald, David. *Charles Sumner and the Coming of the Civil War*. New York, 1960.

————. *Charles Sumner and the Rights of Man*. New York, 1970.

Duckett, Alvin LaRoy. *John Forsyth, Political Tactician*. Athens, Georgia, 1962.

Farrar, Victor J. *The Annexation of Russian-America to the United States*. Washington, D.C., 1937.

————. *The Purchase of Alaska*. Washington, D.C., 1935.

Fuess, Claude M. *Daniel Webster*. Boston, 1930. 2 vols.

Galbraith, John S. *The Hudson's Bay Company as an Imperial Factor, 1821-1869*. Berkeley, 1957.

Gibson, James R. *Feeding the Russian Fur Trade*. Madison, Wisconsin, 1969.

Glanz, Rudolf. *The Jews in American Alaska, 1867-1880*. New York, 1953.

Goetzmann, William H. *Exploration and Empire*. New York, 1966.

Golder, F. A. *Guide to Materials for American History in Russian Archives*. Washington, D.C., 1917-1937. 2 vols.

Graebner, Norman A. *Empire on the Pacific*. New York, 1955.

Greenhow, Robert. *History of Oregon and California*. Boston, 1845.

————. *Memoir, Historical and Political on the Northwest Coast of North America*. London, 1844.

Grinnell, Joseph. *Speech on the Tariff, with Statistical Tables of the Whale Fishery*. Washington, D.C., 1844.

Hildt, J. C. *Early Diplomatic Negotiations of the United States with Russia*. Johns Hopkins University Studies in Historical and Political Science 24. Baltimore, 1908.

Hohman, Elmo Paul. *The American Whaleman*. New York, 1928.

Klein, Philip Shriver. *President James Buchanan*. University Park, Pennsylvania, 1962.

LaFeber, Walter F., ed. *John Quincy Adams and American Continental Empire*. Chicago, 1965.

————. *The New Empire, An Interpretation of American Expansion, 1860-1898*. Ithaca, New York, 1963.

Logan, J. A. *No Transfer*. New Haven, 1961.

McCormac, Eugene I. "John Forsyth." In *American Secretaries of State and Their Diplomacies*, IV. Edited by S. F. Bemis. New York, 1928.

Merk, Frederick. *Manifest Destiny and Mission in American History*. New York, 1963.

_____. *The Oregon Question*. Cambridge, Massachusetts, 1967.

Miller, David Hunter, ed. *Treaties and Other International Acts of the United States of America*. Washington, D.C., 1931-1942. 7 vols.

Morison, Samuel E. *The Maritime History of Massachusetts*. Boston, 1921.

North, Douglas. *The Economic Growth of the United States, 1790-1860*. New York, 1961.

O'Connor, Thomas H. *Lords of the Loom, Cotton Whigs and the Coming of the Civil War*. New York, 1968.

Ogden, Adele. *The California Sea-Otter Trade*. Berkeley, 1941.

Okun, S. B. *The Russian-American Company*. Translated by Carl Ginsburg. Cambridge, Massachusetts, 1951.

Perkins, Dexter. *The Monroe Doctrine, 1823-1826*. Cambridge, Massachusetts, 1927.

Pierce, Richard A. *Russia's Hawaiian Adventure, 1815-1817*. Berkeley, 1965.

Pitkin, Timothy. *Statistical View of the Commerce of the United States of America*. New Haven, 1835.

Poore, Benjamin P. *Descriptive Catalogue of the Government Publications of the United States*. Washington, 1885.

Porter, Kenneth W. *John Jacob Astor*. Cambridge, Massachusetts, 1931. 2 vols.

Reid, Virginia H. *The Purchase of Alaska, Contemporary Opinion*. Long Beach, California, 1940.

Scammon, C. M. *Marine Mammals of the Northwestern Coast of North America*. San Francisco, 1874.

Sellers, Charles. *James K. Polk, Continentalist, 1843-1846*. Princeton, 1966.

Shuck, Oscar T., ed. *Sketches of Leading and Representative Men of San Francisco*. San Francisco, 1875.

Silbey, Joel. *The Shrine of Party: Congressional Voting Behavior, 1841-1852*. Pittsburgh, 1967.

_____. *The Transformation of American Politics, 1840-1860*. Englewood Cliffs, New Jersey, 1967.

Smith, Walter B. *Economic Aspects of the Second Bank of the United States*. Cambridge, Massachusetts, 1953.

Sturgis, William. *The Oregon Question: Substance of a Lecture Before the Mercantile Library Association, Jan. 22, 1845*. Boston, 1845.

Sullivan, G. W., ed. *Early Days in California*. San Francisco, 1888.

Tansill, Charles C. *The Purchase of the Danish West Indies*. Baltimore, 1932.

Tarsaidze, Alexander. *Czars and Presidents: The Story of a Forgotten Relationship*. New York, 1958.

Thomas, Benjamin Platt. *Russian-American Relations, 1815-1867*. Johns Hopkins University Studies 48. Baltimore, 1930.

Thomas, Lately. *Between Two Empires*. New York, 1969.

Tikhmenev, Petr Aleksandrovich. *The Historical Review of the Russian-American Company and Its Activity up to the Present Time*. St. Petersburg, 1861-1863. Translated MSS. by Dimitri Krenov, University of Washington Library, Seattle, 1939.

Tompkins, Stuart R. *Alaska, Promyshlennik and Sourdough*. Norman, Oklahoma, 1945.

Tower, Walter S. *A History of American Whale Fishery*. Philadelphia, 1907.

Van Deusen, Glyndon G. *The Jacksonian Era, 1828-1848*. New York, 1959.

————. *The Life of Henry Clay*. Boston, 1937.

————. *William Henry Seward*. New York, 1967.

Whymper, Frederick. *Travel and Adventure in the Territory of Alaska*. London, 1868.

Wickersham, James. *A Bibliography of Alaskan Literature*. Cordova, Alaska, 1927.

William, Mary W. "John Middleton Clayton." In *American Secretaries of State*, VI. Edited by Samuel F. Bemis. New York, 1928.

Williams, William A. *American-Russian Relations, 1781-1947*. New York, 1952.

————. *The Contours of American History*. Chicago, 1961.

Wiltse, Charles M. *John C. Calhoun, Sectionalist, 1840-1850*. New York, 1951.

UNPUBLISHED MANUSCRIPTS

McPherson, Hallie M. "William McKendree Gwin, Expansionist." Ph.D. dissertation, University of California, Berkeley, 1931.

Miller, David Hunter. "The Alaska Treaty." Unpublished manuscript in General Records of State Department (Record Group 59), National Archives, Washington, D.C.
Stanton, John William. "The Foundations of Russian Foreign Policy in the Far East, 1847-1875." Ph.D. dissertation, University of California, Berkeley, 1932.
Wheeler, Mary E. "The Origin and Formation of the Russian-American Company." Ph.D. dissertation, University of North Carolina, Chapel Hill, 1965.

ARTICLES

Andrews, C. L. "Alaska under the Russians: Industry, Trade, and Social Life." *Washington Historical Quarterly* 7 (October 1916): 278-295.
————. "Alaska Whaling." *Washington Historical Quarterly* 9 (January 1918): 3-10.
————. "Some Russian Books on Alaskan History." *Pacific Northwest Quarterly* 28 (January 1937): 75-87.
Bailey, Thomas A. "Why the United States Purchased Alaska." *Pacific Historical Review* 3 (March 1934): 39-49.
Belov, Mikhail, "Sale of Alaska." *Alaska Review* (Spring-Summer 1967): 8-19.
Blue, Verne, "The Oregon Question—1818-1838." *Oregon Historical Quarterly* 23 (September 1922): 193-219.
Bolkhovitinov, N. N. "Russia and the Declaration of the Non-Colonization Principle: New Archival Evidence." *Oregon Historical Review* 72 (June 1971): 101-127.
Bourne, Edward Gaylor. "Aspects of Oregon History Before 1840." *Oregon Historical Review* 6 (September 1905): 255-275.
Buzanski, Peter M. "Alaska and Nineteenth Century American Diplomacy." *Journal of the West* 6 (July 1967): 451-467.
Caruthers, J. Wade. "The Sea Borne Frontier on the Northwest Coast, 1778-1850." *Journal of the West* 10 (April 1971): 211-251.
Cleland, R. G. "Asiatic Trade and the American Occupation of the Pacific Coast." *American Historical Association, Annual Report* 1 (1914): 283-289.
Coleman, Evan J. "Gwin and Seward—A Secret Chapter in Ante-Bellum History." *Overland Monthly* (November 1891): 465-471.
Coughlin, Magdalen. "Commercial Foundations of Political Interest in

218   Selected Bibliography

the Opening of the Pacific, 1789-1829.'' *California Historical Society Quarterly* (March 1971): 15-33.

Davidson, Donald C. ''Relations of the Hudson's Bay Company with the Russian-American Company on the Northwest Coast, 1829-1867.'' *British Columbia Historical Quarterly* 5 (January 1941): 33-51.

Dennett, Tyler. ''Seward's Far Eastern Policy.'' *American Historical Review* 28 (October 1922): 45-62.

Deppermann, W. H. ''Two Cents an Acre.'' *North American Review* 245 (Spring 1938): 126-132.

Dmytryshyn, Basil. ''Admiral Nikolai S. Mordvinov: Russia's Forgotten Liberal.'' *Russian Review* 30 (January 1971): 54-63.

Dozer, Donald M. ''Anti-Expansionism During the Johnson Administration.'' *Pacific Historical Review* 12 (September 1943): 253-275.

Dubofsky, Melvyn. ''Daniel Webster and the Whig Theory of Economic Growth.'' *New England Quarterly* 42 (December 1969): 551-571.

DuFour, Clarence J. ''The Russian Withdrawal from California.'' *California Historical Society Quarterly* 12 (September 1933): 240-276.

Dunning, W. K. ''Paying for Alaska.'' *Political Science Quarterly* 27 (September 1912): 285-298.

Dviochenko-Markov, Evfronsina. ''John Ledyard and the Russians.'' *Russian Review* 11 (October 1952): 211-222.

Farrar, Victor J. ''The Background of the Purchase of Alaska.'' *Washington Historical Quarterly* 13 (April 1922): 93-104.

————. ''Joseph Lane McDonald and the Purchase of Alaska.'' *Washington Historical Quarterly* 12 (April 1921): 83-90.

————. ''The Reopening of the Russian-American Convention of 1824.'' *Washington Historical Quarterly* 11 (April 1920): 83-88.

————. ''Senator Cole and the Purchase of Alaska.'' *Washington Historical Quarterly* 14 (October 1923): 243-247.

Ford, Worthington C. ''John Quincy Adams and the Monroe Doctrine.'' *American Historical Review* 7 (October 1902): 28-52.

Gibson, James R. ''Food for the Fur Traders: The First Farmers in the Pacific Northwest.'' *Journal of the West* 7 (January 1968): 18-30.

Gilbert, B. F. ''The Alaska Purchase.'' *Journal of the West* 3 (April 1964): 163-174.

Golder, F. A. ''Mining in Alaska Before 1867.'' *Washington Historical Quarterly* 7 (July 1916): 233-238.

————. ''The Purchase of Alaska.'' *American Historical Review* 25 (April 1920): 411-425.

Graebner, Norman A. ''Maritime Factors in the Oregon Compromise.'' *Pacific Historical Review* 20 (November 1951): 331-345.

_____. "Politics and the Oregon Compromise." *Pacific Northwest Quarterly* 52 (March 1961): 7-14.

Huttenbach, Henry R. "Sale of Alaska: A Reply to a Soviet Commentary." *Alaska Review* (Spring-Summer 1970): 33-45.

Jensen, Billie Barnes. "Alaska Pre-Klondike Mining." *Journal of the West* 6 (July 1967): 417-432.

Keithahn, E. L. "Alaska Ice, Inc." *Pacific Northwest Quarterly* 36 (April 1945): 121-131.

Kushner, Howard I. " 'Hellships': Yankee Whaling Along the Coast of Russian-America, 1835-1852." *New England Quarterly* 45 (March 1972): 81-95

_____. "The Oregon Question Is . . . a Massachusetts Question." *Oregon Historical Quarterly* 75 (December 1974): 316-335.

_____. "The Russian Fleet and the American Civil War: Another View." *The Historian* 34 (August 1972): 633-649.

_____. "Visions of the Northwest Coast: Gwin and Seward in the 1850s." *Western Historical Quarterly* 4 (July 1973): 295-306.

Latourette, Kenneth S. "The History of the Early Relations Between the United States and China." *Transactions of the Connecticut Academy of Arts and Sciences* 22 (1917).

Luthin, Reinhard H. "The Sale of Alaska." *Slavonic and East European Review* 16 (July 1937): 168-182.

McPherson, Hallie M. "The Interest of William McKendree Gwin in the Purchase of Alaska." *Pacific Historical Review* 3 (March 1934): 28-38.

Mazour, Anatole G. "The Prelude to Russia's Departure from America." *Pacific Historical Review* 10 (September 1941): 311-319.

_____. "The Russian-American and Anglo-Russian Conventions of 1824-1825." *Pacific Historical Review* 14 (September 1945): 303-310.

Mosse, W. E. "Russian and the Levant, 1852-1862: Grand Duke Constantine Nickolaevich and the Russian Steam Navigation Company." *Journal of Modern History* 26 (March 1954): 39-48.

Nichols, Irby C. "The Russian Ukase and the Monroe Doctrine: A Reevaluation." *Pacific Historical Review* 36 (February 1967): 13-26.

_____, and Ward, Richard A. "Anglo-American Relations and the Russian Ukase: A Reassessment." *Pacific Historical Review* 41 (November 1972): 444-459.

Ogden, Adele. "Russian Sea-Otter and Seal Hunting on the California Coast, 1803-1841." *California Historical Quarterly* 12 (September 1933): 215-227.

Pierce, Richard A. "Prince D. P. Maksutov: Last Governor of Russian Alaska." *Journal of the West* 6 (July 1967): 395-415.

————. "Two Russian [Alaskan] Governors: Hagemeister and Yanovskii." *Alaska Journal* 1 (Spring 1971).

Saul, Norman E. "Beverley C. Sanders and the Expansion of American Trade with Russia, 1853-1855." *Maryland Historical Magazine* 67 (Summer 1972): 156-170.

Schroeder, John H. "Rep. John Floyd, 1817-1829: Harbinger of Oregon Territory." *Oregon Historical Quarterly* 70 (December 1969): 333-346.

Shippee, Lester B. "Federal Relations of Oregon." *Oregon Historical Quarterly* 19 (June, December, September 1918): 89-133, 189-230, 283-331.

Smith, T. C. "Expansion After the Civil War." *Political Science Quarterly* 16 (September 1901): 412-436.

Stanley, Gerald. "Senator William Gwin: Moderate or Racist." *California Historical Society Quarterly* 50 (September 1971): 243-255.

[Sturgis, William.] "Examination of Russian claims to the Northwest Coast of America." *North American Review* 15 (October 1822): 370-401.

Sturgis, William. "The Northwest Fur Trade." *Merchants Magazine* 14 (June 1846): 532-538.

Van Alstyne, R. W. "International Rivalries in the Pacific Northwest." *Oregon Historical Review* 46 (September 1945): 185-218.

Vevier, Charles. "The Collins Overland Line and American Continentalism." *Pacific Historical Review* 28 (August 1959): 237-253.

Welch, R. E. "American Opinion and the Purchase of Russian-America." *American Slavic and East European Review* 17 (December 1958): 481-494.

Wheeler, Mary E. "Empires in Conflict and Cooperation: 'Bostonians' and the Russian-American Company." *Pacific Historical Review* 40 (November 1971): 419-441.

Index

221

ABOUT THE AUTHOR

Howard I. Kushner is assistant professor of history at the State University of New York at Fredonia. He did his undergraduate work at Rutgers University and obtained his Ph.D. at Cornell University. He has contributed numerous articles to scholarly journals. At present he is completing a biography of John Milton Hay.